Scrum® in Action: Agile Software Project Management and Development

Andrew Pham
Phuong-Van Pham

Course Technology PTR
A part of Cengage Learning

WASHINGTON
TECHNOLOGY
UNIVERSITY

COURSE TECHNOLOGY
CENGAGE Learning™

Australia • Brazil • Japan • Korea • Mexico • Singapore • Spain • United Kingdom • United States

COURSE TECHNOLOGY
CENGAGE Learning

Scrum® in Action: Agile Software Project Management and Development
Andrew Pham and Phuong-Van Pham

Publisher and General Manager, Course Technology PTR: Stacy L. Hiquet

Associate Director of Marketing: Sarah Panella

Manager of Editorial Services: Heather Talbot

Marketing Manager: Mark Hughes

Senior Acquisitions Editor: Mitzi Koontz

Project Editor: Jenny Davidson

Technical Reviewer: Ben Oguntona

Copy Editor: Sandy Doell

Interior Layout Tech: MPS Limited, a Macmillan Company

Cover Designer: Mike Tanamachi

Indexer: Broccoli Information Management

Proofreader: Sara Gullion

For product information and technology assistance, contact us at **Cengage Learning Customer & Sales Support, 1-800-354-9706**

For permission to use material from this text or product, submit all requests online at **www.cengage.com/permissions**
Further permissions questions can be emailed to **permissionrequest@cengage.com**

Scrum is a registered trademark of Scrum Alliance.

All other trademarks are the property of their respective owners.

All images © Cengage Learning unless otherwise noted.

Library of Congress Control Number: 2010942047

ISBN-13: 978-1-4354-5913-7

ISBN-10: 1-4354-5913-X

Course Technology, a part of Cengage Learning
20 Channel Center Street
Boston, MA 02210
USA

Cengage Learning is a leading provider of customized learning solutions with office locations around the globe, including Singapore, the United Kingdom, Australia, Mexico, Brazil, and Japan. Locate your local office at: **international.cengage.com/region**

Cengage Learning products are represented in Canada by Nelson Education, Ltd.

For your lifelong learning solutions, visit **courseptr.com**

Visit our corporate website at **cengage.com**

Printed in the United States of America
1 2 3 4 5 6 7 13 12 11

To our family with love.

This book is dedicated to all the professionals throughout the world whose intelligence and hard work have made, and will make, the world a better place.

"A journey of a thousand miles begins with a single step."
—Lao-tzu, Chinese philosopher

FOREWORD

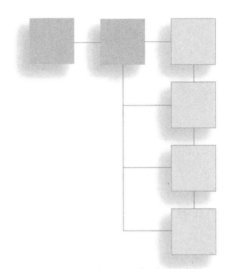

This book is a valuable, practical, no-nonsense addition to the Agile literature. Co-authors Andrew and Phuong-Van quickly get down to brass tacks in covering a very broad software development and management landscape. In valuable detail, they cover Agile foundations, finance, management buy-in, Agile requirements, architecture vision, product owner role, focused testing, teamwork, Agile management, and how to adapt Scrum without destroying it, and they top it off with a readiness assessment tool.

I see two major groups of people who will find this book really useful: those coming from a more traditional plan-driven mindset and those coming from a newer Agile mindset. The strength of this tome is that it is practical without being dogmatic, and therefore provides a bridge to the others' thinking for people in both these groups.

For those of you coming from a traditional, plan-driven background, there are several wonderful sections of information. The material on visioning architecture; creating smart requirements for the Scrum Product Backlog; being an effective product owner in true Agile, servant leader mode; focusing on automated, regression, and integration tests; being an enthusiastic and productive team member; and adapting Scrum without killing its Agile core will serve two purposes. On one hand, it should provide warmth and comfort if your heart has been chilled by myths that Agile teams are lacking in essential software development disciplines. On the other, it will expose you to some of the really critical soft stuff: the wonderful people, team and leadership elements of Scrum that have made it so popular with the rank and file and enlightened managers alike.

For those of you coming from a newer Agile mindset, especially if you may not have been exposed to more traditional rigor, the material that covers considering earned value in particular and finance in general, creating an architecture vision and applying it to the Scrum product backlog, and performing criteria-based estimation as an addition to planning poker should help expand your thinking without raising your hackles. The treatment of traditional rigor here is quite sensible and appropriate, and I really believe that you should have no issues with finding a way to apply some of these proven traditional techniques almost immediately on your projects.

If you're a project manager, developer, tester, product manager, business analyst, or in fact, anyone involved with software development, you will find that this book helps you understand the nitty gritty of work on Scrum teams with a very focused practicality. It is a comprehensive work that I believe you will enjoy, no matter where your starting point.

I met Andrew in one of my ScrumMaster classes, and was quickly impressed by the depth of his knowledge and the sincerity of his viewpoints. Quite frankly, he could have taught the class, and his humility in sharing his knowledge was remarkable. Along with co-author Phuong-Van, Andrew invites you on an exciting journey into Agile management and development. I hope you will accept the invitation.

Sanjiv Augustine
Author, *Managing Agile Projects*
Certified Scrum Trainer
Co-Founder, Agile Project Leadership Network
President, LitheSpeed

FOREWORD

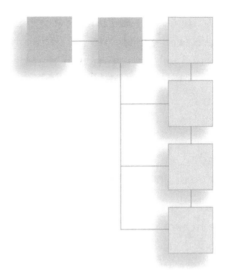

Agile, as a software development process, is frequently misunderstood to mean no requirements, we'll figure out the design as we go, and anything remotely resembling a planning meeting is simply out of the question. This book very effectively puts that misconception to rest.

For those new to Agile and Scrum development practices, it's frequently difficult to discern not only what you need to be doing but how to tell if you're doing it correctly. Without spending real sprints with experienced practitioners, it's difficult to understand the impact of trade-offs that occur constantly during real-world project development. Are your sprints too long? Too short? Are you spending too much time doing retrospectives? Why exactly are you doing them to begin with? Andrew Pham's and Phuong-Van Pham's book not only helps explain why you should be doing a particular Agile or Scrum practice, but also provides hard-earned experience in helping you understand if you're doing it properly. This book provides the desperately needed straw man for activities that are frequently new to everyone on the team.

One of my favorite parts of the book is the time spent looking at Agile from the non-developer perspective. What does it mean to you, as an enterprise architect, if your organization has decided to start using Scrum for its development process? What if you're the customer? What if you're in charge of the effort and need to somehow meld the Agile process you want to support with financial and progress tracking information in your department? For as much as some development teams like to think terms like ROI and EVM are for management to deal with, this book helps tie a project together without losing what makes Agile so effective.

Unlike what is sometimes taught in the theoretical classroom, this book is for professionals who would like—and need—to know how to apply Agile and Scrum to real-life situations. This is to say that this is not a book for process dogmatists but for professional pragmatists whose mission is to deliver real software in real companies with real people and real situations.

Deploying Agile, and especially Scrum, processes into an organization is no small feat, given all the constraints we know. This book is a valuable resource to help make that a reality.

Dan Pilone
Author, *Head First Software Development* and *Head First iPhone Development*
Founder and Managing Partner of Element 84, LLC

ACKNOWLEDGMENTS

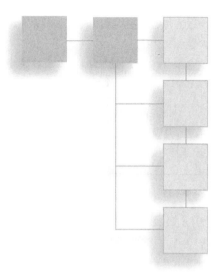

We owe a tremendous amount of thanks and gratitude to many people who have helped us with the writing of this book.

First, there is our family with all their unwavering and unconditional love and support.

Next, we would like to thank the team at Course Technology PTR. And to begin with, there is Mitzi Koontz, senior acquisitions editor, who believed in our book from day one; next Sandy Doell, copy editor, who did a wonderful job in making the book flow much better than when we first started; and finally, Jenny Davidson, project editor, who made it all happen by ensuring a remarkable co-ordination between all of us.

Next, we would like to extend a technical thank you to:

- David K Pham, Formerly CTO with KTD Media Corporation and Founder of 7billion, LLC, for having tested all the ideas in this book and helped improve them even more.

- Scott Booth, MCP, Manager with Pariveda Solutions, a Texas-based consultancy, who not only attended Andrew's presentation on the Influence of Architecture Vision on Team Velocity and Software Quality at the DFW Scrum User Group, but also took quite a lot of time to review the book for us.

- Sameer Bendre, CSM and PMP, a Senior Consultant with 3i Infotech Consulting, who was so enthusiastic about the book and who also put some of his friends in contact with us.

- Mike Vizdos, a Certified Scrum Trainer based in Richmond, Virginia, who took time to give us his feedback despite his busy teaching schedule.

- Linda Rising, author, who did not hesitate to take time out of her busy schedule to give us some quick feedback for an early draft on her way to catch a flight to Germany.

- Henrik Kniberg, author of *Scrum and XP in the Trenches* and a Certified Scrum Trainer, based in Stockholm, Sweden, who was the first one who made us think of a better title for the book.

- Anwar Bardai, a Senior Computer Specialist with Compucom, Inc., who worked with Andrew Pham a few years ago in successfully using some elements of Scrum and Agile to implement an ERP package in record time for a large computer retailer.

- Benjamin Oguntona, Senior System Manager with AT&T, who worked with Andrew Pham when Andrew was Technical Director with SBC and then Principal and Chief Architect with Cingular Wireless, for enthusiastically taking the time to review and to edit the book.

- Dennis Palmer, a product owner with Esquire Innovations, Inc., a software company based in California, who took time to review the book when it was still at an early stage.

- Dennis Simpson, IT Rescue Mission Specialist, based in Dallas, Texas, who not only took time to review the book at length but also helped edit the book to make it more polished.

- Harold Thomas, CBAP, a Business Analyst with the Ohio State Department of Job & Family Services, who did not hesitate to take time from his own writing schedule to review our book and help edit it.

- Sanjiv Augustine, Certified Scrum Trainer, co-founder of the Agile Project Leadership Network (APLN), and author of *Managing Agile Projects*, who not only took the time out of his busy schedule to review the book but was also very kind in writing a foreword for our book.

- Dan Pilone, author of *Head First Software Development* and *Head First iPhone Development*, and Managing Partner with Element 84, LLC, for having taken the time to review the book and for writing the foreword for it.

Last but not least, our thanks also go to all the authors whose works we have cited here. To those we have not mentioned, please know that we have made every effort to trace all the copyright holders, but if any have been inadvertently overlooked, please let us or our publisher know so that we can make the necessary amendments at the earliest opportunity.

Andrew Pham
Phuong-Van Pham

About the Authors

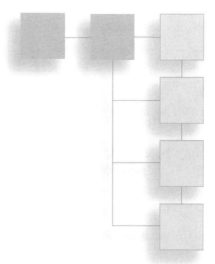

Andrew Pham is a Certified ScrumMaster (CSM), a Certified Scrum Product Owner (CSPO), and a Certified Scrum Professional (CSP).

In addition to this, he is also a PMP (Project Management Professional), a longtime Architect for Java Technologies certified by Sun Microsystems, and an early OOAD (Object-Oriented Analysis and Design) UML professional certified by IBM.

An elect-senior member with IEEE and member of the PMI, Andrew Pham has held top positions in project management, enterprise architecture, and software development in start-up, mid-sized, and multi-billion-dollar corporations. An experienced Agile and Lean coach, Andrew has helped numerous companies successfully use Agile (Scrum) and Lean (kanban) on real-world projects as well as taught development teams both in the USA and abroad.

An entrepreneur at heart, Andrew Pham is also President of Agile Enterprise Consulting, LLC, a consulting, training, and software development company. You can contact him at andrew@agileenterpriseconsulting.com.

Phuong-Van Pham   is currently project manager in a multi-billion-dollar company. Phuong-Van is also a PMP (Project Management Professional), a Certified ScrumMaster (CSM), a Certified Scrum Practitioner (CSP), and a Certified Project Manager for Technology (Project+) by the Computer Technology Industry Association (CompTIA).

In addition to her responsibility at work, she is also an active member with the Association of University Women (AUA), the Project Management Institute (PMI), the PMI New York Chapter, the New York Scrum User Group, the Agile Project Leadership Network (APLN), and the Women in Project Management Special Interest Group (SIG).

Contents

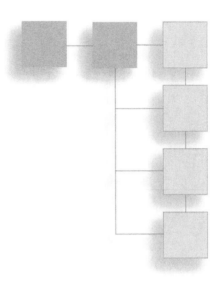

Introduction xvii

Praise for the Book xxxiv

Chapter 1 **Setting the Stage: Agile and Scrum** **1**

What Is the Foundation of Agile Software Development
and Project Management? 3

Scrum Origins 5

    How Scrum Works 6

Why Are Agile and Scrum Effective in Software Project
Management? 12

Summary 15

Chapter 2 **Finance Speak** **17**

Calculate Project Costs 17

Select Project Investments 18

    The Payback Period 18

    Buy Versus Build 19

    Net Present Value (NPV) 21

    Internal Rate of Return (IRR), or Return on Investment (ROI) . . . 22

Monitor Project Performance 24

    Cost Performance 25

    Schedule Performance 26

    Project Budget Forecasting 27

Summary 29

Chapter 3   **Secure Top Management Support but Make
Sure to Obtain Middle Management Buy-In. 31**
Working with Top Business Management 32
Working with Top IT Management. 35
    Program Management Office 35
Working with IT Middle Management 36
    Quality Assurance 38
    Operations Management. 39
    Enterprise Architecture (EA) 40
Turning Your Direct Management into an Ally 43
Summary 44

Chapter 4   **A Visual Requirements Gathering for the
Product Backlog 47**
A New Visual Requirements Gathering Process for Agile
and Scrum 47
    First Step: Identify the Stakeholders and Their Goals 47
    The SMART Rules 48
    Second Step: Gather Requirements for the Product Backlog 49
    The CUTFIT Rules 51
An Example 54
Summary 59

Chapter 5   **Making the Story Point Estimate Comparable
for Scrum Enterprise-Wide Implementation 61**
Problems with a Non-Comparable Story Point. 61
Cultural Problems with Planning Poker 62
An Objective Criteria-Based Estimating Process 62
    Example 71
Summary 73

Chapter 6   **The Influence of Architecture Vision on Team Velocity
and Software Quality 75**
The Importance of Architecture Vision 77
How to Identify Architecture Vision 78
Another Benefit of Having an Architecture Vision 82
Summary 92

Chapter 7 **From Architecture Vision to Release and Sprints Planning to Parallel Software Development** **93**

From Architecture Vision to Release and Sprints Planning 93

From Incremental to Parallel Software Development 103

Summary 105

Chapter 8 **Did You Say Product Owner?** **107**

Managing Stakeholders' Expectations and Prioritization 109

Having a Clear Product Vision and Knowledge 109

Knowing How to Gather Requirements for the Product Backlog . . 111

Making Oneself Always Available 111

Knowing How to Be a Good Organizer 111

Knowing How to Communicate Better Than the Average Person . 112

Knowing That It Is All About Servant Leadership 112

Summary 112

Chapter 9 **The Importance of Automated, Regression, and Integration Tests** **113**

The Importance of the Definition of *Done* 115

The Most Important Tests 117

Automated Testing 118

Continuous Integration Testing 119

Organizing the Testing Infrastructure 119

Summary 121

Chapter 10 **The Importance of Teamwork** **123**

The Individuals 124

The Group 125

The Team 126

The Keirsey Temperament Types 126

The Five Team Stages 129

Techniques to Resolve Team Conflicts 129

Conditions of Great Teamwork 131

Summary 132

Chapter 11 **The New Nature of Management and Leadership on a Scrum Project** **135**

Coaching for Superior Performance: The GROW Model 141

Traits of a Caring Leader and Manager 143

Summary 144

Chapter 12 How to Adapt Scrum (Without Destroying Its Agile Foundations or Doing Negative ScrumButs) . . . 145

How to Adapt Scrum Without Doing Negative "ScrumButs"
with Excuses 146

Examples of Situational Scrum Adaptations 147

    Organization Dimension 147

    Infrastructure Dimension 151

    Team Dimension 152

    Technology Dimension 152

    Process Dimension 153

    Business Dimension 154

Summary 154

Chapter 13 Scrum Project Readiness Self-Assessment 157

A Simple Tool for Your Scrum Readiness Assessment 157

    Organization Dimension 160

    Infrastructure Dimension 160

    Team Dimension 161

    Technology Dimension 161

    Process Dimension 162

    Business Dimension 162

Example 164

Putting It Together 169

Summary 170

Chapter 14 When Do You Need a ScrumMaster? 173

In Depth Theoretical and Practical Knowledge of Scrum 174

Great Servant-Leadership Ability 175

Strong Organizational Skills 175

Great Communication Skills 175

Excellent Presentation Skills 176

Conflict Resolution Skills 176

Great Human Development Skills 176

Summary 176

Chapter 15   Parting Thoughts **177**

Appendix A   Two Real-World Software Product Development
Case Studies **181**
Introduction.   181
Ruby and Ruby on Rails (RoR)   181
Ruby, the Language   181
Ruby on Rails (RoR), the Web Framework   185
Version Control and Testing for Web Development with RoR   189
Git—Version Control   189
Testing and Testing Framework   189
Case Study 1 (Noshster)   192
Product Vision and Goal   192
Requirements Gathering Using the Book's Visual Technique. . .   192
Architecture Vision and Release/Sprint Planning   192
Project Estimation Using the Objective Criteria Technique   197
Noshster Development   199
Case Study 2 (Conferous)   242
Product Vision and Goal   242
Requirements Gathering Using the Book's Visual Technique. . .   242
Architecture Vision and Release/Sprint Planning   242
Project Estimation Using the Objective Criteria Technique   244
Conferous Development   246

Appendix B   Could You or Should You Have an Abnormal
Termination of a Sprint? **265**
Introduction.   265
When Can a Sprint Be Terminated Earlier Than Planned?   265
How to Avoid Terminating a Sprint Earlier Than Planned   266
How to Restart After Terminating a Sprint Earlier Than Planned . .   267

Glossary **269**

References **275**

Index **277**

Introduction

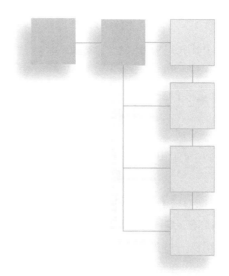

What Is This Book About?

While there are some good books on Scrum out there, we believe none of them deal with all the essentials a software project team needs to know in order to begin and complete a Scrum software project within corporate constraints (by corporate constraints, we mean in companies where Scrum or Agile has not been successfully deployed enterprise-wide).

In order to help these teams succeed, sometimes in navigating treacherous corporate constraints, we set out to write a practical book on Scrum using the knowledge we essentially acquired from the trenches.

To this end, the 15 chapters of this book will provide you with all the knowledge you need as if an experienced ScrumMaster were advising you in person. In addition to this, you will also find in Appendix A two case studies for two software products that had been successfully built and deployed using the techniques and advice outlined in this book.

Chapter 1: Setting the Stage: Agile and Scrum

Chapter 1's focus is the foundation of Agile with emphasis on Scrum as part of the Agile family. Chapter 1 also serves as an introduction to the fundamentals of Scrum and corrects some of the inaccurate information about Scrum, more or less like Alan Shalloway and his team did in *Lean-Agile Software Development Achieving Enterprise Agility (p. 84–92)*. This is a way for us to get you on the same page with us before we move forward.

Chapter 2: Finance Speak

Whether you are passionate about Agile and Scrum or not, one thing to remember is that the language of business management is finance.

In Chapter 2, you will learn the essentials of finance, what you should know in order to better collaborate with business management in helping them select projects, estimate a project budget, and forecast how much money and time you will need to finish your project.

Chapter 3: Secure Top Management Support but Make Sure to Obtain Middle Management Buy-In

Although it is important to work with top business management to get their approval, it is even more important to work with middle management on a daily basis since middle management is where the rubber meets the road. The goal of Chapter 3 is to give you enough knowledge to be successful at both.

Chapter 4: A Visual Requirements Gathering for the Product Backlog

Once the approval is given to a project team to move forward, there is nothing more important than a good set of requirements. Chapter 4 presents a very simple and visual process to gather requirements for a Scrum project that any of us can use.

Chapter 5: Making the Story Point Estimate Comparable for Scrum Enterprise-Wide Implementation

As Agile and Scrum become more and more widely accepted, one of the problems we encounter with the current story point system (upon which team velocity is built) is that it does not allow for comparison between teams. This hinders many IT departments' desire to implement Scrum across the board, especially when it comes to overall resource allocation and re-allocation. As in Chapter 4, we present here an approach that has been successfully used on many projects. It will help you estimate your stories and back up what you say, not with your gut feelings but with tangible data as well as make it possible to compare velocity between different teams within the same organization.

Chapter 6: The Influence of Architecture Vision on Team Velocity and Software Quality

For anyone who has ever worked on even one single Scrum project, you should have seen that team velocity fluctuates up and down, often reducing team productivity and ability to deliver. This chapter will walk you through the reasons for fluctuations in team velocity; and it will suggest how to use architecture vision, similar to what others call architecture intent, to remedy it.

Chapter 7: From Architecture Vision to Release and Sprints Planning to Parallel Software Development

In addition to the fact that it can help team velocity, or even increase it over time, a good architecture vision has additional benefits. This may include a positive impact on release and Sprint planning.

Chapter 8: Did You Say Product Owner?

Everyone is important on a Scrum project, but the product owner is the person who can help the team deliver the most value for the business. Chapter 8 reviews the personal and professional qualities a product owner should have to be successful.

Chapter 9: The Importance of Automated, Regression, and Integration Tests

Not all testing is created equal. In this chapter, we will provide an in-depth treatment of a few tests that are, in our opinion, most important to Scrum projects, and explain why they are key to a successful Scrum project team.

Chapter 10: The Importance of Teamwork

Who among us has not heard about teamwork and how important it is. Even if it sounds like an old cliché, Chapter 10 affirms that teamwork is essential in order for the Scrum team to deliver value, especially since the team is now self-organized. Beyond saying that teamwork is important, this chapter offers some insight into human psychology and temperament types that can help co-workers better understand one another and work well together. In addition, this chapter also offers some techniques for conflict resolution, taking into account the stage at which the conflict happens on a project.

Chapter 11: The New Nature of Management and Leadership on a Scrum Project

Even though Scrum teams are self-organizing, there is still a need for project management and team leadership. The ways that project management morphs into something a bit different in the Scrum environment will be explored. The key thing to remember here is that servant leadership will replace the command and control style of the past. Chapter 11 reviews some useful coaching and leadership techniques for Scrum Masters and product owners as they team up to help guide the team toward their final project delivery.

Chapter 12: How to Adapt Scrum (Without Destroying Its Agile Foundations or Doing Negative ScrumButs)

Wouldn't it be wonderful if someone could invent a methodology or process that could fit every company and every problem, that we could use without ever having to adapt it to our environment? The reality is that we must often adapt the methodology to our constraints, to get it to work. This is also true with Scrum.

Unlike the negative "ScrumButs," which are wrong applications of Scrum, we will review here several examples of positive "ScrumButs," or good adaptations of Scrum, in the same way as Jurgen Appelo, CIO at CSM eCompany in the Netherlands, did in his "ScrumButs are the best part of Scrum".

Chapter 13: Scrum Project Readiness Self-Assessment

Chapter 13 provides an example of a Scrum project readiness self-assessment, which you should try to fill out at the very beginning of your Scrum project. This will allow you to identify where the obstacles may be which could hurt your project team's ability to deliver.

Depending on your score, you will know how easy or how hard it is going to be for your team to perform within your current environment and try to improve it so that you can deliver more readily.

Chapter 14: When Do You Need a ScrumMaster?

Unless you or your team is experienced with Scrum, you will need a ScrumMaster to guide you through some of the tribulations that will accompany your first attempts with Scrum.

Even though this book is supposed to serve as your ScrumMaster, Chapter 14 reviews the personal and professional qualities a ScrumMaster should have to be successful.

Chapter 15: Parting Thoughts

Rather than just let you move ahead alone, Chapter 15 provides some suggestions as to what main applications you should draw from the different chapters and the order in which you should apply them to your project situations.

Appendix A: Two Real-World Software Product Development Case Studies

In Appendix A we showcase two successful software products that were built and deployed using the advice given in this book, from requirements gathering to architecture vision to release and Sprint planning and testing.

The first case study provides an example of an application that is developed vertically, while the second case study provides an example of an application that is developed horizontally.

Appendix B: Could You or Should You Have an Abnormal Termination of a Sprint?

Normally, your Scrum project should go smoothly if you have followed all the advice we have given in this book. This being said, there may be instances where you will be experiencing what is called an abnormal termination of a sprint, which is due sometimes to your underestimation of your team's velocity or the complexity of some of your user stories.

To advise you in what to do in this situation, included in this book is also a small chapter on the abnormal termination of a sprint, what the causes are, how to avoid it, how to deal with it and how to restart the project team's work after one.

Glossary

In order to facilitate the understanding of certain key Scrum terms, a glossary is provided at the end of the book.

WHO SHOULD READ THIS BOOK?

Depending on your title or the role you have in your current organization, here are some suggestions as to what chapters you should read and in what order. There are two kinds of people who will find this book useful: (1) those who are new to Scrum and (2) those who already have some experience with Scrum.

If You Are New to Scrum

If You Are a Member of the Management Team

As you are part of management, you should first read Chapter 1 to get familiar with the Agile evolution, how it got started and with Scrum origin as well as its basics. Next, you should read Chapter 3 to see what advice we give to the Scrum team to work with management, with both top business management and middle management. Next, you should read Chapter 8 and Chapter 14, respectively, on the product owner's and ScrumMaster's quality and role.

Scrum or not, we guess you should wonder how you or your team is going to gather requirements for the so-called product backlog which you have heard so much about. If this is the case, then the next chapter you should read is Chapter 4 on how we identify user goals and use a visual technique to gather requirements for Scrum projects. You may also have heard that with planning poker every team's velocity, which is the number of user stories a Scrum team can deliver for every Sprint, is different from one team to another. If this is what you have heard and if you wonder how you could make it comparable for a large-scale implementation across many teams, then you may want to read Chapter 5. It is effectively in Chapter 5 that we present a straightforward way to estimate your requirements, which will make it possible for every team member to back up their estimate and to make the team velocity comparable. This latter is, without any doubt, a key condition for a successful enterprise implementation of Scrum across many teams.

If you have more time, we suggest that you read the book as a whole, from start to finish, including Appendix A where two examples of two software products that had been built and deployed using the advice given in this book are showcased. You will be surprised to see how much you have learned about Agile and Scrum.

If You Are a Member of the Technical Management Team

As you are part of management, you should first read Chapter 1 to get familiar with the Agile evolution, how it got started, and with Scrum origin as well as its basics. Next, you should read Chapter 3 to see what advice we give to the Scrum team to work with management, both top business management and middle management. Next, you should read Chapter 8 and Chapter 14, respectively, on the product owner's and ScrumMaster's quality and role.

Scrum or not, we guess you should wonder how you or your team is going to gather requirements for the so-called product backlog which you have heard so much about. If this is the case, then the next chapter you should read is Chapter 4 on how we identify user goals and use a visual technique to gather requirements for Scrum projects. You may also have heard that with planning poker, every team's velocity, which is the number of user stories a Scrum team can deliver for every Sprint, is different from one team to another. If this is the case and if you wonder how you could make it comparable for a large-scale implementation across many teams, then you may want to read Chapter 5. It is during Chapter 5 that we present a straightforward way to estimate your requirements, which will make it possible for every team member to back up their estimate and to make the team velocity comparable. This latter is, without any doubt, a key condition for a successful enterprise-wide implementation of Scrum.

Since you come from a technical background, we next suggest that you read Chapter 6 on architecture vision and how it can help your team maintain a good velocity and even do a better job at release and Sprint planning (Chapter 7).

If you want to know who is going to drive requirements and the business needs in Scrum, then Chapter 8 on the product owner is for you. Likewise, if you want to know who will be responsible to help the team and the product owner understand and properly apply Scrum, then you will want to read Chapter 14.

Without having to get your hands dirty anymore since you are part of management, you may still want to read Chapter 9 to know what the three most important tests are for us and how to get organized to help your team or organization to deliver. As a member of the management team, we guess you should be curious to know how the team is going to be managed since you have heard that they are now self-managed in Scrum. If this is the case, then Chapter 10 is for you to read. Naturally, since you are a member of the management team, we next suggest that you read Chapter 11 on project management and team leadership. As any seasoned professional who is part of management, you know for a fact that no process or process framework could easily fit into an organization without a certain amount of adaptation. If this is the case, then Chapter 12 is the chapter you should read next. After this, if you wonder how you know where you stand with

Scrum, then Chapter 13 is what you will want to review and start using the questionnaire.

Last but not least, if you have more time, we suggest that you read the book as a whole, from start to finish, including Appendix A where two examples of two software products that had been built and deployed using the advice given in this book are showcased. You will be surprised to see how much you have learned about Agile and Scrum.

If You Are a Project Manager

Since you are someone who may be asked to act as the ScrumMaster on the project and since you are somewhat part of management, or should we say that as a project manager you likely have the same concerns as management, we suggest that you read the entire book.

You will be surprised to see how much you have learned about Agile and Scrum to understand what experts talk about and how to move forward in all confidence.

If You Are a Developer

Since you are part of the technical team, we make the assumption that you are interested mainly in the chapters that can help you understand how to get the development job done. If this is the case, read:

- Chapter 1 (It is all about Agile and Scrum)

- Chapter 5 (Estimating user stories to make the story point comparable for Scrum enterprise-wide implementation)

- Chapter 6 (The influence of architecture vision on team velocity and software quality)

- Chapter 7 (From architecture vision to release and Sprints planning)

- Chapter 8 (Did you say product owner?)

- Chapter 9 (The importance of automated, regression, and integration tests)

- Chapter 10 (The importance of teamwork)

- Chapter 14 (When do you need a ScrumMaster?)

Now, if you have more time, we suggest that you read the book as a whole, from start to finish, including Appendix A, where two examples of two software products that had been built and deployed using the advice given in this book are showcased. You will be surprised to see how much you have learned about Agile and Scrum to understand what experts talk about and how to move forward in all confidence.

If You Are a Business Analyst

Like the developer, we make the assumption that you are mainly interested in the non-technical chapters that can help you learn to know what Scrum is and how to get the job done. If this is the case, read:

- Chapter 1 (It is all about Agile and Scrum)

- Chapter 2 (Finance speak)

- Chapter 4 (Requirements gathering for the product backlog)

- Chapter 5 (Estimating user stories to make the story point comparable for Scrum enterprise-wide implementation)

- Chapter 8 (Did you say product owner?)

- Chapter 10 (The importance of teamwork)

- Chapter 11 (The new nature of management and leadership on a Scrum project)

- Chapter 14 (When do you need a ScrumMaster?)

If you have some technical background or time, we recommend that you also read Chapters 6 and 7 on architecture vision. We have written them in such a way that they are also understandable to the non-technical team members. They will provide you with the same understanding as the technical folks on the team, allowing you to have the best collaboration with the technical folks.

Now, if you have more time, we suggest that you read the book as a whole, from start to finish, including Appendix A where two examples of two software products that had been built and deployed using the advice given in this book are showcased.

If You Are a Tester

Like the developer and the business analyst, we make the assumption that you are mainly interested in the chapters that can help you learn to know what Scrum is and how to get the job done.

If this is the case, read:

- Chapter 1 (It is all about Agile and Scrum)

- Chapter 4 (Requirements gathering for the product backlog)

- Chapter 9 (The importance of automated, regression, and integration tests)

- Chapter 10 (The importance of teamwork)

- Chapter 11 (The new nature of management and leadership on a Scrum project)

If you have some interest in knowing how your colleagues gather requirements and do their estimate on a Scrum project, read Chapters 4 and 5. If you have some technical background, we recommend that you also read Chapters 6 and 7 on architecture vision. We have written them in such a way that they are also understandable to the non-technical team members. Try to read them and you will not regret it since they will provide you with the same understanding as the technical folks on the team, allowing you to have the best collaboration with the technical folks.

Now, if you have more time, we suggest that you read the book as a whole, from start to finish, including Appendix A where two examples of two software products that had been built and deployed using the advice given in this book are showcased. You will be surprised to see how much you have learned about Agile and Scrum.

If You Are an Application Architect

Like the developer and the business analyst, we make the assumption that you are mainly interested in the chapters that can help you understand what Scrum is and how to get the job done.

If this is the case, read:

- Chapter 1 (It is all about Agile and Scrum)

- Chapter 4 (Requirements gathering for the product backlog)

- Chapter 6 (The influence of architecture vision on team velocity and software quality)

- Chapter 7 (From architecture vision to release and Sprints planning)

- Chapter 10 (The importance of teamwork)

- Chapter 11 (The new nature of management and leadership on a Scrum project)

Next, read Chapter 3, especially section 3.3.

Now, if you have more time, we suggest that you read the book as a whole, from start to finish, including Appendix A where two examples of two software products that had been built and deployed using the advice given in this book are showcased. You will be surprised to see how much you have learned about Agile and Scrum.

If You Are an Enterprise Architect

Unlike the developer, tester, and the business analyst, as an enterprise architect you are mainly interested in ensuring that the Scrum project architecture fits into the overall enterprise architecture. For this, read:

- Chapter 1 (It is all about Agile and Scrum)

- Chapter 4 (Requirements gathering for the product backlog)

- Chapter 6 (The influence of architecture vision on team velocity and software quality)

- Chapter 7 (From architecture vision to release and Sprints planning)

- Chapter 8 (Did you say product owner?)

- Chapter 10 (The importance of teamwork)

- Chapter 11 (The new nature of management and leadership on a Scrum project)

- Chapter 14 (When do you need a ScrumMaster?)

Next, read Chapter 3, especially section 3.3.

Now, if you have more time, we suggest that you read the book as a whole, from start to finish, including Appendix A where two examples of two software products that had been built and deployed using the advice given in this book are showcased. You will be surprised to see how much you have learned about Agile and Scrum.

If You Are a Member of the PMO

As your team is interested in IT alignment on business needs and in IT performance, you will want to read:

- Chapter 1 (It is all about Agile and Scrum)

- Chapter 2 (Finance speak)

- Chapter 3 (Secure top management support but obtain middle management buy-in)

- Chapter 4 (Requirements gathering for the product backlog)

- Chapter 5 (Estimating user stories to make the story point comparable for Scrum enterprise-wide implementation)

- Chapter 6 (The influence of architecture vision on team velocity and software quality)

- Chapter 7 (From architecture vision to release and Sprints planning)

- Chapter 8 (Did you say product owner?)

- Chapter 11 (The new nature of management and leadership on a Scrum project)

- Chapter 12 (How to adapt Scrum)

- Chapter 13 (Scrum project readiness self-assessment)

- Chapter 14 (When do you need a ScrumMaster?)

If you have more time, we suggest that you read the book as a whole, from start to finish, including Appendix A where two examples of two software products that had been built and deployed using the advice given in this book are showcased. You will be surprised to see how much you have learned about Agile and Scrum.

If You Are a Member of Operations

As your team is responsible for the daily running of the organization's software applications, you will want to read:

- Chapter 1 (It is all about Agile and Scrum)

- Chapter 3 (Secure top management support but obtain middle management buy-in)

- Chapter 6 (The influence of architecture vision on team velocity and software quality)

- Chapter 7 (From architecture vision to release and Sprints planning)

- Chapter 8 (Did you say product owner?)

- Chapter 9 (The importance of automated, regression, and integration tests)

- Chapter 14 (When do you need a ScrumMaster?)

If you have more time, we suggest that you read the book as a whole, from start to finish, including Appendix A where two examples of two software products that had been built and deployed using the advice given in this book are showcased. You will be surprised to see how much you have learned about Agile and Scrum.

If You Are a Product Owner

For the responsibility you have on the business of the project, read:

- Chapter 8 (Did you say product owner?)

- Chapter 2 (Finance speak)

- Chapter 3 (Secure top management support but obtain middle management buy-in)

- Chapter 4 (Requirements gathering for the product backlog)

- Chapter 5 (Estimating user stories to make the story point comparable for Scrum enterprise-wide implementation)

- Chapter 9 (The importance of automated, regression, and integration tests)

- Chapter 11 (The new nature of management and leadership on a Scrum project)

- Chapter 14 (When do you need a ScrumMaster?)

If you are interested in seeing the team build a robust application that does not break after you go live, we suggest that you read:

- Chapter 6 (The influence of architecture vision on team velocity and software quality)

- Chapter 7 (From architecture vision to release and Sprints planning)

Now, if you have more time available, we suggest that you read the book as a whole, from start to finish. You will be surprised to see how much you have learned about Agile and Scrum.

If You Are a Business Sponsor

As the person who is behind the business needs for the project and who provides the main funding for it, you should be interested in reading:

- Chapter 1 (It is all about Agile and Scrum)

- Chapter 8 (Did you say product owner?)

- Chapter 2 (Finance speak)

- Chapter 3 (Secure top management support but obtain middle management buy-in)

- Chapter 11 (The new nature of management and leadership on a Scrum project)

- Chapter 14 (When do you need a ScrumMaster?)

If you have more time available, we suggest that you read the book as a whole, from start to finish, including Appendix A, where two examples of two software products that had been built and deployed using the advice given in this book are showcased. You will be surprised to see how much you have learned about Agile and Scrum.

If You Are Already Experienced with Scrum

If You Are a ScrumMaster

As an experienced ScrumMaster, you should read:

- Chapter 14 (When do you need a ScrumMaster?)

- Chapter 2 (Finance speak)

- Chapter 3 (Secure top management support but obtain middle management buy-in)

- Chapter 4 (Requirements gathering for the product backlog)

- Chapter 5 (Estimating user stories to make the story point comparable for Scrum enterprise-wide implementation)

- Chapter 6 (The influence of architecture vision on team velocity and software quality)

- Chapter 7 (From architecture vision to release and Sprints planning)

- Chapter 11 (The new nature of management and leadership on a Scrum project)

- Chapter 12 (How to adapt Scrum)

- Chapter 13 (Scrum project readiness self-assessment)

If you have more time, we suggest that you read the book as a whole, from start to finish, including Appendix A where two examples of two software products that had been built and deployed using the advice given in this book are showcased.

If You Are a Product Owner

As an experienced product owner, you should read:

- Chapter 8 (Did you say product owner?)

- Chapter 2 (Finance speak)

- Chapter 4 (Requirements gathering for the product backlog)

- Chapter 5 (Estimating user stories to make the story point comparable for Scrum enterprise-wide implementation)

- Chapter 6 (The influence of architecture vision on team velocity and software quality)

- Chapter 7 (From architecture vision to release and Sprints planning)

- Chapter 11 (The new nature of management and leadership on a Scrum project)

- Chapter 13 (Scrum project readiness self-assessment)

- Chapter 12 (How to adapt Scrum)

- Chapter 14 (When do you need a ScrumMaster?)

If you have more time, we suggest that you read the book as a whole, from start to finish, including Appendix A where two examples of two software products that had been built and deployed using the advice given in this book are showcased.

If You Are a Member of the (Development) Team

Even though you have had some experience with Scrum, you may find something interesting here in reading:

- Chapter 3 (Secure top management support but obtain middle management buy-in)

- Chapter 4 (Requirements gathering for the product backlog)

- Chapter 5 (Estimating user stories to make the story point comparable for Scrum enterprise-wide implementation)

- Chapter 6 (The influence of architecture vision on team velocity and software quality)

- Chapter 7 (From architecture vision to release and Sprints planning)

- Chapter 8 (Did you say product owner?)

- Chapter 9 (The importance of automated, regression, and integration tests)

- Chapter 10 (The importance of teamwork)

- Chapter 13 (Scrum project readiness self-assessment)

- Chapter 14 (When do you need a ScrumMaster?)

If you have more time, we suggest that you read the book as a whole, from start to finish, including Appendix A where two examples of two software products that had been built and deployed using the advice given in this book are showcased.

PRAISE FOR THE BOOK

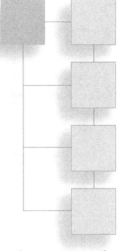

Andrew Pham's book is an answer to the prayers of newbies to Agile/Scrum. Right from assessment techniques for your project/enterprise for agility, to guidance on implementing it—he has included, not only theoretical aspect, but also human and practical aspects. Simply put, for all the impediments he and his team faced over years he has put together a learning guide and answered for us most of the questions which we might face to start with Agile transformation. A great tool for any team trying to explore the Agile path!

Sameer Bendre, Certified ScrumMaster, PMP

3i Infotech Consulting

I have known Andrew Pham for many years and always enjoyed learning something new from him, starting from the time I was still working under his direction at AT&T (formerly known as SBC).

Andrew Pham was particularly clear then in explaining Agile and Architecture Vision to us, something he has done again with this book.

For a technical book, this is a very interesting book with new ideas to look at project management or software development process in general. Very well written and a must-read for those that must improve on current way of doing things and a good reference book for all in IT.

Ben Oguntona, MBA

Senior Systems Manager, AT&T

Andrew Pham takes a different look at Scrum in this book and helps shed light on many of the questions project teams face when beginning to adopt Scrum. Andrew describes many good project management techniques on how to get the most from your project teams. Andrew also bridges the gaps between many Scrum and project management books by addressing how to communicate with executives using financial terms, how to use an objective estimation technique in lieu of the common "poker estimation", and where software architecture fits into Scrum.

A good, quick read to prepare project managers on how to successfully implement Scrum.

Scott Booth, MCP, Manager

Pariveda Solutions, Dallas, Texas

The book was a concise presentation of the steps and concepts that an organization should be aware of when adopting Scrum. The company I work for is currently in our 3rd Sprint of our very first Scrum project. I can't wait for the final version of this book to be released so that I can share it with the rest of my team. In many ways it was good confirmation that we are on the right track and it was a great reminder of the things that we still need to work on. The chapter on what makes a good Product Owner described almost exactly the person who is filling that role in our company. I haven't had the chance to complete the Certified ScrumMaster training yet, so reading about how the ScrumMaster and Product Owner work together to manage the team provided some key insight for me.

Dennis Palmer

Product Manager / ScrumMaster

Esquire Innovations, Inc.

Andrew Pham's book is a very concise reference for Agile and Scrum and is written more on a practical term than just academics. It is an easy read for the novice and advance project managers alike. The language of the book lends itself to showing the fact that Agile and Scrum are absolutely a more natural way of looking at project management.

As Andrew Pham and I had successfully led the first successful PeopleSoft package implementation at Computer City many years ago, I can recognize in this book many Scrum elements he was using then. Essentially, they were to build a good and frequent collaboration with the users, to empower the team while ensuring that they deliver on short demonstrable increments.

The book definitely puts this natural progression in a more formal framework while highlighting the building flexibilities in the process. As a Senior Software Specialist having worked on small and large projects, I feel that this book is a great asset to the project managers regardless of the size and extent of the projects.

Anwar Bardai, Senior Software Specialist

CompuCom, Inc.

I found Andrew Pham and Phuong-Van Pham's book to be immensely practical. It answers in a concise manner what is the minimum I need to do. Of course you can read the entire book, and it is well worth it. But today, many feel they don't have the time to read a book, they just want the answer. And a book is way too general, containing things that are not pertinent to you. But each team's situation is different. This book is the answer. Given your situation, it tells you which chapters should be read. Just look down the list of situations, pick yours, write down the chapters to read, and now the book is customized to your situation.

Other books on Agile/Scrum I've read typically gloss over the complaints or shortcomings of Agile/Scrum that are usually given when a company might initially consider Agile/Scrum. Andrew addresses these questions or difficulties head on, and gives practical advice on what your options might be and how to implement them to help assure a successful project.

Dennis Simpson, Systems Crisis Resolution, MBA, MS, CCP

Andrew and Phuong-Van Pham's book is a clear, concise presentation of Agile and Scrum concepts for professionals and executives who are wondering whether their IT projects can benefit from them. While it provides excellent technical advice on project management and business analysis issues, it also has the rare virtue of addressing financial and human resource issues that affect business management. If one book can make Agile work for an organization, this is it.

Harold Thomas, CBAP

Ohio State Department of Job & Family Services

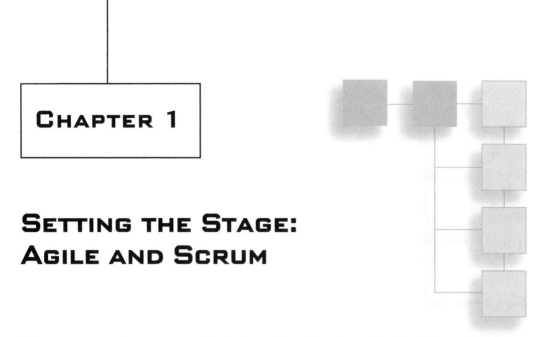

CHAPTER 1

SETTING THE STAGE: AGILE AND SCRUM

Like many people, we are excited about the adoption of Agile (adaptive) project management and development in general, and about the adoption of Scrum in particular.

Unlike many people who are so dogmatic about Agile or Scrum, however, we do not believe that the current corporate world has been reorganized completely for Scrum. Maybe some commercial software companies have done that, but the large majority of corporations have not fired all their specialists or given them a new generalist title as some Scrum dogmatists believe they should. Most of these companies still have their current organizations the way they are, with many separate functions in their IT departments. CapitalOne, one of the companies that has adopted Agile often cited by many Scrum trainers, is still hiring business analysts, business systems analysts, and project managers. This is also true of many large companies known for having transitioned into Scrum, such as Sabre, Verizon, NBC Universal, General Dynamics, Texas Instruments, and American Airlines.com, just to mention a few.

We will talk more about Scrum's origin and fundamentals later in this chapter but for now, let's say that Scrum, as in the sport of rugby, is a way of restarting the rugby game, either after an incident or after the ball is out of play. The idea is to keep the game (software development) rolling.

Even though Scrum can be used outside of software development, we will focus in this book on Scrum as an Agile process framework for software project management and development alone.

Having managed projects in the traditional command and control style for a long time, we have both witnessed, time and again, that Agile and Scrum seem to help our teams produce software results more effectively than their command and control counterparts.

This is not to say that the traditional plan-driven style no longer works in any circumstances; there is much rigor in the traditional approach that even Agile and Scrum can benefit from. What we are simply saying is that we can do better if we know how to take a few steps back to reflect on what we do and learn to improve our techniques and processes with new ideas and concepts.

Because people and companies tend to embrace change slowly, the fact that the Agile movement, and especially Scrum, has taken off and generated this much excitement is a very good sign. Together, we hope to contribute to spreading the adoption of Agile and Scrum with this book, which is derived from many years of experience in software project management and development in real-life.

Like many of us, if you can get past obstacles, you will find Agile and Scrum amazingly refreshing and you will learn how to successfully implement them on a project. Otherwise, your road can be littered with difficulties, which ultimately may cause your project to fail.

There are many reasons why teams sometimes fail with Scrum. One of the most common reasons is that many professionals are still unaccustomed to Scrum, even after taking a Scrum class or reading a few white papers about it. The second reason may be that their project is so complex that more advanced techniques are needed to reduce the project's complexity and get it under control. A third could be that their organization is not yet set up for Scrum, or that the teams do not know how to use Scrum within a company's current constraints. This could either be because of lack of experience or because the team has been ill-advised by dogmatic ScrumMasters or coaches, something we address in this practical guide.

Whatever the reason, Agile and Scrum come with change, and change is always difficult unless properly managed. But with good management these difficulties can be turned into opportunities.

One of our goals in this book is to prepare you for the changes you and your team will go through with Agile and Scrum. We want to help you make the process as smooth as possible while giving your team a chance to adapt to, embrace, and succeed in your Scrum project.

WHAT IS THE FOUNDATION OF AGILE SOFTWARE DEVELOPMENT AND PROJECT MANAGEMENT?

The foundations of Agile Software Development and Project Management are, without a doubt, the Agile Manifesto and the Declaration of Inter-Dependence.

In 2001, a group of software experts got together in the Snowbird resort of Utah to draft what is known as the Agile Manifesto (www.agilemanifesto.org):

"We are uncovering better ways of developing software by doing it and helping others do it. Through this work we have come to value:

- Individuals and interactions over processes and tools
- Working software over comprehensive documentation
- Customer collaboration over contract negotiation
- Responding to change over following a plan

That is, while there is value in the items on the right, we value the items on the left more."

[© 2001 Kent Beck, Mike Beedle, Arie van Bennekum, Alistair Cockburn, Ward Cunningham, Martin Fowler, James Grenning, Jim Highsmith, Andrew Hunt, Ron Jeffries, Jon Kern, Brian Marick, Robert C. Martin, Steve Mellor, Ken Schwaber, Jeff Sutherland, Dave Thomas.]

Along with these four values, the Agile Manifesto has twelve principles:

1. Our highest priority is to satisfy the customer through early and continuous delivery of valuable software.

2. Welcome changing requirements, even late in development. Agile processes harness change for the customer's competitive advantage.

3. Deliver working software frequently, from a couple of weeks to a couple of months, with a preference to the shorter timescale.

4. Business people and developers must work together daily throughout the project.

5. Build projects around motivated individuals. Give them the environment and support they need, and trust them to get the job done.

6. The most efficient and effective method of conveying information to and within a development team is face-to-face conversation.

7. Working software is the primary measure of progress.

8. Agile processes promote sustainable development. The sponsors, developers, and users should be able to maintain a constant pace indefinitely.

9. Continuous attention to technical excellence and good design enhances agility.

10. Simplicity—the art of maximizing the amount of work not done—is essential.

11. The best architectures, requirements, and designs emerge from self-organizing teams.

12. At regular intervals, the team reflects on how to become more effective, then tunes and adjusts its behavior accordingly.

Although the Agile Manifesto was drafted in 2001, a few years after Scrum was announced at Object Oriented Programming, Systems, Languages, and Applications (OOPSLA) in 1996, it is a well-known fact among experts that it has great influence on Scrum. This influence was obvious in Ken Schwaber's second book, *Agile Project Management with Scrum*, in which he wrote that Scrum is one of the Agile processes with values and principles as described in the Agile Manifesto.

While the Agile Manifesto dealt with software development, the Agile Project Management "Declaration of Interdependence" which another group of experts pulled together in 2005 focused more on the project management side (http://pmdoi.org):

"We are a community of project leaders that are highly successful at delivering results. To achieve these results:

■ We **increase return on investment** by making continuous flow of value our focus.

- We **deliver reliable results** by engaging customers in frequent interactions and shared ownership.

- We **expect uncertainty** and manage for it through iterations, anticipation, and adaptation.

- We **unleash creativity and innovation** by recognizing that individuals are the ultimate source of value, and creating an environment where they can make a difference.

- We **boost performance** through group accountability for results and shared responsibility for team effectiveness.

- We **improve effectiveness and reliability** through situationally specific strategies, processes and practices."

[©2005 David Anderson, Sanjiv Augustine, Christopher Avery, Alistair Cockburn, Mike Cohn, Doug DeCarlo, Donna Fitzgerald, Jim Highsmith, Ole Jepsen, Lowell Lindstrom, Todd Little, Kent McDonald, Pollyanna Pixton, Preston Smith and Robert Wysocki.]

Whether the Agile Manifesto and the Declaration of Interdependence (DOI) came to the experts' minds first or after they had been somewhat influenced by Scrum or by any other then existing Agile processes, it does not really matter.

What matters is that if your truly understand the meaning of the Manifesto and the DOI, you will have a leg up in adapting Scrum, should the need arise, without betraying its Agile foundation.

SCRUM ORIGINS

Historically, the term Scrum comes from an article published by Hirotaka Takeuchi and Ikujiro Nonaka in the Harvard Business Review in 1986. In that paper, entitled "The New New Product Development Game," Takeuchi and Nonaka described a holistic approach in which project teams are made up of small cross-functional teams, working successfully toward a common goal, which the authors compared to the Scrum formation in rugby.

While working on building an Object Oriented Analysis and Design (OOAD) tool at Easel, Jeff Sutherland, then VP of Engineering at Easel, Inc. realized that his software team would need an enhanced version of rapid application development. What he wanted was a process similar to Scrum where at the end of short iterations, the CEO at Easel would see working code demonstrated, rather than paper Gantt charts.

During more or less the same period, Ken Schwaber (see recommended further reading in the bibliography) was actively looking into how he could help his company, Advanced Development Methods, Inc. (ADM), enhance their software process in order to improve their teams' productivity.

After further analyzing how other successful independent software vendors (ISV) built software, Ken came to realize that all their development processes were similar in that they all used empirical processes, which requires constant inspection and adaptation.

At the request of the Object Management Group (OMG) in 1995, Jeff and Ken worked together to summarize what they had learned throughout the years; they created a new methodology, which they named Scrum, and described in Schwaber's article, "Scrum and the Perfect Storm," at www.controlchaos.com/my-articles.

How Scrum Works

Notice in Figure 1.1 that the Scrum team, which should be a cross-functional team, is composed of a ScrumMaster, a product owner, and the development team (or simply, "the team"), with all the skills needed (such as requirements gathering, designing, coding, and testing) to build the software product.

Even in the best situations, when the Scrum team composition is fully cross-functional, it does not necessarily follow that the Scrum project members are, organizationally and hierarchically, all part of the permanent Scrum project team structure. Unless your company is a resolute proponent of enterprise-wide Scrum deployment and has completely reorganized itself, following Scrum organizational structure recommendations, Scrum teams are still borrowed from different organizations to which they belong, such as QA, Enterprise Architecture, Pre-production, or DBA.

Even some of those companies often cited as having adopted Scrum still have Project Management, QA, Pre-Production, Business System Analysis Groups, and Enterprise Architecture working as separate functions in IT, and project teams have to negotiate with these groups to get their Scrum projects going. Very rarely does a company fire all its project managers (Scrum does not have a project manager per se) or change their title to ScrumMaster or reorganize all its separate IT groups around multi-disciplinary Scrum project teams. That would be the dream, but it is not the current reality yet.

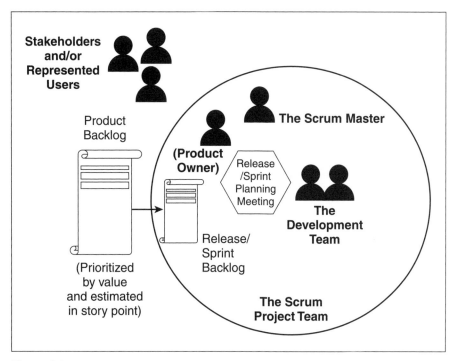

Figure 1.1
Product backlog, release backlog, and Sprint backlog.

In Figure 1.1, you can see how a Scrum project gets started. As you can see in the diagram, it all begins with the product owner who is responsible for taking input from different stakeholders, or users who represent them, to elaborate a list of requirements to create a product backlog.

Simply put, the product backlog is a prioritized list of requirements, which can include everything from business features to technologies to technical issues to bug fixes.

Some practitioners and authors, such as Henrik Knitberg in his book, *Scrum and XP from the Trenches* would prefer to keep the product backlog at the business level to include only business requirements, as we do.

As you will learn in Chapter 4, "A Visual Requirements Gathering for the Product Backlog," the user requirements for Scrum product backlog are usually gathered as short user stories during a one- or two-day requirements workshop prior to the release and Sprint planning meeting.

While release planning in Scrum was somewhat optional in the early days, it has proven to help many Scrum teams become even more effective throughout the years. Thus, we strongly recommend that the product owner go through release planning with the team even if this is a difficult exercise, as it will require you to learn about the product prior to the planning meeting.

The more you, as the product owner, know the product, the more you can help the team. The key goal of release planning is for the Scrum team to identify all the releases the software product should have, along with a probable delivery schedule. Normally, release planning should last four hours for a Scrum team with four-week Sprints.

Besides release planning, the Scrum team should also go through some Sprint planning, either as part of the release planning process or independently after the release planning is done.

Normally, the Sprint planning meeting should be around eight hours for Sprints of four weeks and should be adjusted to four hours for Sprints of two weeks.

As a common practice, the Sprint planning meeting should be divided into two equal four-hour meetings.

During the first part of the meeting, the product owner will go through the requirements, as user stories, to decide, with the team's feedback, which ones should be part of which Sprints and what their goals are. The first of the two-part meeting is mainly to answer the "What" question.

During the second part of the Sprint planning meeting, which focuses on the "How," the Development team will try to identify tasks from the previously chosen stories and deduce how much time (in hours) it will take them to turn these tasks into potentially shippable product increments. Unless the team uses some kind of planning software, all the development tasks that are part of the Sprint will normally be consigned to a Task Board, some kind of white board on a wall, for easy team allocation and tracking.

As soon as the release and Sprint planning meeting is done, then starts the actual sprinting work (Figure 1.2) along with its 15-minute daily Scrum, or Daily Standup.

Originally, the Daily Standup could last up to 30 minutes, but as part of Scrum evolution, or adjustment, which we will talk more about in Chapter 12, "How to

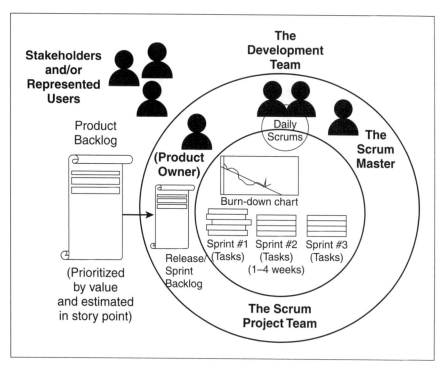

Figure 1.2
Sprints, a burndown chart, and daily Scrums.

Adapt Scrum (Without Destroying Its Agile Foundations or Doing Negative ScrumButs)," its duration has been reduced more and more in practice, to around 15 minutes today.

Normally, the duration of a Sprint will be from one to four weeks. Except under very special circumstances, no additional items should be added to or deleted from the Sprint backlog while the Sprint is underway, unless the team and the product owner agree to them, but this is something like an exception rather than the norm.

Unlike the traditional process where the project manager is responsible for organizing weekly status meetings to track project status, with Scrum, the team will get together every day to inspect, not the project status, but the team's progress toward the Sprint goal. This is the reason you often hear people say that the daily Scrum is not a status meeting.

To keep track of the team progress towards the Sprint goal, a burndown chart will be created by the team to show how much work remains until the team is

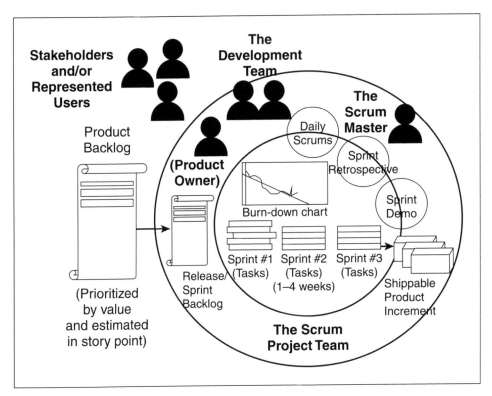

Figure 1.3
Sprint review and retrospective.

done with the Sprint. Even though the creation of this burndown chart is the team's responsibility, it can be updated by the ScrumMaster whenever the team does not have time to do so.

Just before the end of every Sprint, the team will meet with the product owner, as part of Scrum's Inspect and Adapt mechanism, to go through what is known as a Sprint review organized by the ScrumMaster (Figure 1.3). This is another time-boxed meeting, which normally lasts four hours for a four-week Sprint or two hours for a two-week Sprint.

The objective of this meeting is multi-fold: The first is for the Scrum team and the product owner to discuss what was done and what was not done. The second is for the team to demonstrate what was built to the product owner and get her feedback. Finally, the third objective is to get updates from the product owner regarding any new changes to the product or market direction.

Right after the Sprint review and prior to the next Sprint, the Scrum team will also meet to go through a Sprint retrospective to identify what worked and what did not work during the current Sprint. The intent is to see how they could make their collaboration even more effective going into the next Sprint.

As a common practice, the retrospective meeting should normally last three hours for a monthly Sprint but its duration should be adjusted, as is the case for all the other timed-box meetings, in proportion to the length of the Sprint, such as two hours for a two-week Sprint.

Figure 1.4 provides an overall graphic of the collaborative responsibilities of Scrum team members.

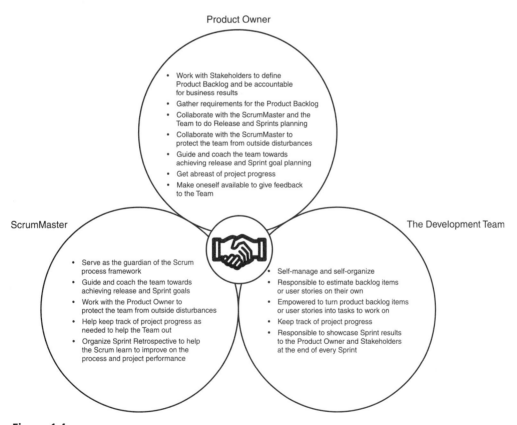

Figure 1.4
It's all about collaboration between the team, the ScrumMaster, and the product owner.

Overall, Scrum does not sound too complicated as a general project framework, right? Yes, but while Scrum sounds simple in theory, it can be very difficult to implement, especially if your company is still new to Scrum practice or if you want to turbo-charge your Scrum project with some of the current practices.

WHY ARE AGILE AND SCRUM EFFECTIVE IN SOFTWARE PROJECT MANAGEMENT?

Even though Agile and especially Scrum can be difficult to implement, it has proven to be extremely effective when properly deployed.

As you read this book, you will see many reasons why Agile and Scrum are normally more effective in project management and development. There are, however, four advantages that we would like to emphasize up front:

- A systematic risk reduction mechanism: All of us who are responsible for project planning and execution know how important it is to reduce the level of risk or uncertainty to zero or to the lowest level possible.

  While there are as many as four different ways to deal with risks (avoidance, transfer, accept, and mitigate), project managers often end up having to mitigate risks in the end. This is where Scrum excels with its frequent Inspect and Adapt cycle.

- A leaner software development life cycle:

  In Figures 1.5 and 1.6, we see the large difference in timeline, with one of the teams using a longer life cycle (Figure 1.5) while another team is

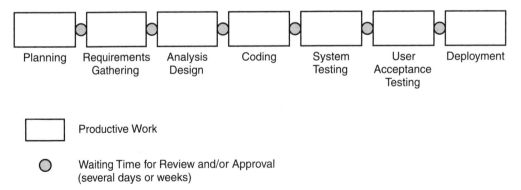

Figure 1.5
Traditional value stream.

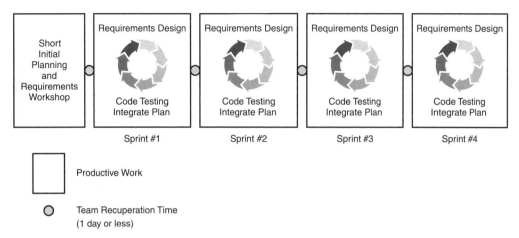

Figure 1.6
Scrum value stream.

using a leaner life cycle (Figure 1.6), making more efficient use of productive time.

- A more adaptive project management process. Unlike the sequential process used within the waterfall environment, which considers project stability as the foundation (Figure 1.7), Scrum will look more like Figure 1.8, in which change is considered to be the only constant.

- A project management and development process framework based on people's motivation and pride. More than anything else, this may be one of the most powerful tenets of Agile and Scrum. The new focus is not on having the manager dictate to team members what they should be doing, but to let the teams decide for themselves how they would go about accomplishing their work on their own.

Scrum proposes a new software management framework, which is based on a project team's self-organization, motivation, ownership, and pride in their achievement.

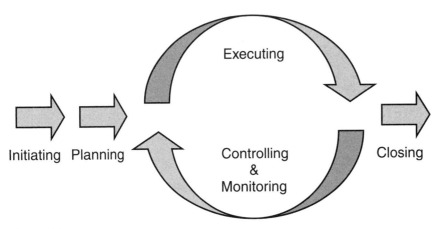

Figure 1.7
The traditional project management process.

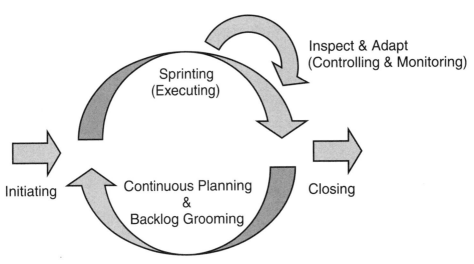

Figure 1.8
Adaptive project management framework with Scrum.

This introduction to Agile and especially to Scrum, although short, will provide you with enough understanding to be able to move forward with the rest of this book.

But before doing this, let's also say that since our focus is on Scrum, we will, therefore, refer only to Scrum for the rest of this book.

Summary

The Agile was born in 2001 when a group of experts got together in Utah to draft what is now known as the Agile Manifesto, the focus of which is on the software development side.

As a complement to the Agile Manifesto, another group of experts came together in 2005 to draft another document called the PM Declaration of Interdependence (DOI), the emphasis of which is on the project management side.

Together, the Agile Manifesto and the DOI form the foundation of the Agile movement and of all Agile development and project management processes, including Scrum.

Since Scrum cannot be used in many contexts without some sort of adaptation, a good knowledge of the foundation of the Agile movement and processes will enable you to know how to adapt Scrum to your environment.

While you will see all the advantages of Scrum during the course of this book, four of them are worth pointing out right away: (1) a risk reduction mechanism, (2) a leaner software process, (3) a more adaptive software project management process, and (4) a framework based on a team's self-organization, motivation, ownership, and pride.

Since the focus of this book is on Scrum, we will refer only to Scrum from now on throughout this book.

Chapter 2

Finance Speak

Although not often addressed in Scrum literature, an understanding of finance will enable you and your team to have a more successful dialogue with business people.

It will not be enough to tell the business and management team to trust that your project is a good investment and that your software product will be better if you use Scrum. You need numbers to support your business case.

To avoid spending more time than needed on finances, we have selected a few key financial concepts and formulas to help you get your project approved; you can also use the information in this chapter to keep track of your project's financial health.

Calculate Project Costs

Even though it is not a value or an artifact, one concept that is essential to Scrum is team velocity. *Team velocity* is the number of user stories or product backlog items, in number of points, that the team can deliver during a Sprint.

We will discuss team velocity in more detail in Chapter 5, "Making the Story Point Estimate Comparable for Scrum Enterprise-Wide Implementation," but it is pertinent here due to the role it plays in the calculation of the human resource cost of the project.

For illustration purposes, let's assume that your project team's velocity is 20 story points per Sprint and a Sprint lasts 4 weeks. So, if your project is estimated at 160 points, you can guess that it will take your team around 8 Sprints, or 32 weeks, to finish the project.

Assume that your project team costs are $150,000 per year including salary and benefits. This means that the team cost for this project would be equal to $92,308 ([$150,000 $\times$ 32 weeks]/52 weeks).

Now, if you add the other project costs, such as computer equipment and telecom, to this human resource cost, you will be able to obtain the overall project cost.

From this discussion, you can guess that the sooner you know your team velocity, the better you will be able to estimate your project team cost with Scrum. Otherwise, you will still need to use the technique or approach that currently exists in your company.

SELECT PROJECT INVESTMENTS

Now that we have seen how to calculate project human resource costs using team velocity, let's see how to calculate project returns before a company can make the decision to invest in a project or not.

There are many ways to calculate project returns, but the most frequently used are Payback Period, Buy Versus Build, Net Present Value (NPV), and Return on Investment (ROI).

The Payback Period

To convince business people that your project is worth investing in, you will need to know the payback period. In simple terms, the *payback period* is the length of time it takes a company to recoup the initial investment; this is also referred to as the break even point.

This technique contrasts the investment cost (equipment and human resource costs, etc.) with the cash flow or revenue expected over the life of the new software product, as shown in Figure 2.1.

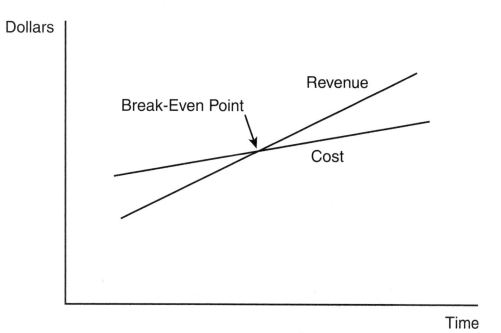

Figure 2.1
Break even point.

As an illustration, let's imagine that your project will require an initial investment cost of $200,000. Per your projections, the cash inflows, or revenue, will be around $28,572 for every quarter.

Given the calculations, it will take 7 quarters ($200,000/$28,572 = 7), or 21 months, to break even on this project.

Although this technique does not take into account the value of money over time, it is still used quite often in many companies, especially when it comes to internal software development.

Buy Versus Build

This technique is relatively simple if we follow the procedure in the right order.

First, we must calculate the difference in fixed price between the fixed price to build and the fixed price to buy, which is called the *price difference.*

Next, we have to calculate the difference in monthly fees by subtracting the monthly buy fee from the monthly build fee as follows.

Finally, we will calculate the number of time periods by dividing the price difference by the monthly fee difference.

Price difference / Monthly fee difference = Number of months

More specifically, there are three scenarios:

1. The build fixed cost and the build monthly fee are both higher than the buy fixed cost and the buy monthly fee. In this case, the logical option is for the company to buy.

2. The buy fixed cost and the buy monthly fee are both higher than the build fixed cost and the build monthly fee. In this case, the logical option is for the company to build.

3. The third scenario is more complex and will necessitate some calculation:

   a. The build fixed cost is higher than the buy fixed cost and the monthly buy fee is higher than the monthly build fee. In this case, the company should buy if it intends to keep the software product less than the calculated number of months.

   b. The buy fixed cost is higher than the build fixed cost and the monthly build fee is higher than the monthly buy fee. In this case, the company should build if it intends to keep the software product for less than the calculated number of months.

For an illustration of the third scenario, let's assume that we have two projects, A and B.

For project A, the Build fixed cost is $1,000,000 and the Build monthly fee is $50,000.

For project B, the Buy fixed cost is $900,000 and the Buy monthly fee is $100,000.

If we plug these numbers into the formulas previously reviewed, we will get:

Price difference = Build fixed cost − Buy fixed cost = $1,000,000 − $900,000 = $100,000

Monthly Fee difference = Monthly buy fee − Monthly build fee = $10,000 − $50,000 = $50,000

Now, if we divide $100,000 by $50,000, we will get 2 months, which is the point at which both the build and buy options will have the same cost (fixed cost + aggregated monthly fees).

So the conclusion is if we intend to keep the software for less than 2 months, then we should buy because the total cost of buying ($900,000 + $100,000 = $1,000,000) will be less than the total cost of building ($1,000,000 + $50,000 = $1,050,000). But if, on the contrary, we plan on keeping the software for more than 2 months, then we should build because the total cost of building ($1,000,000 + $50,000 + $50,000 + $50,000 = $1,150,000) will be less than the total cost of buying ($900,000 + $100,000 + $100,000 + $100,000 = $1,200,000). Normally, companies keep software for longer than two months, but this is an example for illustration purposes only.

Net Present Value (NPV)

Let's talk about Present Value before we discuss Net Present Value (NPV) and Return on Investment (ROI) as a way to select projects to invest in.

Present Value (PV) is a more sophisticated technique than the previous payback technique because it takes into account the time value of money. This is important because money received in the future is usually worth less than the same amount of money received today.

The formula to calculate PV is $PV = FV/(1 + i)^n$

FV is the Future Value (the value of the sum of money in the future), PV is the Present Value, i is the interest or inflation rate, and n is the number of time periods during which the interest is paid.

For illustration purposes, let's assume that you have $4,000 and wonder what this will be worth in three years with an interest or inflation rate of 5%.

Using this formula, you will find that FV is equal to $4,630, which is the product of $4,000 multiplied by $(1.05)^3$ or $4,000 multiplied by (1.157625).

In other words, the PV (Present Value) of $4,630.50 in the future is $4,000 in today's dollars.

So, if you have to choose between two projects with two different values or yields in the future, what you should do is choose the project that has the higher Present Value (PV).

To apply this technique to the project selection process, let's assume that you must choose between two projects, A and B. Project A has a PV of $70,000 and project B has a PV of $80,000. By applying the PV rule, based on a purely financial perspective, you should select project B because it has a higher Present Value (PV) than that of project A.

In the same way Present Value (PV) gives today's value of future cash flows or revenue, Net Present Value (NPV) is the present value of the total revenue minus the present value of the investment cost over a period of time.

By the end of the calculations, you will have three situations to choose from:

- If the NPV of a project is greater than zero, the project should be accepted.

- If the NPV is less than zero, the project should be rejected.

- If there are two or more projects to choose from, choose the project with the highest NPV.

For illustration purposes, let's suppose that we need to calculate the NPV of a project with a 10% interest rate over a period of three years. Given the estimated revenue of $25,000, $100,000, and $200,000, respectively, for the first, second, and third year and the annual calculated project cost of $100,000 per year for the next three years, as shown in Figure 2.2, we will have:

Difference NPV = Revenue NPV − Project cost NPV

Difference NPV = $252,046 − $281,654 = −$29,608

Given that the NPV is a negative number, business management should not invest in this project.

Internal Rate of Return (IRR), or Return on Investment (ROI)

Calculating the IRR, or ROI, is rather complex and will require a computer or a sophisticated calculator. However, there is a practical way CEOs often use to calculate ROI by using only two concepts: velocity and profit margin.

Period	Revenue	Revenue NPV (interest at 10%) PV=FV/(1+i)n	Project Cost	Proj. Cost NPV (interest at 10%) PV=FV/(1+i)n	Difference NPV (interest at 10%)
0	0	0	100,000	100,000	-100,000
1	25,000	18,783	100,000	99,009	-82,226
2	100,000	83,000	100,000	82,645	+335
3	200,000	150,263	0	0	+150,263
		252,046		281,265	-29,608

Figure 2.2
Net present value (NPV).

The first concept, velocity, is practically the same concept as Scrum velocity. In business, velocity defines how quickly a company can make enough revenue (or reduce costs) to pay for the cost of its investment (or asset or inventory), plus the profit it hopes to realize.

The second concept, profit margin, is the money, or profit, the company makes after paying all its expenses, costs associated with making and selling its products or services as well as taxes and loan interest.

To calculate the ROI on your project, you will only need to know the project velocity and your company's profit margin. The finance department should have calculated this for your company and will provide it to you if you ask.

$$ROI = Velocity \times Margin$$

Let's assume that your project can bring in $4 million in revenue for a total cost of investment of $2 million, and if your company's profit margin is 10 percent, then, using the above formula, the ROI for this project will be equal to:

$$ROI = (4,000,000/2,000,000) \times 10\%$$

$$ROI = 20\%$$

When having to compare between different projects, remember to select the project which has the highest ROI.

MONITOR PROJECT PERFORMANCE

Earned Value is used to measure the performance of a project team's work against what was planned, in order to identify variances, or risks of deviation, both in schedule and cost.

Earned Value (EV) is the sum of work that has been accomplished up to date and the authorized budget for that work. So, if a project has a budget of $100,000 and 30% of the work has been completed, its EV is $30,000.

For this book's practical purposes, we will review the following three formulas that are of interest to the project team.

1. Formulas for Cost Performance:

   Cost Variance (CV) = Earned Value (EV) − Actual Cost (AC)

   Cost Performance Index (CPI) = Earned Value (EV)/Actual Cost (AC)

2. Formulas for Schedule Performance:

   Schedule Variance (SV) = Earned Value (EV) − Planned Value (PV)

   Schedule Performance Index (SPI) = Earned Value (EV)/Planned Value (PV)

3. Project Budget Forecasting:

   Estimate at Completion (EAC) = Budget at Completion (BAC)/Cost Performance Index (CPI)

   Estimate to Complete (ETC) = Estimate at Completion (EAC) − Actual Cost (AC)

   Variance at Completion (VAC) = Budget at Completion (BAC) − Estimate at Completion (EAC)

Cost Performance

The goal of cost performance is primarily to calculate the project performance in terms of cost efficiencies. It can also be used to predict trends in future cost performance.

Cost Variance (CV)

Cost variance is the difference between the value of work accomplished (EV) and the actual cost (AC) of the project.

If you wonder what AC is, it is the actual cost, or the actual amount of money that has been spent on the project so far. For example, if a project has a budget of $100,000 and $40,000 has been spent on the project so far, then the AC of the project is $40,000.

Knowing EVC and AC will make it possible to calculate project variances, schedule, and performance indexes, thus allowing the project manager to determine any new course of action or whether the project should be continued.

A positive CV implies that the project is under budget, while a negative cost variance means that the project is over budget.

Cost Variance (CV) = Earned Value (EV) − Actual Cost (AC)

Cost Performance Index (CPI)

While a variance is an actual number, negative or positive, such as −$25,000, an index, like the Cost Performance Index (CPI), is a ratio that should be between 0 and 2.

The formula to calculate the Cost Performance Index (CPI) is as follows.

Cost Performance Index (CPI) = Earned Value (EV)/Actual Cost (AC)

A CPI greater than 1 indicates that we get more value for work performed than the cost incurred. A CPI less than 1 implies that the value of the project work accomplished is less than the cost incurred. In other words, the project team is burning cash faster than they are creating value, and therefore, will probably be over budget. The graph in Figure 2.3 shows how the CPI varies with the changing EV and AC.

So, a CPI equal to 0.90 would mean that the project is over budget.

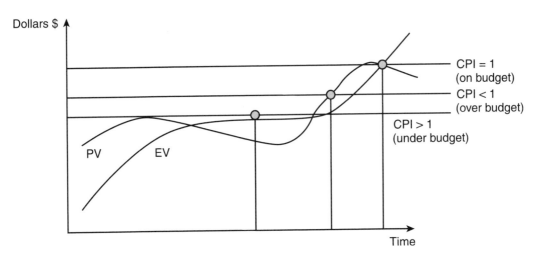

Figure 2.3
Cost Performance Index (CPI).

Schedule Performance

The goal of schedule performance is primarily to calculate the project perform-ance in terms of schedule efficiencies. It can also be used to predict trends in schedule performance.

Schedule Variance (SV)

While AC refers to cost, Schedule Variance (SV) gives us an indication as to whether the project is behind or ahead of schedule.

Schedule Variance (SV) = Earned Value (EV) − Planned Value (PV)

Planned Value (PV) is the work that had been planned given the authorized budget. For example, if a project has a budget of $500,000, and it had been planned that 50% of the project would be accomplished by a certain date, then PV will be equal to $250,000 on that date.

A negative Schedule Variance means that the project is behind schedule, while a positive Schedule Variance means that the project is ahead of schedule.

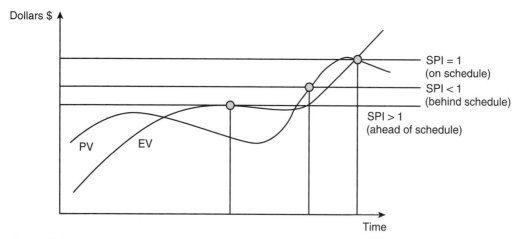

Figure 2.4
Schedule Performance Index.

To illustrate this, let's assume that instead of accomplishing 50% as had been planned, the team only achieved 40% of the work, in which case EV would be equal to $200,000.

As a result, SV will be equal to −$50,000 ($200,000−$250,000), which means that the project is behind schedule.

Schedule Performance Index (SPI)

SPI is close to CPI in principle, but unlike the CPI, which tracks the cost performance, the SPI tracks the project schedule.

The formula to calculate the Schedule Performance Index (SPI) is as follows.

Schedule Performance Index (SPI) = Earned Value (EV)/Planned Value (PV)

As with the CPI, the SPI is a ratio, which should be between 0 and 2 as shown in Figure 2.4.

An SPI greater than 1 indicates that the team performs better than scheduled, whereas an SPI less than 1 implies that the project team is behind.

So, an SPI equal to 0.70 means that the project team is way off target.

Project Budget Forecasting

The idea behind project budget forecasting is to use Earned Value (EV) to forecast what your project will actually cost when it is done.

For the valuable help they can bring to the project team, we will review three of these values in the following pages, namely the EAC (Estimate at Completion), the ETC (Estimate to Complete), and the VAC (Variance at Completion).

Estimate at Completion (EAC)

If you know your cost performance index (CPI), you should be able to forecast how much your total project cost will be when completed. The formula is

EAC = BAC/CPI (with BAC being the original budget)

So, if BAC = $200,000 and CPI = 0.85, then EAC = $200,000/0.8 = $235,294.

What this means is that originally you had asked for $200,000, but given the current state of the project, it is likely to cost a total of $235,294, or $35,294 more than originally had been planned.

Estimate to Complete (ETC)

The Estimate to Complete (ETC) is how much money will be needed to complete the project for the work that remains to be done, the same thing as indicated by the Scrum Burndown chart. The formula is

ETC = EAC − AC.

Assume that EAC = $500,000, which is the total amount you will have to spend on this project. Now, if AC, the actual cost of what you have already spent, is equal to $450,000, then ETC will cost you another $50,000 (ETC=$500,000−$450,000) to get the remaining work be done.

Variance at Completion (VAC)

The Variance at Completion (VAC) calculates the difference between what had been planned, the original budget (as indicated by BAC), and what is estimated at completion (EAC). The formula is

VAC = BAC − EAC

So, if BAC = $25,000 and EAC = $13,400, then VAC = $11,600 ($25,000−13,400). This means that someone must come up with $11,600 to pay for the variance.

Summary

Unlike many books on Agile or Scrum in which almost no mention is made of finance, we believe that knowing the basics of finance can only enhance your chance of a successful dialogue with business management.

Without wanting to turn this book into a treatise on finance, we have chosen to cover in this chapter only a few useful concepts and formulas relating to project finance. Some are to justify project investments, some to calculate the project costs, and some are to be used during project execution to estimate how much more you will need to spend to get the job done.

As software professionals, most of us will not need to become experts in finance, but we believe you will, at least, need the basics, which are covered here. Knowing some of these essential financial concepts and formulas will help you to better communicate with business management.

A few key things to remember about EV are that:

- When it comes to variance, it is EV subtracted by either AC (cost) or PV (schedule).

- When it comes to index, it is EV divided by either AC (cost) or PV (schedule).

- When the variance is negative, it is bad, but if the variance is positive, it is good.

- When the index is less than 1, it is bad, but when the index is more than 1, it is good.

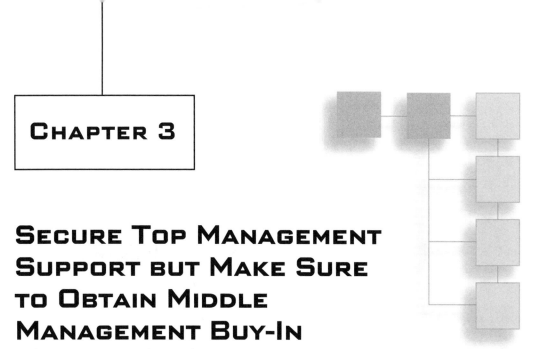

CHAPTER 3

SECURE TOP MANAGEMENT SUPPORT BUT MAKE SURE TO OBTAIN MIDDLE MANAGEMENT BUY-IN

Unless you are working alone or in a small start-up company, the project manager will have many people to deal with, within an organization, to move the project forward (see Figure 3.1).

Even though Scrum does not have a project manager per se, that does not mean that project management has been abandoned. For those of us who have some deeper experience with Scrum, we know that project management responsibility in Scrum is simply transformed and divided among the product owner, the team, and the ScrumMaster. You can learn more about this in Ken Schwaber's seminal book, *Agile Project Management with Scrum, p.15.*

What Ken says in his book is that rather than having one single project manager (or ScrumMaster) taking care of all the interaction with the outside actors like in the old command and control environment, the responsibility of project management is now shared by the development team, the product owner, and the ScrumMaster as shown in Figure 3.2.

We will talk about the specifics of the ScrumMaster's and the product owner's responsibility in leading and managing a Scrum project in a later chapter. This chapter is mainly to raise your awareness about what you should do when interacting with the rest of the company, especially if your company is new to Scrum or if it has not chosen to adopt Scrum enterprise-wide on a large-scale.

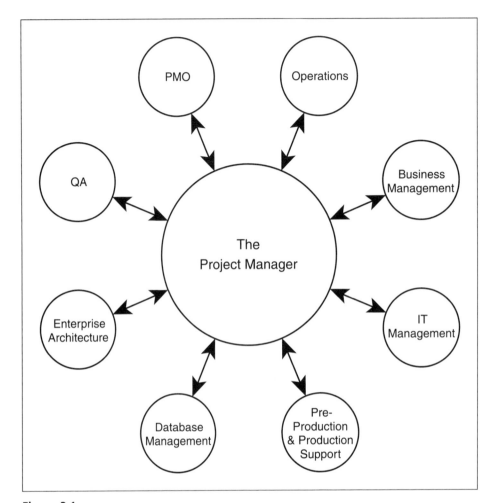

Figure 3.1
The traditional role of project manager within a company.

As we discussed in Chapter 2, you will need to speak to top business or IT management in terms they can understand (the language of finance), because they will have to give the green light before you can do anything else.

WORKING WITH TOP BUSINESS MANAGEMENT

When interacting with top business management, such as your CEO, President, CFO, or Senior Vice President of a Business Unit, we recommend that you avoid talking about how much Scrum will help you to build better software faster.

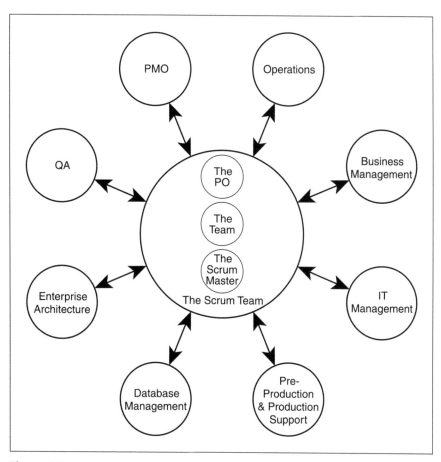

Figure 3.2
The changing role of project management with Scrum.

As business executives, they will be polite, but they will ultimately reject you while wondering why someone has ever hired you into the company—who wastes their time talking in general terms, rather than presenting the ideas to them in financial terms that they can more easily understand.

Although building better software or improving programmer productivity is important to executives, they are more interested in the company's overall market share, large scale savings, or overall profit margin.

So, despite your excitement for Scrum, do not let yourself get carried away talking with top business management about how wonderful your software will be or how fast you will be able to build it if they will only allow you to use Scrum.

Instead, always relate your technical prowess and passion to an executive's financial concerns in terms of numbers or at least to their overall business strategy.

Whenever you are talking to anyone in the organization, you must consider the point of view of the listener and speak to those concerns.

To help you better interact with top business executives, we have reproduced an example of the balance scorecard (Figure 3.3) for a fictional company, quite similar to one you may encounter in real life situations. The balance scorecard is a well-known concept among business executives.

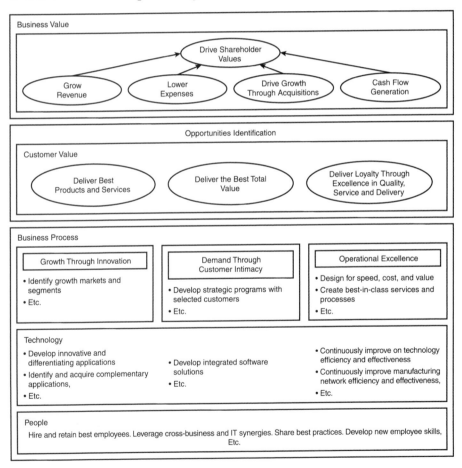

Figure 3.3
Top business management balance scorecard.

The balanced scorecard for this fictional company shows what top business management considers to be their main business goals and strategy.

In this example, their goals are to:

1. Grow revenue

2. Lower expenses

3. Drive growth through acquisitions

4. Generate cash flows

What follows is their strategy in terms of customer value and what they think the company should do in terms of business processes, IT projects, and human resources.

Knowing how IT projects will fit into your business executives' overall vision and strategy will help you communicate more effectively to them how your project will contribute to the overall strategy of the firm. Always remember that it is important to relate your project's contribution to the company in terms of finance, which is the language of business. Your executives will thank you for that.

WORKING WITH TOP IT MANAGEMENT

In some companies, the program management office (PMO) is not considered part of top IT management. We have listed it here because it is the Chief Information Officer (CIO)'s main representative in the IT department's effort to align IT on business strategies and to continuously improve and track IT performance.

Program Management Office

As the group responsible for IT performance and alignment with a company's business needs and strategy, the program management office, or PMO, is the first group that you should try to meet and work with.

If you understand the PMO's concerns, you should not have any difficulty turning the PMO into an ally, since its mission is to ensure that IT projects bring the most value to the business. This is, after all, what we all have learned the product owner's mission should be on a Scrum project, right?

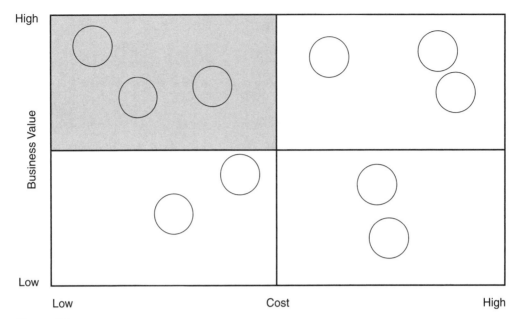

Figure 3.4
IT business prioritization matrix.

Figure 3.4 shows one of the many matrices maintained by the PMO. The upper left quadrant is the most desirable because it has high business value and low cost. Use this matrix to quantify your project in order to gain a realistic view of the true business value and cost associated with your project. If it falls into the upper left quadrant for high business value and lower cost, your project has a good chance of being approved.

The PMO's other responsibility is IT project governance. Figure 3.5 should give you an idea of the overall process that goes from the time a project is approved until the post-implementation meeting where the project is reconciled with the original targets to ensure the project's goals were met. So, verify your product owner has solid criteria and goals for you to work with to ensure that you can meet their expectations.

WORKING WITH IT MIDDLE MANAGEMENT

Before we get too deep into the discussion about the functions of middle level or operational management, we should make it clear that these are the people whose job will be most impacted by your project(s) in terms of daily

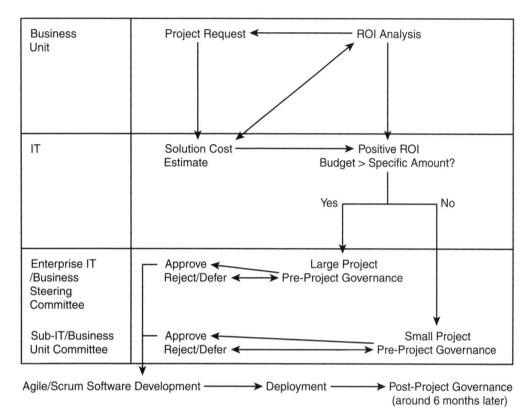

Figure 3.5
PMO IT project governance.

responsibility. It is, therefore, necessary that you obtain their buy-in to successfully get the project to the finish line.

Remember that middle management's role is not to rock the boat, but to keep it going.

Their concern is to keep issues to a minimum, look like a winning team, and do things at the right time.

Change is always difficult and needs to be properly managed. You, as the person who brings change along with your project, should know the process of how people normally experience change (Figure 3.6). You must know how to communicate with middle management and give them enough reasons to think that these changes will result in something good for them.

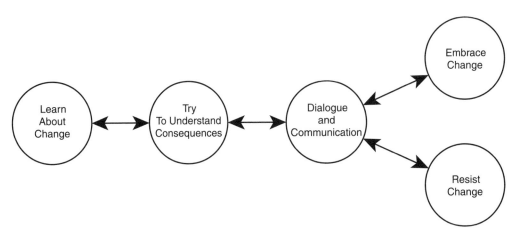

Figure 3.6
Stages of the change process.

When people hear that change is coming, the best you can expect is that they will try to understand the consequences those changes will bring with them. Hopefully, their response will not be outright fear and resistance.

Next, depending on the quality and quantity of communication and information they receive, they will either resist, directly or indirectly, or they will embrace change if they think it will be good for their work or career. So, when communicating, keep the interests of the other party in mind to ensure that your communication produces the result you hope for and provides you the support you need from these people.

You should plan to contact, stay in touch with, and communicate with the people who will be affected by the change your project will bring, and you should communicate in such a way that they can clearly see that this is good for them.

Quality Assurance

Given the importance and changing nature of testing with Scrum, you will want to build a good relationship with the Quality Assurance team.

Depending on whether your company is already set up for common Scrum practice, mainly in terms of testing infrastructure, you may need to do more or less here. If Scrum is part of the culture, then you may only need to know the procedures and learn to follow and leverage them.

If Scrum isn't already part of the company's culture, you might need to explain Scrum to Quality Assurance management, especially to those who are in charge of testing, and ask for their support. You might request that they make someone available from their team to work on your project throughout the life cycle, and/ or help set up the appropriate testing environment for your project, which you will learn more about in Chapter 9, "The Importance of Automated, Regression, and Integration Tests." This way you can be ready quickly with automated, regression, and continuous integration testing.

Operations Management

Like it or not, you cannot avoid Operations management. They are the people who are in control of all the pre-production and/or production activities. Make sure to pay them a visit to explain to them what you need, so that the code you deliver at the end of every single Sprint will be to the level they expect. First and foremost, remember that the development and operations departments have different, and sometimes opposite, objectives.

The objective for you, as part of the development organization, is to produce a continuous stream of well-perceived value to the business. But in so doing, you bring about change; whereas the objective of operations is to produce a continuous stream of value while making sure that everything stays stable.

By the very nature of Scrum development, there will be more software releases, often in many smaller updates, as opposed to a few larger ones, which the operations team will need to handle.

Operations will not and cannot drop their control procedures for you just because your updates are small. To do so would lead to an increase in interruptions in running business systems. The operations team simply has to remain as strict as ever before applying their pre-production verification tests. The entire change process has to remain intact, even for smaller updates.

So, unless your company is ready for some sort of self-service deployment or more precisely the automation of the self-service deployment process, try to work out some sort of schedule arrangement with operations since that will help them deal with frequent updates. In return, they will help as well as thank you for it.

In time, operations will find that it has more time to complete its other work and will be glad to support change for the development department while, at the same time, retaining all the control over their production environment.

Enterprise Architecture (EA)

If your company has a group called enterprise architecture, try to find out where they fit in or how much clout they have in the IT organization.

Take the time to understand the concerns of this group and work with them to show how your application will fit into their enterprise architecture.

Find out what they need from you but avoid being dragged to many meetings without any tangible results to show.

If the enterprise architecture team is seriously in the process of moving towards a Service-Oriented Architecture (SOA), your company's EA overall diagram may look like that shown Figure 3.7.

In this case, make sure to explain your needs to the enterprise architecture team in a timely manner and request that they deliver or help deliver the other services, so that you can get all the pieces connected before the end of the iteration or deadline.

If, however, your company is still leveraging a more traditional architectural style, then the EA framework might look like that shown in Figure 3.8.

Every layer of the enterprise architecture framework shown in Figure 3.8 can fill a whole book by itself, but for the purpose of this book, let's focus only on the last layer, the data architecture layer.

Whether your background is in data architecture or application architecture, there should be no doubt in your mind that data architecture is an important topic within a company. Data architecture is also an often quite messy issue that leads the enterprise data warehouse team to produce reports that cannot be

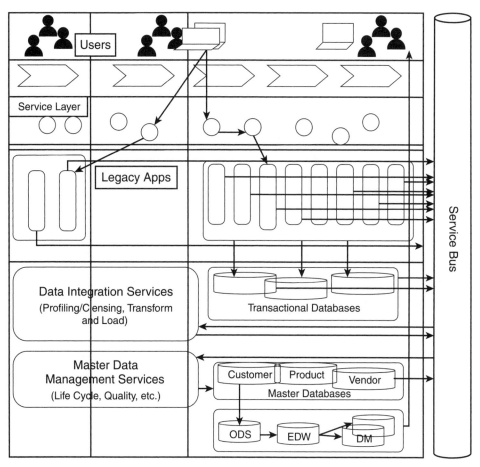

Figure 3.7
Your project and the SOA enterprise architecture.

counted on. There are many examples of this, but the most commonly cited one is that the values of the reports often vary from one department to another, even when it comes to the same so-called sales figures.

Based on the illustration in Figure 3.9, there should be no surprise that the reports are often conflicting and the data unreliable.

This situation often frustrates business executives, especially the CFO. As a result, IT usually tries to turn it into something more organized like the diagram in Figure 3.10, by creating a new Master Data Management layer, or MDM for short.

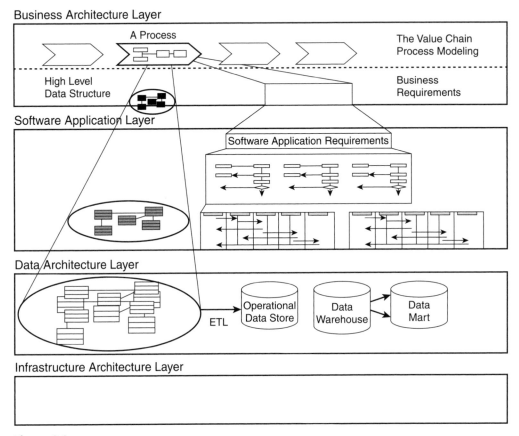

Figure 3.8
Your project and the traditional enterprise architecture.

You need to know what your company's enterprise data architecture currently looks like and what the future enterprise data architecture plan is.

Knowing this will help you make sure that your new application's data architecture will be designed in such a way that it fits into or contributes to the creation of the future enterprise data architecture.

As you will see in Chapter 6, "The Influence of Architecture Vision on Team Velocity and Software Quality," and Chapter 7, "From Architecture Vision to Release and Sprints Planning to Parallel Software Development," the architectural approach we recommend is very much based on core business data elements, and is therefore stable. This is why it can very much help contribute

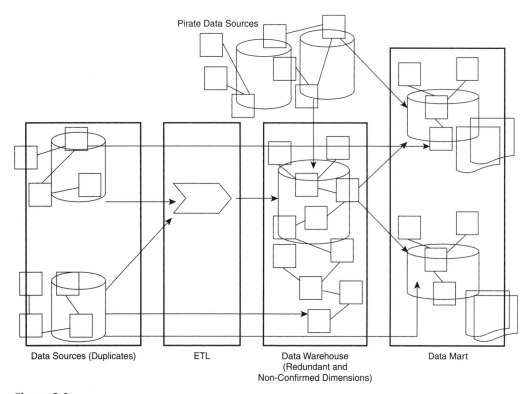

Pirate Data Sources

Data Sources (Duplicates)   ETL   Data Warehouse   Data Mart
                                                (Redundant and
                                            Non-Confirmed Dimensions)

Figure 3.9
Current enterprise data chaos.

to the creation of the Master Data Management (MDM) layer (Figure 3.11), a key ingredient to better enterprise data or information management.

TURNING YOUR DIRECT MANAGEMENT INTO AN ALLY

As known in the industry, the goal of middle management is to keep going and to avoid rocking the boat, so unless you report to the CIO or CEO, make sure that you spend time with your middle manager to ensure that she fully understands Scrum and what it entails.

If your manager doesn't understand how Scrum works and your project doesn't go well or lags behind schedule, there is a risk that your direct management will want to revert to the old command and control style very quickly.

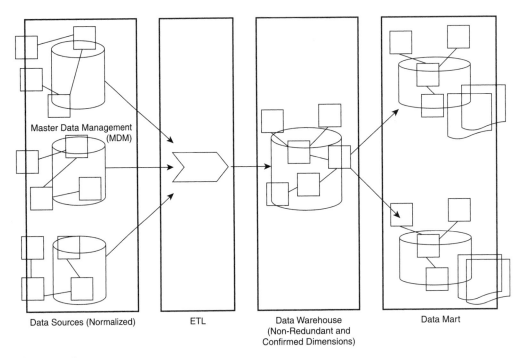

Figure 3.10
Re-architecting the enterprise data architecture.

You must do what you can to educate your management before you start: about what Scrum is, how Scrum works during the daily execution of the project, and how it works when things go well and how it works when things do not go well.

SUMMARY

Besides the obvious need for you to secure agreement from top business management for your project funding, it will be critical for you to gain middle management buy-in, as it is with these same people that you, as part of the Scrum team, interact with most on a day-to-day basis. It is, as the popular saying goes, where the rubber meets the road. These people will either make or break your project.

Unlike the dialogue with business management, which is based mainly on financial numbers, the relationship with middle management requires more

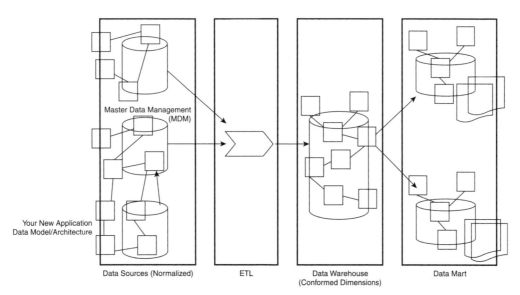

Figure 3.11
Fitting into the new enterprise data architecture.

finesse. Finances are the concern of executives in your company. Middle managers are more concerned with workload, recognition, and job safety, to name a few.

Before you start your project, and while working on your project, do not just inform middle management of the changes that will take place as you implement Scrum; try also to help them with the new workload or the new changes. This, along with an effective communication strategy, will help you obtain their support, a necessary condition for your project's success.

For this same reason, remember to work closely with the enterprise architecture group to ensure that your new application architecture fits into the enterprise architecture group's plan and vision, especially with regard to the data architecture, which is often in a chaotic situation in many companies and a headache for the CFO.

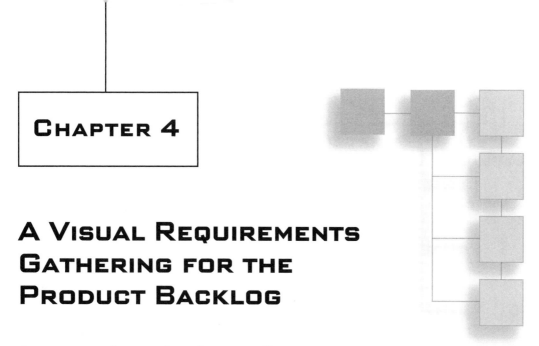

CHAPTER 4

A VISUAL REQUIREMENTS GATHERING FOR THE PRODUCT BACKLOG

Assume now that you have been so effective in presenting your project to top business management that they have given your project their full support, and you are eager to move forward. What else do you think you still need to have for your project?

The answer is a good product backlog and, to create this backlog, a good way to capture requirements in the form of user stories, which are called in this case Product Backlog Items (PBI).

Below is an approach we have used to help many teams capture user stories for their product backlog. Given the complexity of some other techniques, it is a small contribution we are making to the Agile community, hoping that you will find it useful, as many people do.

A NEW VISUAL REQUIREMENTS GATHERING PROCESS FOR AGILE AND SCRUM

This two-step process first helps identify the stakeholders and their goals. Then, using a "forest and tree" analogy, it helps gather requirements for users who represent the stakeholders and links those requirements back to the stakeholders' goals for prioritization.

First Step: Identify the Stakeholders and Their Goals

Identify the different categories of stakeholders of the new software product.

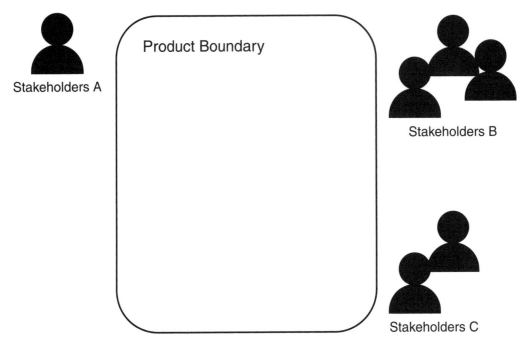

Figure 4.1
Product boundary and its stakeholders.

When you first start your project, make an effort to identify all parties who have an interest or stake in, or need for, your software product (see Figure 4.1).

Next, inventory stakeholders and their goals. Identify their goals by asking questions such as "What are your business objectives or goals?" "Why would you need the new software product?" and "How do you measure your goals accomplishment?"

The SMART Rules

There are many ways to help identify goals, but one of them is known as the SMART rules, which we used extensively to help set goals for many teams:

- **Specific**: Everyone will have the same understanding as to what the goals are.

- **Measurable**: We can objectively determine if the goals have been reached.

Stakeholders	Goals	Measures
1. Business Development	Increase market share by 15% to reach 200,000 customers by year end	Increase the number of users by 10,000 every month
2. Customer Service	Reduce customer calls by 20% every quarter	Number of calls received at the Call Center
	Reduce the time to resolve a complaint by 50% of the current time	The time spent over the phone with the customer for one single complaint

Figure 4.2
Stakeholders' goals and measurements. Measures can be criteria such as cost savings (30%), number of service calls (35%), or the number of registered users (35%).

- **Achievable**: The stakeholders agree as to what the goals are.
- **Realistic**: We shall be able to achieve the goals for the project with the resources we have.
- **Time-Based**: We will be given enough time to achieve the goals.

An example of the stakeholders' goals and measurements is presented in Figure 4.2.

Second Step: Gather Requirements for the Product Backlog

During this step, you will meet with the stakeholders' representative users, each in her individual role, to try to understand the needs of some of the users and turn those needs into requirements for the new software product.

Our technique, called "the trees and the forest" and illustrated in Figure 4.3, is visual and easy to use.

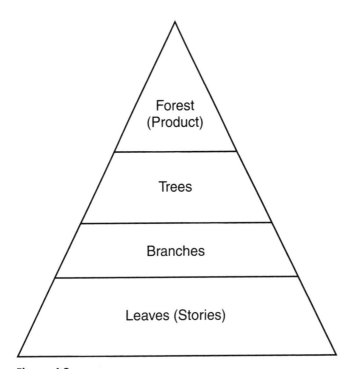

Figure 4.3
The trees and the forest analogy.

Start at the forest, or overall product, level. Ask yourself what your new product should be composed of. In other words, how many "trees" should be in your "forest"?

Next, further divide a tree into its branches (Figure 4.5).

Then, divide the branch into leaves as shown in Figure 4.6.

In addition to going top down like this, you may also ask the users to list all the stories, or leaves, they can think of first, then try to group them together, using this tree and forest analogy to get from the leaves to the branches, then from the branches to the trees, and then from the trees to the forest.

In the same way that the product owner can use the SMART rules to verify the stakeholders' goals, he and the team can use the CUTFIT rules listed in the next section to verify that their stories, or PBIs, are properly written, ready for the development team to estimate and develop.

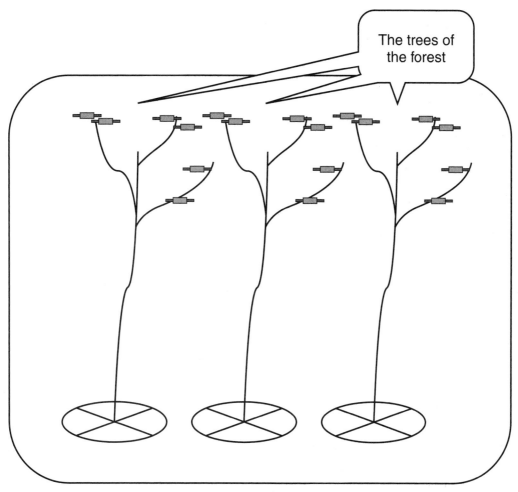

Figure 4.4
A view of the forest.

The CUTFIT Rules

There are many ways to help verify that the requirements are well written, but one of them is known as the CUTFIT rules, which we used extensively to help validate the user stories.

- **Consistent**: A consistent requirement does not conflict with another requirement.

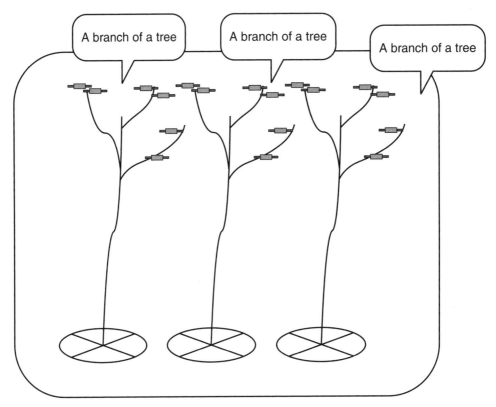

Figure 4.5
Tree branches.

- **Unambiguous**: The reviewers of a requirement statement should be able to draw only one interpretation of it, regardless of their role.

- **Testable**: We should be able to create test cases for a requirement. If a requirement is not testable, trying to determine whether it is correctly implemented is a matter of opinion.

- **Feasible**: It must be possible to implement each requirement within the known capabilities and limitations of the system environment.

- **Independent**: No user story (PBI) should be dependent on another user story (PBI).

- **Traceable**: You should be able to link each requirement to a user and to his goals.

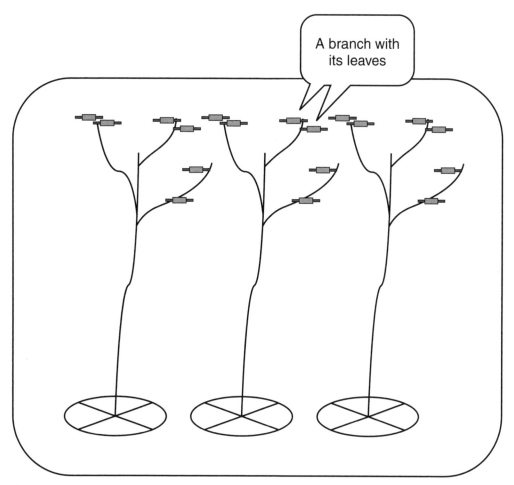

Figure 4.6
A branch with its leaves.

A question often asked of us is how someone knows whether she is done with writing a user story, without having to flesh out all the details, as we had traditionally done within the waterfall environment. The answer we usually give is that one can stop writing the story when:

1. The user cannot decompose that story into more end-to-end stories, meaning stories that touch all the layers of the application.

2. The team can derive tasks, ranging from 4 to 8 hours, from those stories to start their development work.

3. When the team can start estimating the point of that story using the criteria-based technique we will be presenting in Chapter 5 to estimate the number of points of the story.

An Example

Following is a simple example that illustrates our visual requirements gathering (or elicitation) process, not to show all of its strengths (especially in helping correct errors made with other requirements gathering techniques), but only to show how it is easy to use.

Let's start with Figure 4.7, which shows the product boundary and its stakeholders.

Next, by talking with the stakeholders, we can identify some of the key goals, as listed in Figure 4.8, which also shows how they can be measured.

By following the technique as laid down in the previous section, we can identify three trees (or areas of interest) for this new software product, as demonstrated in Figure 4.9.

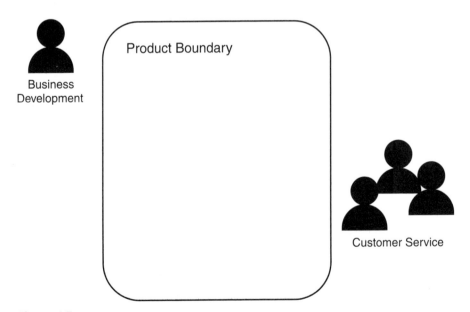

Figure 4.7
Product boundary and its stakeholders.

Stakeholders	Goals	Measures
1. Business Development	Allow customers to register without calling customer service	The GUI should allow users to register in less than 2 minutes
	Allow customers to log conference room issues with our software by themselves	Allow customers to log conference room issues with our software in less than one minute
2. Customer Service	Allow customers to be billed to a different bank than their own	The system should allow customers to edit their billing info 24x7

Figure 4.8
User's goals and their measurements.

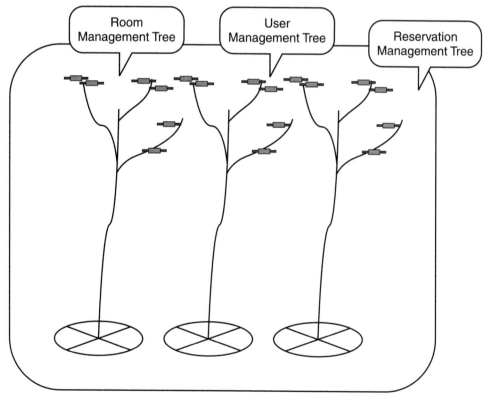

Figure 4.9
Private Room Reservation software product and its trees.

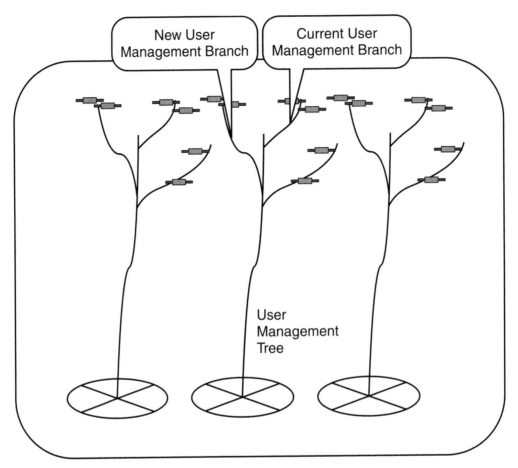

Figure 4.10
User Management tree and its branches.

More specifically, the trees in this software product are called user management, room management, and reservation management.

By looking at the "User Management Tree," we can see that it has two branches, the "New User Management Branch" and the "Current User Management Branch," as can be seen in Figure 4.10.

Finally, by looking at all the leaves on all the branches, we should be able to list them all as shown in Figure 4.11.

As to Figure 4.12, it is how the software product will look like with all the leaves, all the branches, and all the trees within the forest.

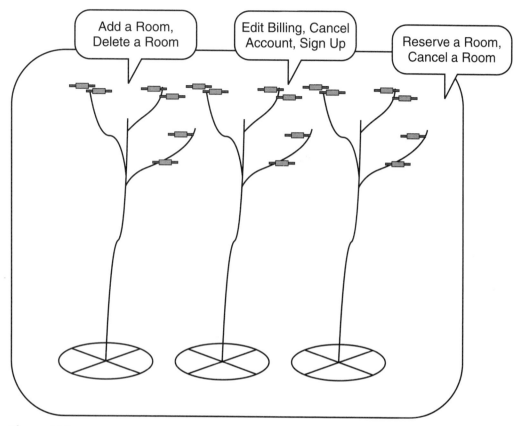

Figure 4.11
The Private Room Reservation software product and its leaves.

As a result of their prioritization, we can assume that the stakeholders will first want to focus on the user stories that bring in the most value to their company or business unit.

After this decision is made, a story card, as shown in Figure 4.13, can be used to describe some high level tasks that the users would want to perform along with all the test cases ("verify that ....") that should be performed for that user story.

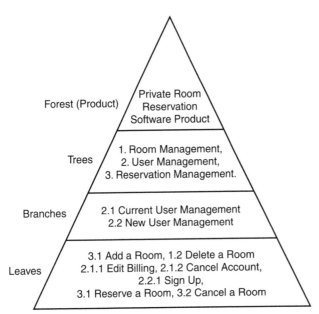

Figure 4.12
The trees and forest approach applied to software product development.

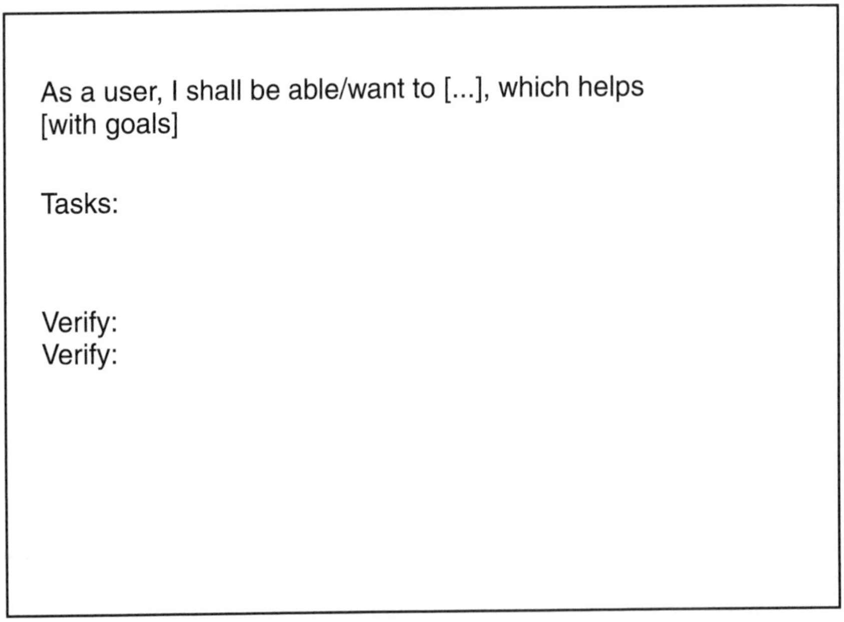

As a user, I shall be able/want to [...], which helps
[with goals]

Tasks:

Verify:
Verify:

Figure 4.13
An original story card.

SUMMARY

One of the Scrum project team's most critical tasks is to identify the stakeholders and their goals in order to capture requirements for these stakeholders' representative users, each in their specific role.

While different approaches exist, we offered here a simple and visual two-step process which all of us can use. The first step is to identify the stakeholders and their goals. The second step is to identify the users who will represent these stakeholders, along with their requirements. We did all of this using a visual technique called the Forest and the Tree approach.

To verify that the stakeholders' goals are well written, they can use a series of rules called the SMART rules. These rules require that the goal be specific, measurable, achievable, realistic, and time-based, meaning achievable within a given timeframe.

To verify that the requirements (user stories or PBIs) are properly written and ready for development, the product owner and the team can use the CUTFIT rules. These rules require that the story point be consistent, unambiguous, testable, feasible, independent, and traceable.

When asked how someone knows if she is done with writing user stories for release and sprints planning, meaning without having to flesh out all the details, a three-point test was given in this chapter to help make that determination.

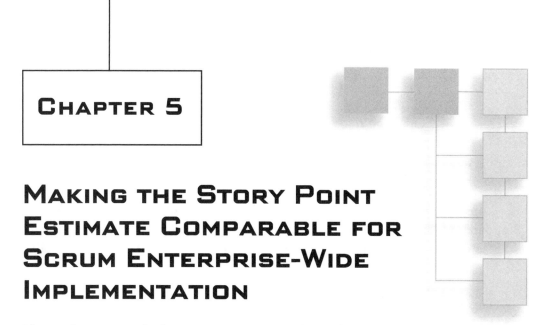

CHAPTER 5

MAKING THE STORY POINT ESTIMATE COMPARABLE FOR SCRUM ENTERPRISE-WIDE IMPLEMENTATION

If you have ever had any experience with Agile or Scrum estimation and planning, you should have surely heard or read about planning poker. In a nutshell, planning poker is an estimation technique used by agile project teams to collectively estimate the relative size of their stories using a measurement called story point.

To be effective with planning poker, the project team is supposed to be composed of generalists who have experience with the different software development tasks such as requirements, analysis, design, coding, and testing.

PROBLEMS WITH A NON-COMPARABLE STORY POINT

As long as Agile or Scrum was implemented on some isolated project and there was no need for an enterprise-wide implementation of Agile or Scrum across many teams, everything was acceptable. But now that the subject of enterprise-wide implementation of Agile or Scrum has become of interest, it is clear that the fact that the story point is not comparable between the different teams risks having a negative impact on a successful enterprise-wide implementation of Agile or Scrum.

To be clear, what we are referring to here is not some unhealthy or unnecessary comparison or competition among teams. What we're simply saying is that when Scrum is deployed across different teams, the least we should expect is to be able to update management when there is a change in a project team composition, as a result of some transfer of personnel, and whether that change will affect the project deadline or not.

Unless you work in a company where you are the only member of the staff, how can you give an estimate to complete (ETC) to business or IT management when members resign from the company or transfer out of a project, if nothing is comparable between different teams?

As a consequence, you can see why it has become a problem for some PMO to plan on an enterprise-wide deployment of Scrum or Agile when the story point, and, therefore, the team velocity as it is based on story point, are not comparable between teams.

CULTURAL PROBLEMS WITH PLANNING POKER

In addition to the above, as Agile and Scrum spread beyond the border of the United States into other countries, we have observed that planning poker does not always work well in non-Western cultures, especially Asian, where we come from. The reason is in many non-Western cultures, the respect for older people and for people in leadership roles often inhibits team members from coming up with an estimate that is different from that of their older or higher ranking team member.

Despite these above shortcomings, we have to say that planning poker has had a very good impact on our community as a whole, especially at the early stage of Scrum or of the Agile movement. This being said, the time seems to have come for us to find another, more objective approach, especially with the need we have for Agile or Scrum enterprise-wide deployment and resource allocation.

AN OBJECTIVE CRITERIA-BASED ESTIMATING PROCESS

It would not be truthful if we said that we invented the estimating approach that follows after many years in a prestigious research lab to impress you. Instead, we will simply say that the approach we present here is a combination of ideas that originated with remarkable professionals we learned from after many years of managing and performing estimation for numerous projects of all kinds. The

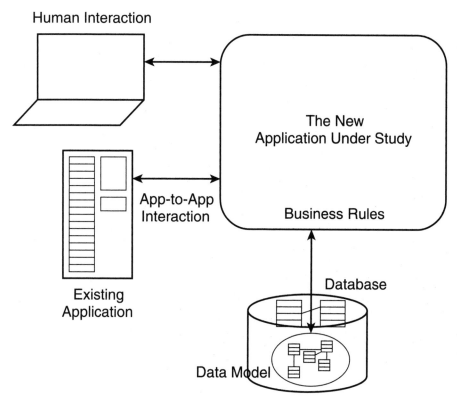

Figure 5.1
Different aspects of an application.

other thing we will say is that this method has worked on real projects that have been actually deployed.

In Figure 5.1, you will see that an application is nothing more than (1) some business users trying to interact with some working code that implements (2) some business rules running against (3) a model containing some business entities, whose values are stored in the physical database (4) which it is to create, read, update, or delete.

So, if we all agree, this is how we are going to estimate the user story or Product Backlog Item, one type at a time (Figure 5.2).

1. Interaction type
2. Business rules

Interaction Type	Description	Value
Simple	Well Defined Interface	1
Average	Dynamic Interface	2
Complex	Human Interaction	3

Figure 5.2
Interaction type.

3. Number of entities manipulated

4. Data to be created, read, updated, and deleted (CRUD)

The table in Figure 5.2 means that if the story you are looking at requires a human interaction, you should give it a value of 3. If it requires, however, only an interaction with another application, according to a well defined protocol, then that user story should get a value of 1 for the interaction.

Next, let's calculate the complexity based on the number of business rules to be applied (Figure 5.3).

Business Rules	Description	Value
Simple	1 Rule	1
Average	1–3 Rules	2
Complex	>3 Rules	3

Figure 5.3
Business rules complexity.

If there is only one business rule, then you should give the story a value of 1. If there is more than one rule but less than three, then that story should get a value of 2. If there are more than three rules, give the story a value of 3.

Although the table in Figure 5.3 on the interaction type is rather obvious, we can already hear your question about what is a business rule. A business rule is a statement that tells you when you may or may not do something.

What then is the difference between a business rule and a business requirement? To simplify, a business requirement is what you need to do to enable the implementation of and compliance with a business rule as dictated by the law or by a company's policy.

Example of a business rule:

A patron should be 18 years or older.

A possible business requirement to enforce this rule:

The patron must be in possession of a valid driver's license or a valid US passport with photo to verify that he is at least 18 years old.

Next, we need to determine the number of data entities needed to execute this user story (Figure 5.4).

The number of entities manipulated means that if the number of data entities is only one, then you should give that story a value of 1, but if it is between two and three, then that story should get a value of 2, and so on.

Entities	Description	Value
Simple	1 Entity	1
Average	1–3 Entities	2
Complex	>3 Entities	3

Figure 5.4
Number of business entities manipulated.

High Level Business Entities

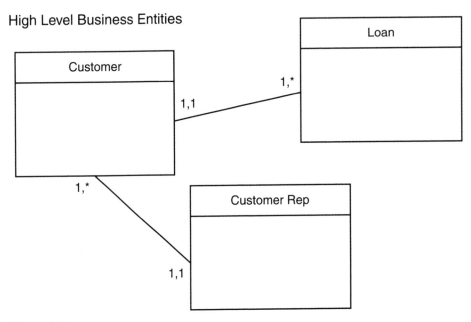

Figure 5.5
A simple data structure with three business entities.

Following is an example of what we mean by business entities. In this small data model (see Figure 5.5), we can see that there are three data entities total, which are 1) the customer, 2) the loan, and 3) the customer representative serving that customer.

Finally, we need to determine the data manipulation (CRUD) factor.

Create, Read, Update, Delete (CRUD), is illustrated in Figure 5.6:

Data Manipulation Type	Description	Value
Simple	Read, Delete	1
Average	Create	2
Complex	Update	3

Figure 5.6
CRUD.

Let's now imagine that one of the user stories is called "add a (conference) room." Let's try together to calculate its Unadjusted Points (UP) before we take into account the project's environment dimensions (ED):

A.   Interaction Type = 3 points
B.   Business rules = 1 point
C.   Number of entities manipulated = 1 point
D.   Create, Read, Update, Delete (CRUD) = 2 points

UP = 7 points (for the Unadjusted Points for the "add a room" story or PBI).

Next, let's take into account the Environment Dimensions (ED), which can have either a negative or positive impact on the team in its effort to deliver the "add a room" story:

1. Organization Dimension

2. Development Infrastructure Dimension

3. Team Dimension

4. Technology Dimension

5. Process Dimension

6. Business Dimension

For each of these dimensions, a higher value indicates higher team ability or capability, whereas a lower or minus value indicates a lower team ability or capability. A zero will mean the lowest score, while a positive value indicates a high level of ability or capability with 2 being the maximum. As you did with the previous tables, you should go through these dimensions, one by one, and see what value you should give to a question.

Toward the end of these tables (Figures 5.7–5.12), you will total the estimate in points for the story for all the environment dimensions (ED). It will vary between 0 for the minimum and 36 for the maximum.

Factor	Value Range (0/2)
1. Have different departments worked successfully together on a Scrum project previously?	
2. Does some strong resistance exist within the organization with regard to Scrum?	
3. Does a great support for Scrum exist between different departments within the company?	

Figure 5.7
Organization dimension.

Factor	Value Range (0/2)
1. Is automatic testing already in place and a common practice?	
2. Is continuous integration testing already in place and a common practice?	
3. Is daily build environment already in place and a common practice?	

Figure 5.8
Development infrastructure dimension.

Depending on this total value, three scenarios will be possible:

1. **If the ED value is between 0 and 11, then the multiplication coefficient C will be 2.** This implies that the environment dimensions are such that the team will not be able deliver as many stories during the Sprint than if the ED score had been higher.

Factor	Value Range (0/2)
1. Is the team completely new to Scrum?	
2. Have the team members successfully worked together before?	
3. Do team members know well and appreciate one another?	

Figure 5.9
Team dimension.

Factor	Value Range (0/2)
1. Is the development team very experienced in the programming language?	
2. Are development team members very experienced in the technology to be employed?	
3. Is a Scrum production environment already ready?	

Figure 5.10
Technology dimension.

2. **If the ED value is between 12 and 23, then the multiplication coefficient C will be 1.** This implies that the environment makes the team job neither difficult nor easy.

3. **If the ED value is between 24 and 36, then the multiplication coefficient C will be ½.** This implies that the environment dimensions are such that the team should be able to deliver more stories during the Sprint.

Factor	Value Range (0/2)
1. Is Scrum the company's adopted process framework?	
2. Is there a good support for Scrum within the company?	
3. Is there strong resistance against Scrum within the company?	

Figure 5.11
Process dimension.

Factor	Value Range (0/2)
1. Is there a Product Owner fully available and completely engaged with the team?	
2. Is the Product Owner familiar with Scrum but has no practical experience?	
3. Has the Product Owner successfully used Scrum before?	

Figure 5.12
Business dimension.

So, to calculate the total value in points for a single story, simply use the following formula:

AP (Adjusted Points) = UP (Unadjusted Points) $\times$ C (Coefficient)

PPS (Points per Story) = (AP $\times$ ED)/36

Example

Let's take the "add a room" feature again and assume that the values of its environment dimensions (ED) are equal to the following coefficient for every dimension listed below:

1.	Organization	= 3
2.	Infrastructure	= 2
3.	Team	= 4
4.	Technology	= 3
5.	Process	= 2
6.	Business	= 4

Adding up all of these values gives us an ED that is equal to 18. Since ED is equal to 18, this would mean, as previously mentioned, that the coefficient of multiplication to be used will be equal to 1.

In other words, the calculation for the story "add a room" will be equal to:

$$AP = UP \times C$$
$$AP = 7 \times 1 = 7$$

(with UP equal to 7 points, as was calculated previously).

Then,

$$PPS = (AP \times ED)/36$$
$$PPS = (7 \times 18)/36 = 126/36 = 3.5 \text{ points.}$$

Using the same formula for every other story or PBI, the table in Figure 5.13 provides the overall estimate for the entire product to be built.

By now, it should be obvious that the advantage of this type of calculation is that it is based on objective criteria; therefore, it is more appropriate for comparison between different teams and even between different members of the same project team.

For what we have just gone through, it looks like we will be able to improve the common story card examples to make them look like that shown in Figure 5.14,

PBIs (Story)	Characteristics				Total UP (Unadjusted Points)	Coefficient	AP (Adjusted Points)	ED (Environment Dimensions)	PPS (=(AP*ED)/36)
	Interaction Type	Business Rules	Entities	Data Manipulation Type					
Sprint 1									
Sign Up	3	1	1	2	7	1	7	12	3.5
Add a Room	3	1	1	2	7	1	7	12	3.5
Delete a Room	3	1	1	3	8	1	8	12	4
Sprint 2									
Edit Billing Information	3	1	1	3	8	1	8	12	4
Cancel Account	3	1	1	3	8	1	8	12	4
Browse Recordings	3	1	1	3	8	1	8	12	4
Total (Sprint 1 + Sprint 2)								108	23

Figure 5.13
Overall estimation matrix.

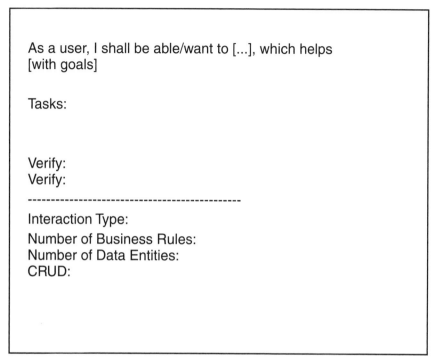

As a user, I shall be able/want to [...], which helps
[with goals]

Tasks:

Verify:
Verify:

Interaction Type:
Number of Business Rules:
Number of Data Entities:
CRUD:

Figure 5.14
Improved story card.

and this, in order to fully take advantage of the estimation process just presented.

SUMMARY

As a consequence of Scrum success, more and more companies are contemplating rolling out Scrum to their entire IT department.

One of the impediments to this is the fact that the story point value is unfortunately not comparable between teams. With the weight of the velocity so different from one team to another, you can see why it has become a problem for many Agile PMOs to plan an enterprise-wide deployment of Scrum.

In this chapter, we offered a new technique based on an objective criteria-based estimating process in the form of a series of relatively straightforward tables to guide the team in their effort to estimate the different stories or PBIs. As simple as it is, this method allows us to make objective comparisons among teams as well as among different members of the same Scrum team.

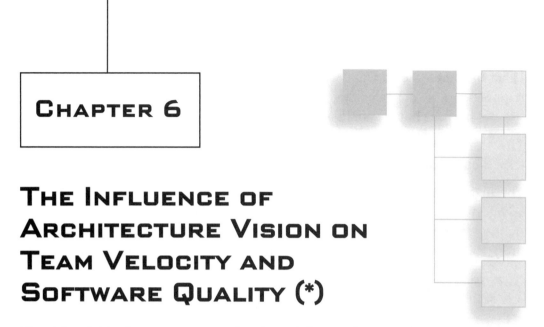

CHAPTER 6

THE INFLUENCE OF ARCHITECTURE VISION ON TEAM VELOCITY AND SOFTWARE QUALITY (*)

The title of this chapter may sound technical, but we hope we have presented the information in such a way that even the nontechnical person can understand the concepts covered in this chapter.

Because it is very important for everyone on the Scrum team to understand what is meant by architecture and architecture vision, let's take a few minutes to define what we mean by these two terms before we move forward.

Imagine for a moment that you are trying to pay for the construction of your dream house (your new software product). Of course, you would not want the construction crew to just show up one day in front of your empty lot and start their building work (coding).

You would first want to meet with the builder team members to tell them what your vision and needs are for the house (the software product). You would tell them, for instance, that your vision is to have a two-story house with as many glass windows as possible (user stories or requirements).

You might also tell them that you plan on having one more child in addition to the two children you already have (another requirement). As for your other requirements (software product requirements), you might also say that you want the children to live downstairs (a constraint) because you cannot bear the noise made by children running and jumping around over your head.

What the builder team will do upon hearing these expressions of your needs or requirements is to create some kind of drawing (architecture vision), at a high level, of how the house should look and how the main elements will be arranged.

This is how the builder (software developer) is going to get some idea of what they should do and where they should do it (architecture built over time).

The high level drawing resulting from this vision of needs is what we call an architecture vision, or high level architecture blueprint, while the end result of the team's construction work will be the house architecture (software architecture), some sort of main frame supporting the house as a whole.

Now, going back to what we were discussing at the beginning of this chapter, one of the most interesting things we have observed on different Scrum projects is that team velocity (the number of user stories the project team can deliver per sprint) often fluctuates for quite a while. And the more complex the project, the more team velocity is going to fluctuate, resulting very often in the reduction of the team velocity and, therefore, their ability to deliver.

There may be many reasons for this but one of the main causes, from an architecture perspective, is that teams are often busy trying to figure out or fix their software architecture on the go. Because of this, their velocity often fluctuates as seen in Figure 6.1.

If you were to build a small website or trivial application (a dog house to continue with the construction metaphor), this fixing may not be too time consuming, but if you are building a large application, these fixes on the go can take a lot of effort and time. They might also cause some of the functionalities previously delivered to need to be redesigned and all the tests to be rerun. The tests themselves might also need to be modified prior to being run again.

Just a few years ago many software teams were excited about drawing architecture and design diagrams using all state-of-the-art tools and UML for Object-Oriented Analysis and Design (OOAD). UML for OOAD is a good technique, but sometimes, too much is too much, especially when all of that hard work only results in beautiful paper documentation and not enough working software.

But having no design at all, even in intent, will be just as harmful to the team productivity and effectiveness, possibly more so.

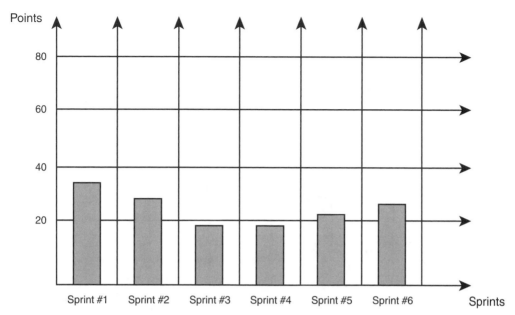

Figure 6.1
Velocity fluctuations due to lack of an architecture intent.

The Importance of Architecture Vision

Scrum or not, you should have guessed by now that a good architecture vision is a key element in software development, even if you have to build it as you go.

With a clear architecture vision, something similar to what others call architecture intent, what happens is that the team may be somewhat slow at the start of the release or sprint. However, their velocity usually goes back up quite quickly and stays at a pretty good level as seen in Figure 6.2. This increases the team confidence and ability to perform over the long run.

From a technical perspective, where there is no architectural vision, what the developers normally get from the Product Owner is a big chunk of user stories (Figure 6.3) to work with without any idea of what the final product will look like or even how the different components will fit together.

From there, the reason team velocity fluctuates so much is because the team will be tempted to try to move all the small rectangles (representing the user stories), very often one by one, into their proper locations. Figures 6.4, 6.5, 6.6, and 6.7 illustrate the time and effort it will take the team to work without architecture vision.

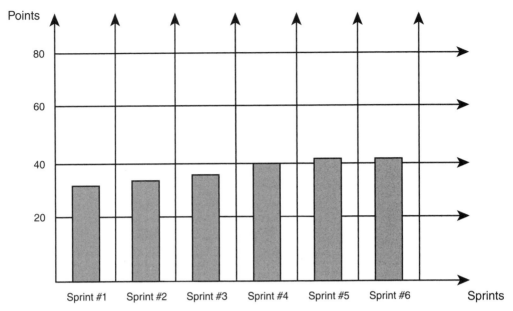

Figure 6.2
A more consistent and increasing velocity with the existence of an architecture intent.

What is interesting to observe is that their effort will ultimately lead them to an architecture (Figure 6.7) that is the same as the architecture which the team could have laid down had they decided to spend a little time at the beginning, figuring out the architecture vision first and not hurrying to get into the sprints with all their detailed stories.

HOW TO IDENTIFY ARCHITECTURE VISION

In order to arrive at this architecture vision, there are two things the team can do. One is to look at the product vision and goal to identify the main business data that would support that product vision, or pertain to that business domain, as some experts put it.

An alternative would be to use the visual high-level requirements gathering technique presented in Chapter 4, "A Visual Requirements Gathering for the Product Backlog," to see which core user-visible stories share the same common business data grouping. For example, all book reservation stories should have some common data related to the book and its characteristics.

Presentation Tier	Application Logic Tier	Business Logic Tier	Data Access Tier	Database Tier

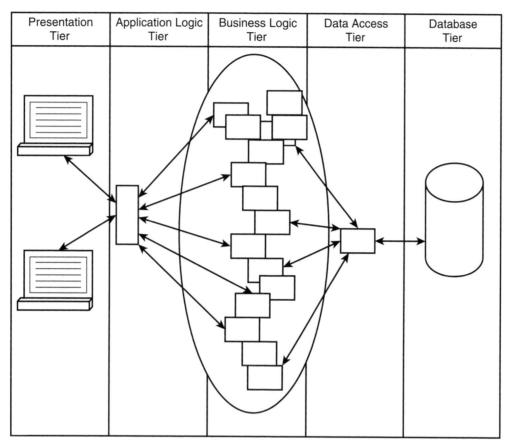

Figure 6.3
Coding application without an architecture plan or intent.

This does not mean that all the user stories with the same data should not necessarily be built together, but they should at least be candidates for being built together.

Following this strategy, the team should be able to identify user stories that can be clustered based on common business, therefore stable, data elements as shown in Figure 6.8, with the core elements being in the middle ring.

After this first grouping, the team will want to split up the stories even more, to separate the ones that are to be created from the ones that are to be updated, read, or deleted. This is illustrated in Figure 6.9.

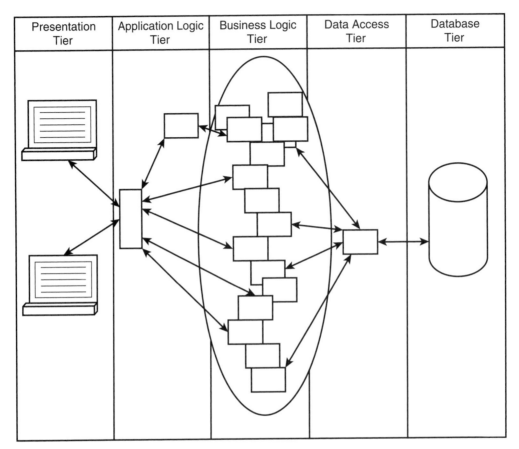

Figure 6.4
Figuring out the architecture during sprint #2.

If they wanted to, the team could next split up the user stories one step further, as shown in Figure 6.10.

The advantage of all of this additional effort is that the team can eventually organize the development in parallel or concurrently, as shown in Figure 6.11. This is similar to the way teams organize their work in kanban, a lean technique, famous for its contribution to Toyota Production System (TPS), and which has attracted quite a bit of interest in software development, especially in software maintenance and support.

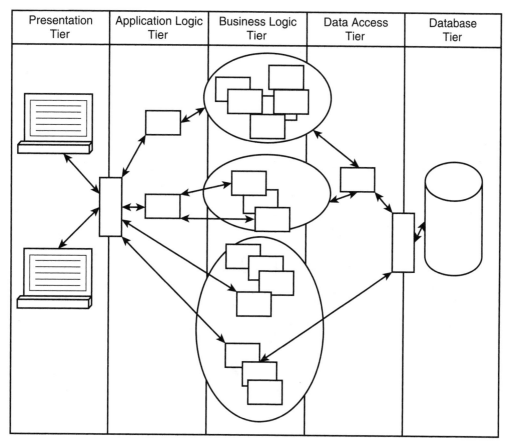

Figure 6.5
Figuring out the architecture during sprint #3.

In addition to this benefit, another advantage of organizing the work by common data elements is that as long as the core data elements are identified and worked on first, the product owner can re-prioritize, switching between detailed user stories as shown in Figures 6.12 and 6.13, without this re-prioritization having an impact on the team velocity. This is true as long as the team had laid down the data foundation by doing all the creations for all the base data entities first.

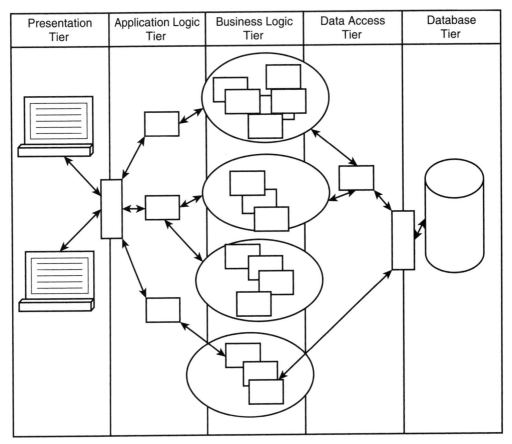

Figure 6.6
Figuring out the architecture during sprint #4.

ANOTHER BENEFIT OF HAVING AN ARCHITECTURE VISION

In addition to the previous benefits, identifying common business data early on can also bring in an additional benefit to the team in that it will likely help the team lay down some kind of good and stable data architecture. This is essential for good data warehouse reporting. Unless your application is the only one that your company has, this will help your application easily fit into the enterprise data architecture along with the rest of the company's applications.

Presentation Tier	Application Logic Tier	Business Logic Tier	Data Access Tier	Database Tier

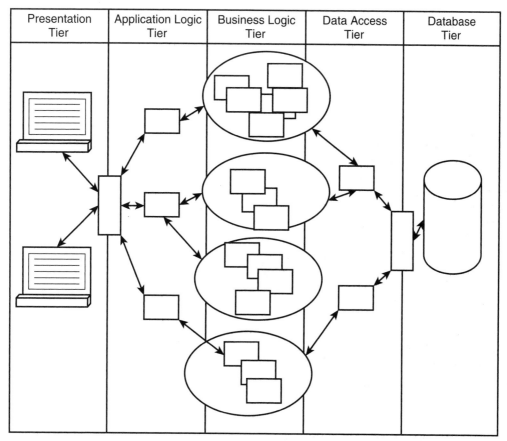

Figure 6.7
Figuring out the architecture during sprint #5.

As before, you have here two possible ways to create the data architecture for your library application. The first is to do it horizontally as shown in Figures 6.14 and especially 6.15. In Figure 6.15, an extension has been made to the first data architecture layer by adding "Teen Book" and "Toddler Book" sub-types to the Book type and by adding the "Woman" and "Girl" sub-types to the Patron type, which already exists in the current data model.

Another way is to work vertically, as shown in Figures 6.16 and 6.17, by working on a new data entity type at every sprint. You would first add the Book concept

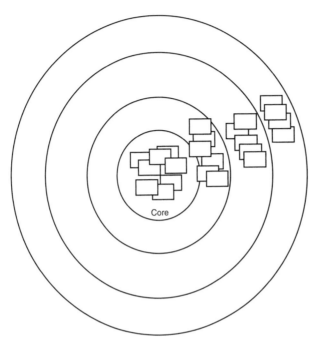

Figure 6.8
Identify common data-based user stories/PBIs clustering.

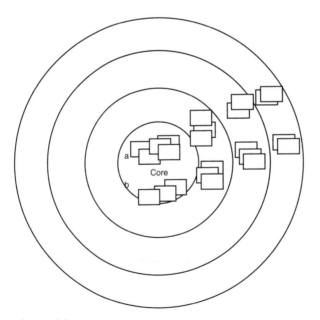

Figure 6.9
Split common business data-based user stories into smaller features clusters.

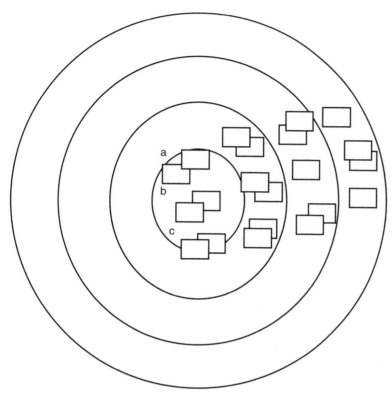

Figure 6.10
Split common business data-based user stories into even smaller features clusters.

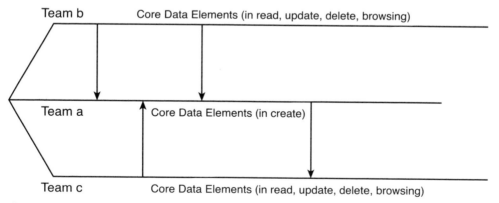

Figure 6.11
Building user stories/PBIs in concurrence.

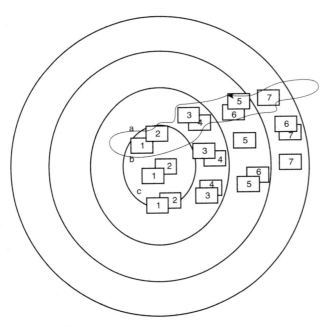

Figure 6.12
Changing product prioritization.

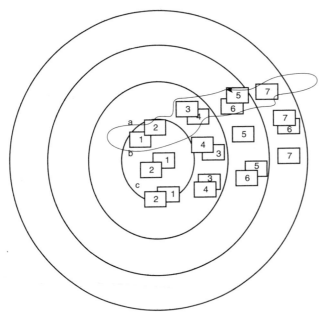

Figure 6.13
Changing product prioritization without impacting teamwork.

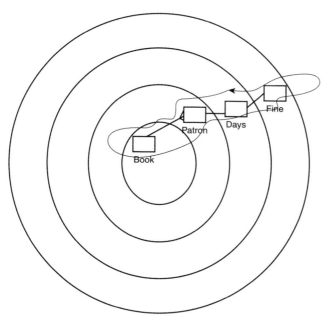

Figure 6.14
A beginning data architecture in progress.

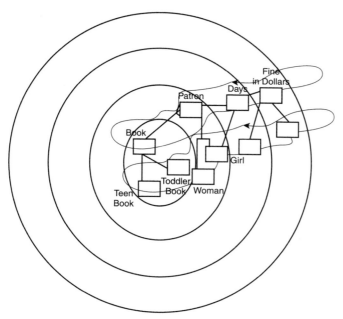

Figure 6.15
A horizontal data architecture in progress.

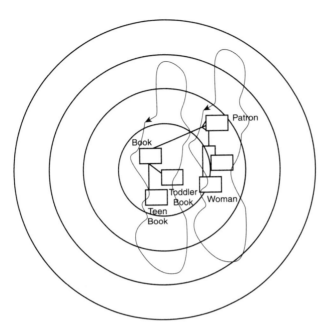

Figure 6.16
A vertical data architecture in progress.

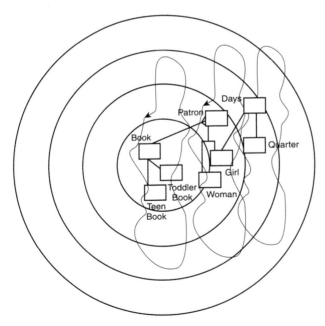

Figure 6.17
A data architecture in progress.

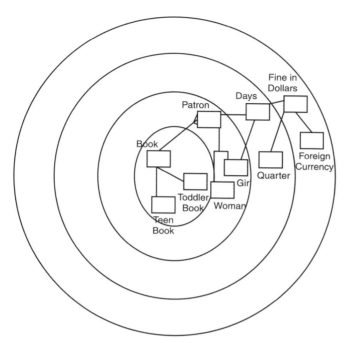

Figure 6.18
Your application final data architecture.

during the first sprint, then add the Patron concept during the second sprint, and then add the Day (Calendar) concept during the third sprint, and so on.

Both strategies will evolve into the final data model shown in Figure 6.18.

When closely examined, we can assume that the data model in Figure 6.18 will have all the relationships and cardinalities as the data model in Figure 6.19.

Figure 6.20 is an extension of the previous transactional data model with two new entity sub-types, Teenager and Adult, added to the Patron type.

Figure 6.21 shows how you could construct the star schema for this application. You first add a Fact table, called Visit, to the middle of the model. You then surround it by the Quarter, the Patron, and the Library Location, called Dimensions, and which came from the transactional data model in Figure 6.20.

Figure 6.22 shows how your application will ultimately fit into the overall enterprise data architecture of the company. Rather than building applications

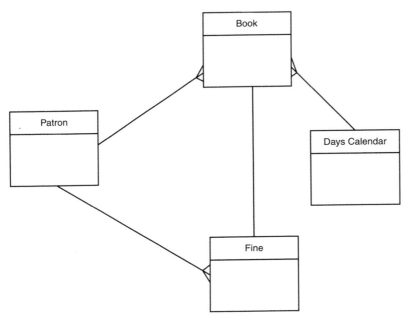

Figure 6.19
Your transactional data model.

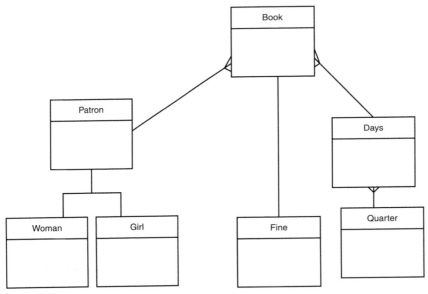

Figure 6.20
Extending your transactional data model into covering Woman and Girl.

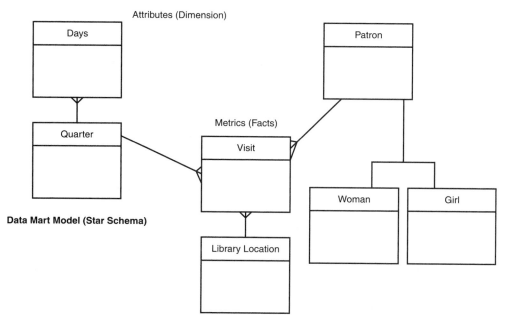

Figure 6.21
Your data mart star schema.

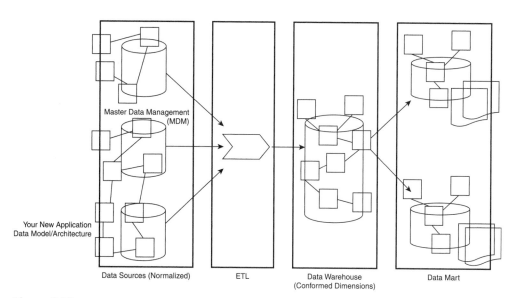

Figure 6.22
Fitting into the new enterprise data architecture.

in such a way that you can only hope they will fit into the enterprise architecture, your effort to lay down some kind of architecture vision could help ensure that your system will fit seamlessly into your company's IT enterprise architecture.

Summary

As software professionals, many of us are accustomed to doing a lot of architectural design using all kinds of tools. Then along came eXtreme Programming, which dictated that we should only design as we go. The success of Scrum seems to have amplified this phenomenon.

Suddenly, no one seems to want to use the term architecture or design any more, lest they be considered to be living in the past.

But as lessons start to emerge from Scrum projects, it has become clear that without an architecture vision, the chunk of user stories the teams get from the product owner will look like a stack of cards, without any clear idea of what the final product will look like.

As a result, the team will have to spend time and effort trying to get the different stories to fit into some kind of blurred image of an ever-changing architecture.

With a clear architecture vision laid down at the beginning, one observes that team velocity does not fluctuate much, but instead increases over time. The team members feel more confident in their ability to deliver.

To arrive at this architecture vision, we must first identify user stories that share common business data and consider building them together. By splitting the user stories along common business data elements, the team will be able to organize their work and develop in parallel. This is something many software managers have dreamt of because they see the potential benefit it can be to team performance.

Working with common business data also allows the team to lay down some sort of stable data architecture, a key ingredient to good data reporting and analytics. Another benefit of this is to allow the product owner to change the project's sequencing without negatively affecting the team's velocity.

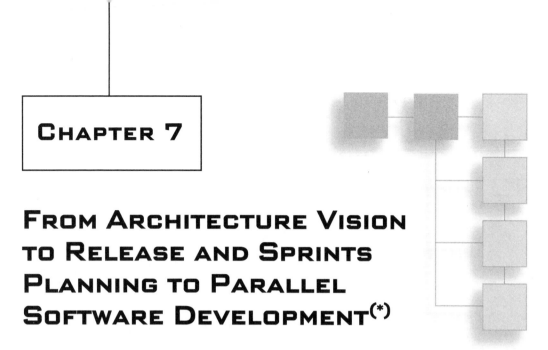

CHAPTER 7

FROM ARCHITECTURE VISION TO RELEASE AND SPRINTS PLANNING TO PARALLEL SOFTWARE DEVELOPMENT(*)

You have learned about the benefits of an early architecture vision, not only in terms of velocity but also in terms of software quality. The benefits of architecture vision for your product, however, do not stop here. They continue into the area of release and Sprint planning.

Armed with this knowledge, you can better work with the product owner to suggest adjustments to the sequence of work that will bring the most value to the business. At the same time, you will be able to maintain a good velocity and progressively build a solid foundation for a good application and data architecture.

Even though the product owner is likely to pay more attention to customer or user requests, a good Scrum product owner will pay attention to suggestions from the development team as well.

FROM ARCHITECTURE VISION TO RELEASE AND SPRINTS PLANNING

Rather than passively letting the product owner decide what she would like the team to work on during a specific sprint, it is our experience that the team would benefit more from the collaboration with the product owner if they have a more proactive attitude.

(*) Pham, Andrew. "Scrum: The Influence of Architecture Vision on Release/Sprint Planning," University of Pennsylvania, June, 2010.

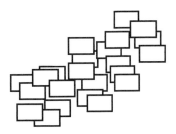

Figure 7.1
Inspecting the set of user stories for a central library system.

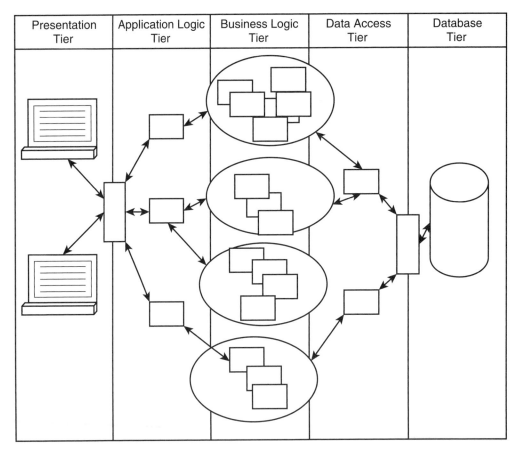

Figure 7.2
Identifying the architecture intent for the central library system.

The team should take an active look at the set of stories prior to the planning and try to see whether they can derive an architecture vision from them.

Let's assume that a recent workshop just concluded and a set of user stories has been identified as illustrated in Figure 7.1.

The team might take a quick look at the set of stories and be able to identify a high level architecture that would look like that shown in Figure 7.2.

Then, using the common data element approach described in Chapter 6, "The Influence of Architecture Vision on Team Velocity and Software Quality," the team will be able to divide the user stories among different rings as shown in Figure 7.3.

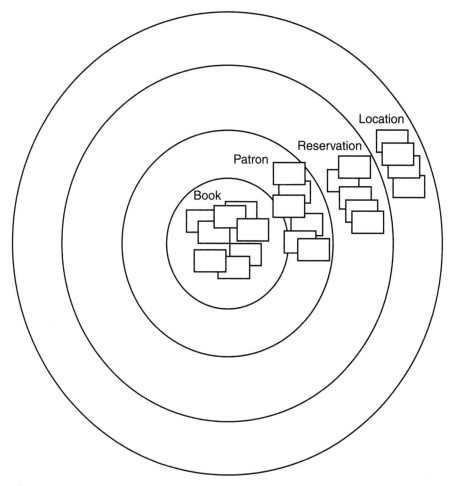

Figure 7.3
Dividing user stories among common data elements.

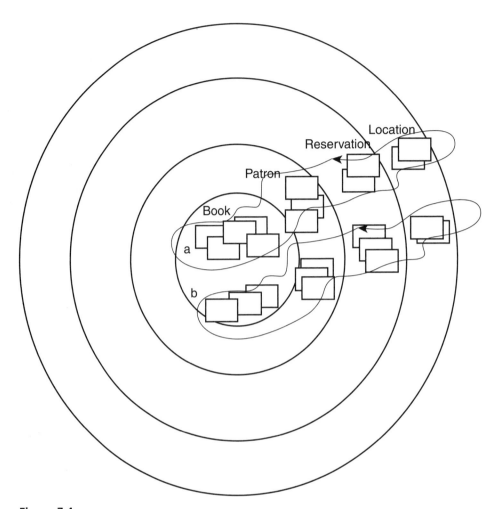

Figure 7.4
Further dividing the user stories among the common data elements.

By continuing to further divide, the team may be able to split the user stories into smaller groups. This results in separating the data elements that would need to be created from the ones that would only need to be read, updated, or deleted as shown in Figure 7.4.

At this point, there will be two options for the team to envision the release, either by horizontally slicing or vertically slicing.

Horizontally slicing means that the team can envision developing the software product by creating the foundation for the key data elements and

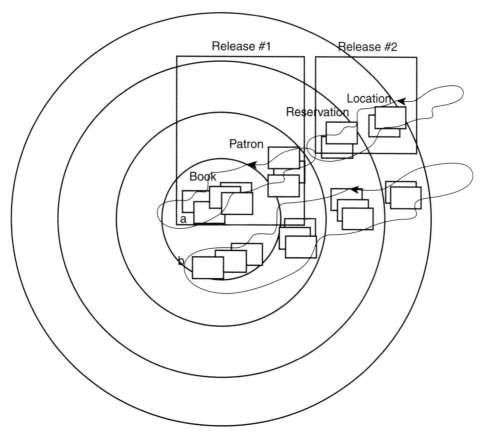

Figure 7.5
Organizing the release by horizontal slicing.

entities across all the rings, starting from the core in the middle to the outermost ring.

In the case of a central library system, that could mean to lay the foundation for the book and patron entities first in release #1, and then reservation and location in release #2, as shown in Figure 7.5.

Next, by virtue of common data (and probably also of team velocity), release #1 can be split into two sprints. Sprint #1 will focus on the first part of the book concept while sprint #2 focuses on the first part of the patron concept.

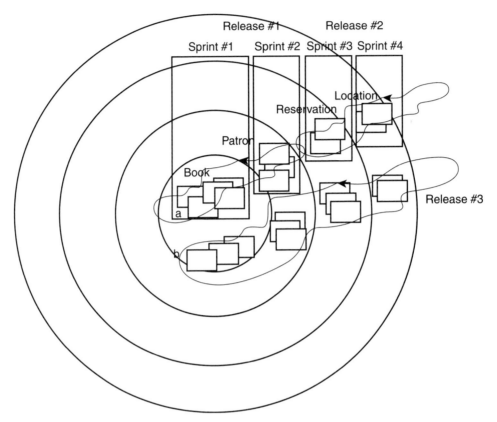

Figure 7.6
Divide the horizontal release into sprints.

The same approach can be applied to release #2, which can also be divided into two sprints, with sprint #3 focusing on the reservation concept while Sprint #4 puts the emphasis on the library location concept (Figure 7.6).

Vertically slicing means the team could develop the software product by creating the foundation for all the data elements and entities, ring by ring. Going back to our central library system, this means that the team could first lay the foundation for everything that relates to the book concept in release #1; then, all the details for the patron concept could be in release #2, and so on (Figure 7.7).

Next, we apply the same virtue of common data (and probably also of team velocity) to this second type of slicing. Release #1 (Figure 7.7), which focuses

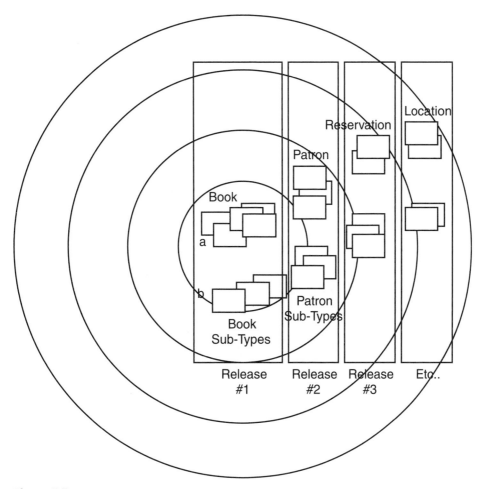

Figure 7.7
Organizing the release by vertical slicing.

completely on the book concept, can be split into two sprints. Sprint #1 will focus on the basics of the book concept, while sprint #2 will focus its extension in terms of sub-types.

The same approach can then be applied to release #2, also shown in Figure 7.7. That can also be divided into two sprints (Figure 7.8), with sprint #3 focusing on the basics of the patron concept while sprint #4 focuses its extension in terms of patron sub-types, and so forth (Figure 7.8).

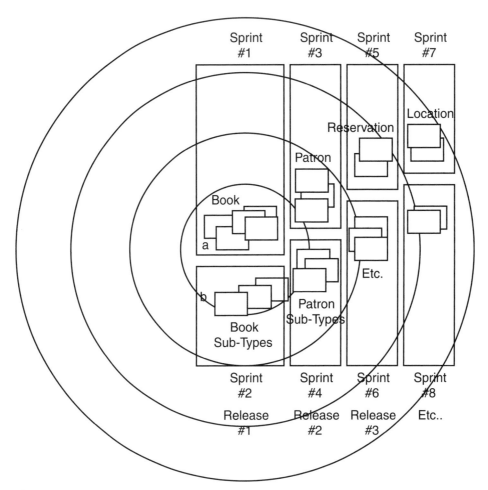

Figure 7.8
Divide the vertical release into sprints.

After a while, if you are concerned that you may lose track of all the release and sprint goals, you may want to organize them, along with their respective high-level stories descriptions, using a matrix like the one in Figure 7.9.

In addition to the benefit it brings to the Scrum team for their release and sprint planning, the diagram in Figure 7.9 can be easily turned into a new and improved sprint backlog (Figure 7.10) to help both allocate teamwork assignments and track team progress.

Release	Sprint	Stories	Goals
1. Release #1			....
	1. Sprint #1 (Book)		....
		1. Story #1	
		2. Story #2	
2. Release #2	2. Sprint #2 (Patron)		....
		3. Story #3	
		4. Story #4	

Figure 7.9
Tracing sprint goals back to release goals (horizontal slicing).

Because we are talking about tracking team progress, we would like to make our position clear with regard to the so-called technical debts, defined as the accumulated amount of technical rework that will be necessary to correct the software design.

From experience, we have found that technical debts are an inverse relationship to software quality (Figure 7.11). Because technical debt hides the fact that a release is actually late, we are absolutely opposed to having it around.

If you are reporting that you are well on track to finish your sprint goals, yet you know that you have a heavy load of technical debt, you are not being honest with yourself and with your team members.

You should therefore strive at any cost to not let technical debt interfere with the tracking of your true project progress.

Backlog	Tasks	Member	Estimate (Hours)	Remaining Work in Hours					
				Day 1	Day 2	Day 3	Day 4	Day 5	Day 6
Release #1	Goal:								
1. Sprint #1	Goal:								
Story #1	.IU Design/Coding .Application Layer	John	4	2	2	:	:	:	:
	Design/Coding .Business Layer	Frank	2	2	1	:	:	:	:
	Design and Coding .Data Access Layer	Andrew	5	2	2				
	Design and Coding .Database Layer	Laura	6	5	6				
	Design and Coding .Etc.	Lola	4	3	3				
Story #n	.IU Design/Coding .Application Layer	John	7	5	:	:	:	:	:
	Design/Coding .Etc.	Andrew Etc.	5	5	:	:	:	:	:
2. Sprint #2	Goal:								
Story #n+1	.IU Design/Coding .Etc.	John Etc.	3	2	1	:	:	:	:
	Total								

Figure 7.10
A sprint backlog organized by sprints and by release.

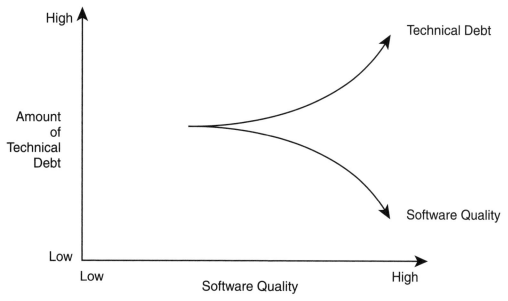

Figure 7.11
The inverse relationship between technical debt and software quality.

FROM INCREMENTAL TO PARALLEL SOFTWARE DEVELOPMENT

In addition to the helping hand an architecture vision can bring to the whole Scrum team in terms of release and sprint planning, there is one more concept the team could greatly benefit from: parallel software development (even within the seven-member Scrum team).

In other words, by organizing work around common data elements and the CRUD concept, you will be able to speed development by having small sub-teams (even within the current seven-member Scrum team) work in parallel on specific and self-contained user stories as shown in Figure 7.12. This, along with an effective continuous integration mechanism (using a tool such as Git), should allow the Scrum team to tremendously speed up their velocity.

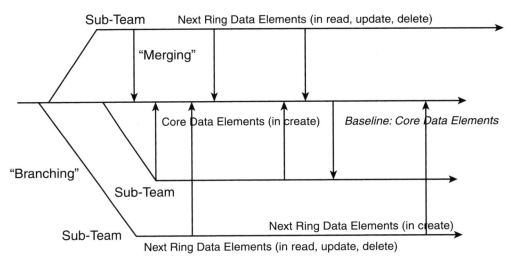

Figure 7.12
Sub-teams developing in parallel.

Because more than one team is working together, you should modify the questions you ask during your daily Standup (still called daily Scrum).

In addition to the three well-known questions which are asked during these meetings:

1. What did you do yesterday?

2. What do you plan on doing tomorrow?

3. What prevents you from making progress?

We suggest that you add two more questions, which should allow the sub-teams to be easily synchronized:

1. What are you doing that can help my sub-team?

2. What are you doing that slows down my sub-team?

To remind everyone on the Scrum team of their responsibility with regard to what they have to do, a summary is provided in Figure 7.13.

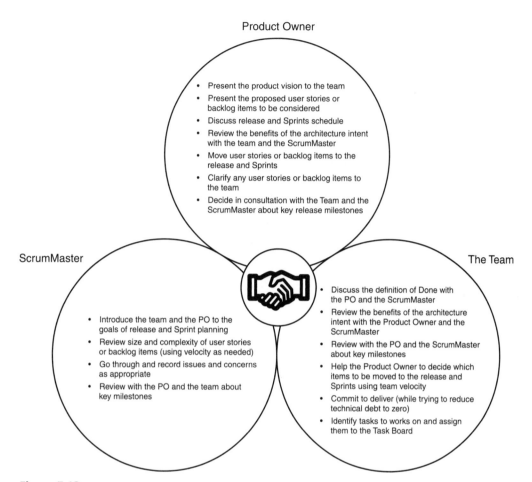

Figure 7.13
Collaboration for release and sprint planning.

Summary

Identifying architecture vision early on not only helps the team avoid velocity fluctuation but can increase software quality and lay down the foundation for a good application and data architecture.

In addition, it can help the development team have a more active, better collaboration with the product owner during the release and sprints planning meeting.

As a result, the Scrum team can increase both stakeholders' business value and the robustness of their application while experiencing more satisfactory team-work and effective collaboration.

Finally, using the common data architectural approach presented in this book can allow the team to speed up development by splitting the Scrum team into smaller size teams (which can be referred to as feature teams) that can perform work in parallel. This along with an effective continuous integration mechanism should allow the team to speed up their velocity or ability to finish their work even earlier than planned. With or without Scrum, this is something that has been the dream of software project managers and software managers for years.

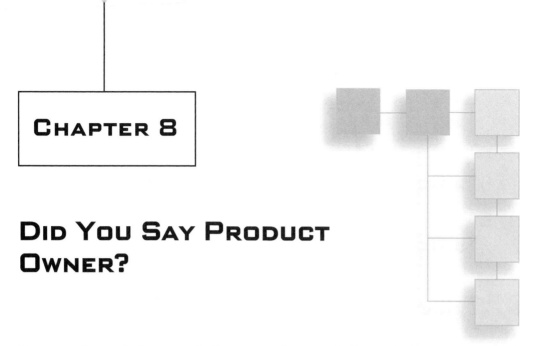

CHAPTER 8

DID YOU SAY PRODUCT OWNER?

Everyone is needed on an Agile project but an Agile project cannot succeed without a good product owner, who is the guardian of the product vision and goals, because the focus on an Agile or Scrum project is to deliver business results and values.

More than that, an Agile or Scrum project needs not just a good, but a great, product owner.

So the question is how can one be the best product owner possible?

We believe, based on our experience, that a product owner should possess seven key qualities. These qualities are listed in Figure 8.1.

The seven qualities of a great product owner are:

1. Know how to successfully manage the stakeholders' expectations and sometimes conflicting priorities.

2. Have a clear vision and knowledge of the product.

3. Know how to gather requirements to turn the product vision into a good product backlog.

4. Be fully available to actively engage with the team, not only during the sprint, but also during the release and sprint planning.

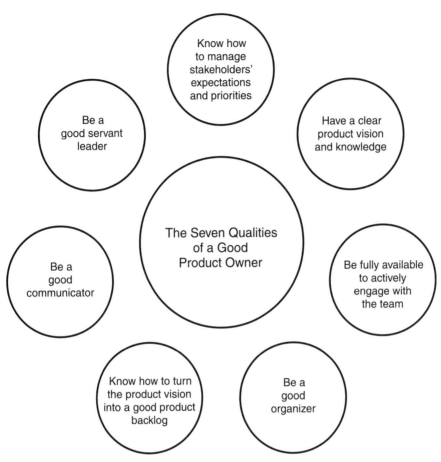

Figure 8.1
The seven qualities of a product owner.

5. Be a good organizer who can juggle multiple activities, while keeping things in perspective and maintaining her composure.

6. Know how to communicate the product vision; not only to the team, but also with the business, so their trust in the team remains intact throughout the life of the project.

7. Be a good leader, able to guide, coach, and support the team as needed while making sure that the business gets the value they expect out of IT.

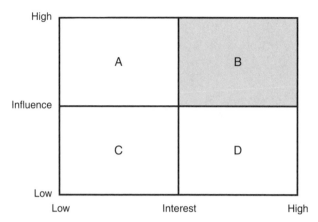

Figure 8.2
Stakeholder management matrix.

Let's now review these qualities, one by one:

MANAGING STAKEHOLDERS' EXPECTATIONS AND PRIORITIZATION

One of the most important activities for the product owner is to interact with and manage stakeholders' expectations and often conflicting priorities.

Since you may not have the time needed to spend with the stakeholders, we suggest that you learn to know and manage them differently depending on their influence on the future success of your project (Figure 8.2).

This is to say that most of your time should be spent working with the category B stakeholders who have a lot of influence and interest in your project. At the same time, you should try to get the A category to move towards the B category and, to a lesser extent, the C category to move towards the D category.

HAVING A CLEAR PRODUCT VISION AND KNOWLEDGE

If the product owner has a clear vision about the product that will help her easily set goals and priorities, it brings a lot to the project team in its effort to create a good release and sprint plan.

Everyone has a different way to come up with a product vision, but what we use is a simple technique called the 5W, which is:

- Whom? (The customer target.)
- Why? (In what way is this product special?)
- What? (What does the product offer?)
- Where? (Location.)
- When? (Time zone.)

For illustration purposes, an example would be to build a website which answers those questions in the following way as shown in Figure 8.3.

- **Whom?** All foodie gourmets.
- **Why?** Find the best dishes around the world.
- **What?** The dishes are being rated, rather than by restaurants.
- **Where?** All regions of the world.
- **When?** 24/7

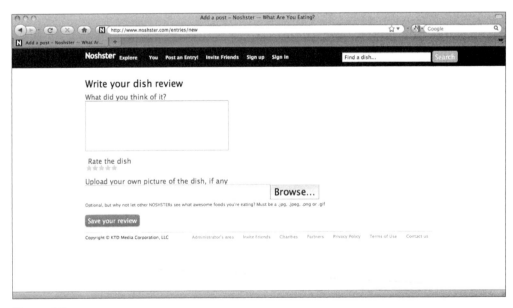

Figure 8.3
Noshter: A worldwide foodie social network.

Knowing How to Gather Requirements for the Product Backlog

Even though having a product vision is important, maybe even more important is the product owner's ability to come up with a good list of user stories for the product backlog.

So if you feel that you or your product owner are not skillful at gathering requirements (yet), do not hesitate to go back to Chapter 4, "A Visual Requirements Gathering for the Product Backlog" to review how to gather requirements that can easily be understood by developers and converted into tasks.

Making Oneself Always Available

Perhaps you are lucky enough to work with a product owner who has a clear product vision and who knows how to gather requirements and backlog items.

However, that will not be enough if the product owner is not available to work and dialogue with the development team.

The product owner should be someone who is available, ideally on a daily basis, to interact with the team and attend each review meeting.

If you find yourself in a company where there is no such product owner, you should then make it a priority to explain to management that the team needs one and why the team will need to have someone who is both business savvy and empowered to interact regularly with the team and to make decisions for the business.

Knowing How to Be a Good Organizer

Unless you are lucky enough to work in a small company where the product owner has plenty of time, chances are that she is someone busy dealing with all kinds of priorities, from working with the marketing department to dealing with business issues within her own department.

If this is the case, you should be diplomatic but do not hesitate to remind the product owner that her active participation is critically necessary as part of the process.

Knowing How to Communicate Better Than the Average Person

Besides having a good product vision and the ability to write requirements that are doable and easy to understand, the best thing a product owner can do is to be an active advocate for the team with business management.

For this, he or she will need to actively work with management and users alike, always helping them to understand the team's status relative to release goals and business value.

Knowing That It Is All About Servant Leadership

Finally, the product owner should be someone who knows how to be a good servant leader, someone who can guide, support, mentor, and, as needed, coach the team towards achieving the project vision and goals.

By looking at these qualities, you can ask yourself whether the product owner has all the qualities needed to be effective.

If the answer is a resounding yes, then there is nothing for you to do or to worry about.

However, if you see a gap, then it may be time for you to work with the ScrumMaster to help educate or remind the product owner of her role.

Summary

Everyone on the Scrum team has a role to play. The question is to know who can bring the most value to the business to justify the project. It should be the product owner.

The next question is how one can be the best product owner possible.

From our experience on real-life projects, the product owner should possess the seven qualities outlined in this chapter.

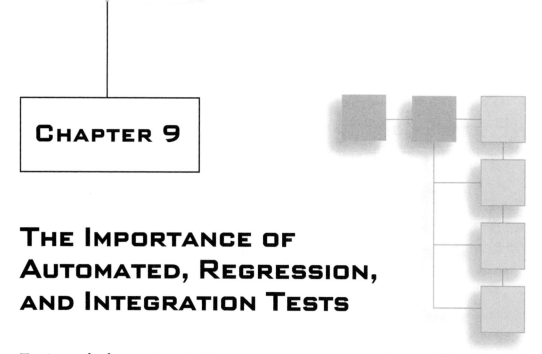

CHAPTER 9

THE IMPORTANCE OF AUTOMATED, REGRESSION, AND INTEGRATION TESTS

Testing, whether system testing or user acceptance testing, traditionally was done at the end of the waterfall life cycle, as illustrated in Figure 9.1.

Without further questioning the effectiveness of this model, let's simply say that in an Agile or Scrum project, testing is no longer performed at the end of the life cycle but is "baked" throughout the different iterations or sprints, as shown in Figure 9.2.

Without doubt, testing is one of the things that make the most difference in Scrum development. Whether or not the team is capable of producing regular shippable increments will most likely be determined by how well testing is organized and run.

Even on a small Scrum project, it is difficult to conceive how teams can regularly deliver without some kind of automated testing mechanism already in place and fully functioning.

The more automated testing infrastructure is in place, the more the team's velocity is likely to increase in the long run (Figure 9.3).

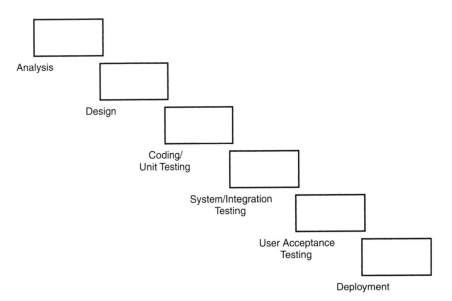

Figure 9.1
Testing within the traditional waterfall software process.

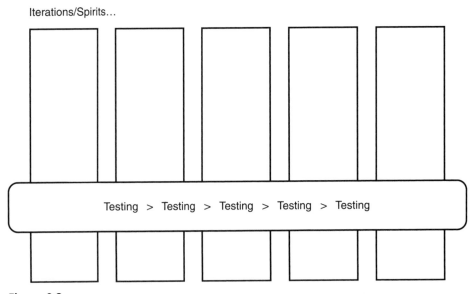

Figure 9.2
A new place for testing in the new Agile/Scrum process framework.

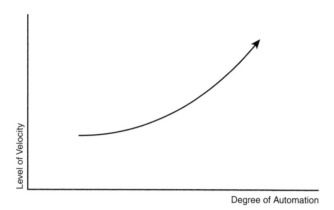

Figure 9.3
Degree of automation.

THE IMPORTANCE OF THE DEFINITION OF *DONE*

Before we go further with our discussion of testing, let's first talk about the definition of the word *done*. This is what will determine which types of testing should be done by the team. By testing types, we referred to something like user-acceptance or technical testing.

Like most experts, including Henrik Kniberg, in his book, *Scrum and XP from the Trenches*, we prefer *done* to mean "ready to deploy to production." But also like Kniberg, we sometimes have to accept that the definition of done can be somewhat different.

The definition of done often differs depending on the project situation. In the following sections, we will review two or three definitions of done as we have seen on real-life projects.

The first definition of done in Figure 9.4 shows that the team has decided to consider their work done by the end of coding and unit testing.

In the example illustrated in Figure 9.4, many teams are working in parallel on the same product line. The teams decided that it would be most beneficial for them to deliver their different work results after unit testing, so that integration and stabilization work can be done before they move into the next iteration.

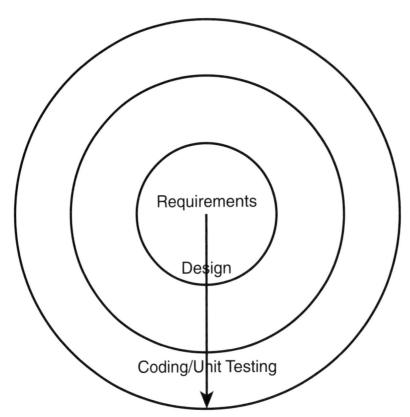

Figure 9.4
A definition of done.

This is a situation you are likely to encounter in real-life—that the done is declared at the unit testing level. This approach is fine as long as the team has also accounted for the additional integration and testing effort that will be needed before deployment.

Figure 9.5 shows a common scenario where the team considers that they are done only after all new stories have been integrated and tested before they do their sprint demo.

Figure 9.6 shows the best scenario, in which some business users are part of the Scrum team, where they are responsible for performing acceptance testing before done is certified. Whether or not a project is using Scrum, user

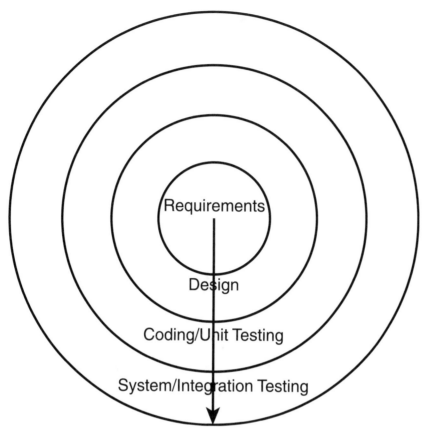

Figure 9.5
Another definition of done.

acceptance test development has become more and more a widespread practice which should be incorporated into release iterations as early as possible in the process.

THE MOST IMPORTANT TESTS

Because Scrum is mainly a project management framework, it is silent about the engineering practices related to coding and testing.

However, in our experience, the following testing should be in place in your organization to sustain your Scrum effort:

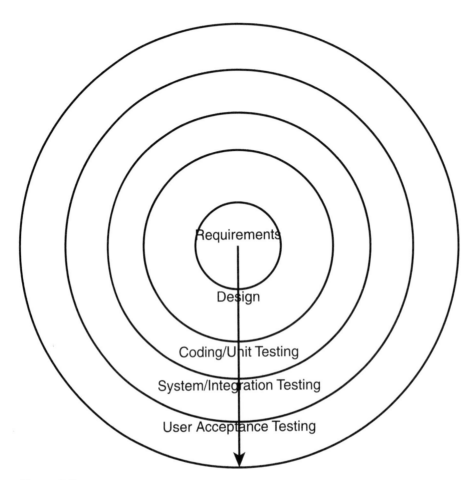

Figure 9.6
Another definition (still) of done.

1. Automated testing

2. Continuous integration testing

Automated Testing

The reason we list automated testing first is because as soon as you start seeing your team churn out regular software increments, you will realize that you cannot really sustain their pace unless some kind of automation is in place.

Automated testing will save you time and will enable your team to cruise along quite smoothly.

Unlike manual testing where you are required to go through all the test cases yourself manually, automated testing can take hours, even days, depending on your code base. One of the main benefits of automated testing is that a software program will handle all the testing for you.

Of course, in order to do automated testing, you must do a little more work and have bought a tool and have got all the test cases created. But that is only a fraction of time compared to all the time it will take should you have to do everything manually.

Continuous Integration Testing

Another type of test that we think is critical to your Scrum project success is continuous integration testing.

The reason this test is important to perform regularly is that you want to make sure that your software product is always shippable.

ORGANIZING THE TESTING INFRASTRUCTURE

Now that we have covered the different testing types and the ones we consider to be most fundamental, let's turn our attention to organizing the testing.

If you are lucky and the company where you work is fully committed to Scrum, you would not need to do anything more than working and communicating closely with the quality assurance department. Otherwise, if you are like us, you may find yourself in companies that have not implemented Scrum throughout the enterprise and, because of that, little or no infrastructure has been set up in terms of automated and continuous integration testing for Scrum.

In case this happens, this chapter provides you with some idea of what you should see in terms of testing infrastructure, either for your own needs or for the company, should they ask you.

Figure 9.7 shows a very decent environment, in which the software is organized around three different environments: development, testing, and production.

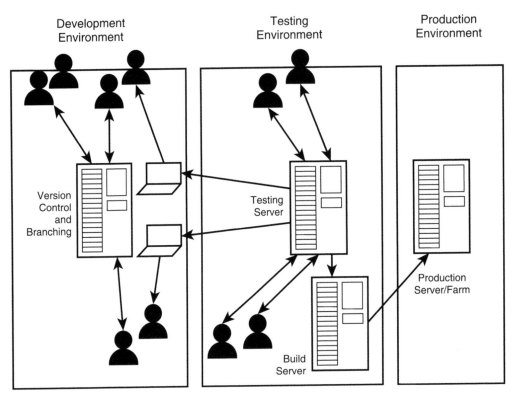

Figure 9.7
From development to testing to production.

There is a natural flow from development to testing and from testing to production.

Perhaps you are not so fortunate as to be in a company where everything is set up like this. We suggest that you get together with your technical team members at the very beginning of your project, and see how they can set up a makeshift testing environment within your project's own development environment, as shown in Figure 9.8.

We know from experience that many teams do not start with this, but, it has been an essential part of all the successful Agile or Scrum projects we have worked on. This is why we include this information here to help save you time and headache. We think that you will thank us later.

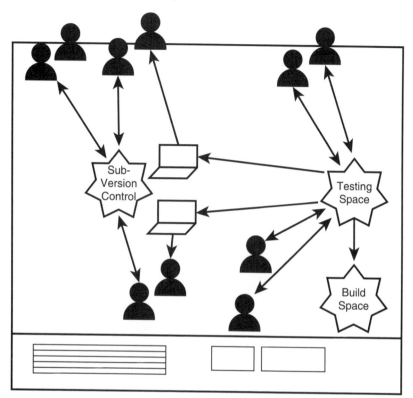

Figure 9.8
Organize testing in your development environment.

Unless you have taken the time to organize your testing strategy and organization, you will not be able to deliver with Scrum if your testing does not follow or support you.

SUMMARY

Testing no longer takes place at the end of the software life cycle. We have emphasized in this chapter just a few tests, which are critical to your Scrum project success. This is why you do not hear about test-driven development (TDD), despite its remarkable effectiveness for the average programmer team to churn out good code. Instead, this chapter focused more on automatic and continuous integration testing, the two most important types of testing for every Scrum project team to set up as soon as possible.

This chapter then focused on testing organization.

If you do not work in a company where a good testing infrastructure has been set up, we recommend that you work with technical team members at the beginning of your project to set up a makeshift testing environment—if necessary within your project's development environment. This testing environment will provide an indispensible support for the development team as they turn out new increment after new increment, sprint after sprint.

Because the definition of *done* has a large impact on how much of a testing type you would need to do, this chapter also covered some different definitions of done in order to give you an idea of what you may need to do on your project.

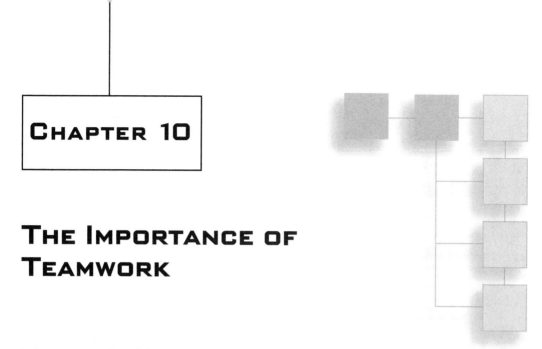

CHAPTER 10

THE IMPORTANCE OF TEAMWORK

We are sure that, like most people, you have heard a lot about teamwork, and you might be wondering what new information we have to share on the subject.

As we value your time, we are not going to repeat the things you have heard a hundred times already. That being said, teamwork is still a very critical element on a Scrum project.

Even if you have had support from management and pulled together the best possible product backlog, you can still fail if your team members do not work well together. From our experience, we do not remember any successful project where the team did not work well together but still delivered.

For a short project, it may not be that important due to the limited duration. But when people are required to work together every day for a long period of time on a mid- or large-sized project, it takes more than luck to make good teamwork happen.

If a project's team members do not get along and nothing is done about it, we have seen that the project almost always ends in trouble. This is true with traditional projects and even more so with Agile and Scrum since these two process frameworks rely heavily on team self-management and team accountability.

One of the Scrum engagement rules is that everyone is supposed to rely on everyone else to perform as a team. While this topic may sound cliché, nothing is more important to a Scrum project than to get team members to work well together.

In the following pages, we will provide you with some ideas and techniques we have learned throughout the years that will help you, as a team, avoid conflicts, or at least learn to resolve them as much as you can, before they break your project.

Before talking about the team, though, let's talk about the individuals on the team because all teams consist of individuals.

THE INDIVIDUALS

Computers are complex machines, but there is nothing more complex than a human being.

Fortunately, learning more about humans has always been a subject of study, which has provided us with a good understanding of ourselves as human beings.

We won't turn this book into a treatise on human psychology, but we will discuss those elements of human nature that can help the Scrum team work well together.

First, let's mention the study done by Abraham Maslow, still known as Maslow's Pyramid, or hierarchy of needs, which sheds some light on human needs as individuals.

Viewing the pyramid in Figure 10.1 from the bottom, we see that an individual must first satisfy some bodily needs, such as food and water.

Once these needs are fulfilled, one next needs to feel safe. Safety can be provided by a roof to live under or a place to protect oneself from weather or external dangers.

After this, the individual needs to have some social contact.

The last levels of the pyramid, the self-esteem and self-actualization layers, are what the Agile gurus and Scrum experts count on the most for a team to be empowered to do their work and self-manage. This is exactly why we ended up in Scrum with team self-management and empowerment to select their tasks and do whatever they like to accomplish their commitments.

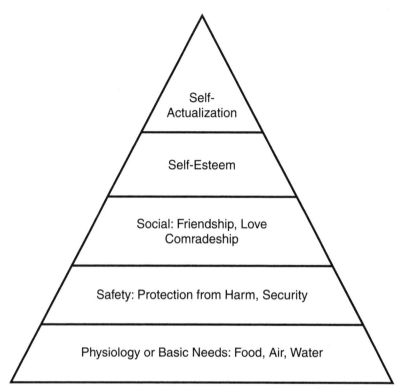

Figure 10.1
Maslow's Hierarchy of Needs.

So much for the individuals, but before we study the team in detail, let's talk about the group.

THE GROUP

Whenever an individual feels the need for some sense of belonging or to share a common need or ideas, he tends to find other people with whom he can associate.

A group, however, has no common goal that will unite individuals; no goal for which they will be held accountable.

Going back to what we understand about teamwork and team performance, whenever a project team fails, when it is not due to some other reason, it may well be because the project team has performed at the level of the group, not feeling accountable for something together.

THE TEAM

When a group of people comes together to achieve a common goal, there is the beginning of a team. Whether the team is a high-performance team or a low-performance team depends on their ability to work together as a self-organized team and on the people who lead them in the traditional command and control environment.

As soon as we say that there is a team, or a group of people with a goal to accomplish, disagreements as to who should do what, how long, how much, and why will begin.

In paraphrasing Patrick Lencioni, in *Five Dysfunctions of Teams*, it is teamwork, not finance or technology, that gives us the competitive advantage.

Therefore, it is critical for all members of the team to know how to work well together.

Among all the things you can know about your teammates, nothing is more important than knowing their personality type. Having that knowledge enables you to communicate with teammates in such a way that they understand and accept what you say more easily. Likewise, this knowledge allows you to hear and more easily accept things from them. This will help you avoid misunderstanding and potential conflict.

THE KEIRSEY TEMPERAMENT TYPES

Tracing the idea of temperament back to the ancient Greeks, David Keirsey developed a modern temperament theory, which is composed of 16 temperament types, called the Keirsey Temperament Sorter (Figure 10.2).

The Keirsey Temperament Types Sorter is designed to help people better understand themselves and contains a total of 16 temperament types:

1. **Inspectors** are careful and meticulous. These individuals are extremely dependable on following through with things, which they promise to get done.

IS_IT_EJ	IS_IF_EJ	IN_IF_EJ	IN_IT_EJ
Inspector	Protector	Counselor	Mastermind
IS_ET_IP	IS_EF_IP	IN_EF_IP	IN_ET_IP
Crafter	Composer	Healer	Architect
ES_ET_IP	ES_EF_IP	EN_EF_IP	EN_ET_IP
Promoter	Performer	Champion	Inventor
ES_IT_EJ	ES_IF_EJ	EN_IF_EJ	EN_IT_EJ
Supervisor	Provider	Teacher	Fieldmarshal

Figure 10.2
The 16 Keirsey temperament types.

2. **Protectors** are warm and kind-hearted. They value cooperation and are sensitive to co-workers' feelings.

3. **Counselors** are gentle, caring, and highly intuitive individuals. Counselors are perfectionist, stubborn, and tend to ignore other people's opinions, thinking that they are right.

4. **Masterminds** are introspective, pragmatic, and attentive. Masterminds observe the world to look for ideas and opportunities. Their minds constantly gather information.

5. **Crafters** have a compelling drive to understand the way things work. They're logical and thrive on action. Usually fearless, crafters are very independent.

6. **Composers** are quiet and reserved, difficult to get to know well. They keep their ideas and opinions to themselves, except from those who they are closest to.

7. **Healers** are introspective and cooperative. They do not like conflict and go to great lengths to avoid it. If they must face it, they will always approach it from the perspective of their feelings.

8. **Architects** are introspective but pragmatic. Their primary interest is to determine how things are structured, built, or configured. They live

primarily inside their own minds, and enjoy analyzing difficult problems to come up with logical resolutions. Not surprisingly, they are very tolerant and flexible.

9. **Promoters** are doers who live in action. Blunt, risk-takers, they are willing to jump into things and get their hands dirty.

10. **Performers** enjoy being the center of attention. In social situations, they are informative and expressive. Lively and fun, performers like to attract the attention of other people. They live in the here-and-now, keeping abreast of the latest trends.

11. **Champions** are enthusiastic people, typically very bright and full of potential. Champions like to make their thoughts known to the world. Big believers in possibilities, their enthusiasm often inspires and motivates others.

12. **Inventors** are less interested in developing plans or making decisions than they are in generating ideas. Intensely curious, they have an entrepreneurial character and are always looking for new projects.

13. **Supervisors** live in the present with their eye constantly observing the environment to make sure that everything is running smoothly and systematically.

14. **Providers** are naturally interested in others. They like people and have a special skill at bringing out the best in others.

15. **Teachers** have excellent people skills. They understand and care about people, and have a special talent for also bringing out the best in people.

16. **Field Marshals** are natural born leaders. They live in a world of challenges and want to be the ones responsible for surmounting them. Their talent for contingency planning is only second to their ability to execute strategy or action plan.

Knowing your team members' personality types helps a lot in learning to know one another and work well together, but sometimes that may not be enough to avoid problems and conflicts.

Depending on the stage at which the problem or conflict occurs, there are techniques that we can leverage to resolve conflicts, something we are going to review next.

But let's review the various team stages and the different conflict resolution techniques before deciding which one would be the most appropriate to use for a good conflict resolution, depending on the team stage.

THE FIVE TEAM STAGES

In 1965, Bruce Tuckman identified five stages a team goes through in coming together:

1. **Forming:** This is when the team is brought together for the first time. At this time, people tend to behave in a formal and reserved manner.

2. **Storming:** In this stage, team members start to position themselves against one another, often in a rather confrontational way. This is where the manager's, or leader's, role is most useful in helping to build the trust between team members. We will review this in greater detail in the next chapter.

3. **Norming:** This is when team members are confrontational with one another as they tackle project issues.

4. **Performing:** This is the time when team members become effective and productive working together. The trust between team members is high.

5. **Adjourning:** The adjourning stage is the last stage just before the team is released after the teamwork is completed.

TECHNIQUES TO RESOLVE TEAM CONFLICTS

Even though none of us likes to have conflict, it is unfortunately something we all have encountered or will encounter during our lifetime at work.

Many conflict resolution techniques exist, but among the most known is the following technique identified by Kenneth Thomas and Ralph Kilmann in the 1970s:

1. **Accommodating** (ACCO): This technique indicates a willingness to meet the needs of others at the expense of one's own needs.

2. **Compromise** (COMP): This happens when everyone in the conflict gives up something to reach an agreement.

3. **Competitive** (COMPE): This is a useful technique when there is an emergency and a decision needs to be made fast or when the decision is unpopular.

4. **Collaborating** (COLLA): All the perspectives of the different team members are examined. This technique normally leads to a good consensus.

5. **Avoidance** (AVOID): One of the parties refuses to discuss the conflict. This is an example of a lose-lose conflict resolution technique.

Now, let's combine the team stage, the project life cycle, and the conflict resolution techniques into a conflict resolution matrix (Figure 10.3) to help guide team members when they go through difficulties.

According to this matrix, if the team is still at the forming stage, and if the project is still at the early initial planning stage, then the two most appropriate techniques to use are either accommodating or competition.

The reason for this is that accommodating will allow people to first get to know one another better, which may be the best thing to do in some cultures such as in Asia. Then, the next best technique to use is competition. Yes, competition, so that people can have a chance to challenge one another's ideas based on factual data, which may be the best thing to do in Western cultures. When this happens early in the life of the project, the confrontation that results will not greatly affect

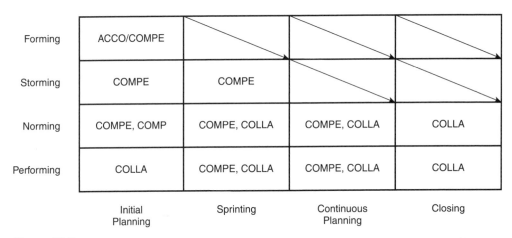

Figure 10.3
The most appropriate resolution techniques to use when conflict arises in a team.

the progress of the project. The good thing after this type of confrontation in the early stage is that people will learn one another's opinion better and tend to move towards a more collaborative approach. If a project team is unable to resolve its own conflicts within the team itself, the ScrumMaster and the product owner should intervene, indirectly of course, to try to get everything on track again.

CONDITIONS OF GREAT TEAMWORK

Work would be wonderful if there were no conflict, but since conflicts happen and they can hurt the team's progress, what should we do to avoid it?

We have seen the same patterns emerge time and again. We call these patterns the (five) conditions of great teamwork, and they can be seen in Figure 10.4. These conditions help team members work well together.

As a team member, you should come to the team with a very open mind and think in terms of team rather than individual. Try to see things from someone else's perspective and have the desire to learn about the other team members.

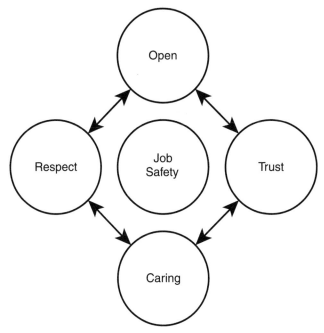

Figure 10.4
Conditions for great teamwork.

Only with this open mindset can you hope to blend successfully into the team with so many different personalities.

Secondly, you should care. You should want everyone to be heard and to have a chance to contribute. The more people feel they are listened to, the more likely it is that the team will function well.

Then, find opportunities to show respect for one another on the team.

Next, remember that trust is the glue we need to get everything to stick together for great teamwork.

Finally, we add job safety, or security, as the central condition of great teamwork because people can't be productive or get along with others when they worry about losing their jobs.

This is where the ScrumMaster and the product owner can help by working closely with the team's direct management to help team members feel safe working together, as we will discuss in the next chapter.

As a result of their collaboration, we can identify three types of teams, based on how successfully they work together: (1) the high-performance team, (2) the average-performance team, and (3) the mediocre or low-performance (political) team.

High-performance teams are fun, open-minded, and caring. By contrast, low-performance teams are usually characterized by silence in meetings, forced smiles, and a cover-up attitude. The team members on an average-performance team just go with the flow at work each day, doing only what is needed to turn in the hours and get paid, but they bring no value to the organization. The only difference between them and the mediocre or low-performance team is that they do not resort to cover-ups and political games.

SUMMARY

The absence of a project manager on a Scrum project does not mean that this responsibility can be abandoned. Nor have we done away with project leadership.

Unlike a traditional project using the command-and-control style, the team is self-organized in Scrum. This means that they are empowered to decide for themselves how they would like to share in the work. No one, no project manager, will tell the team what to do anymore.

Because the team is self-managed, they should learn to resolve conflicts among themselves. This is the reason we have reviewed in this chapter, not only the different Keirsey temperament types for the team to learn to know one another, but also the different techniques for conflict resolution.

Because conflict happens, it is important to consider the stage at which it happens. A conflict that takes place when the team is formed does not require the same resolution techniques as a conflict that occurs in the middle of sprinting.

Because conflicts do hurt a team's progress, we need to ask ourselves how to avoid them. One of the answers to this question is what we call the five conditions of great teamwork. Four of these five elements are Open, Trust, Caring, and Respect, while the last one is Job Safety. While team members have little control over their job safety, the product owner and the ScrumMaster may have more influence over it by working closely with the team's direct management.

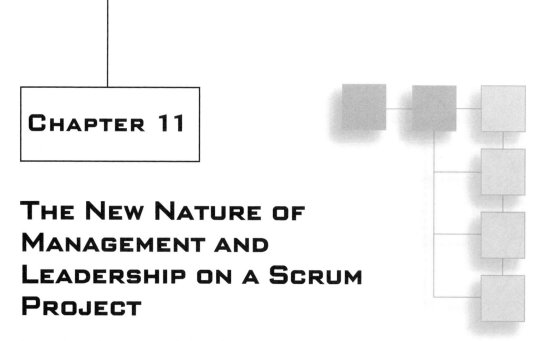

CHAPTER 11

THE NEW NATURE OF MANAGEMENT AND LEADERSHIP ON A SCRUM PROJECT

Even if you have learned that there is no project manager on a Scrum project, that does not mean that there is no management, or especially, leadership on a Scrum project. This misconception was corrected in a discussion by Mike Cohn posted Aug 25, 2009 on InformIT. You can find that article at www.informit.com/articles/article.aspx?p=1382538.

Unlike the traditional command and control environment, management responsibility is now split among the three different components of the Scrum team: the ScrumMaster, the development team and the product owner. Although the ScrumMaster and the product owner do not directly manage the team, they are responsible for project reporting to the management of the business. This is true, according to Ken Schwaber in *Agile Project Management with Scrum*, even if we no longer report by tasks on a Scrum project but only by requirements.

Anyone can be considered a leader on a Scrum project as long as that person has some influence over the team. To the surprise of some purists and our delight, in his blog, Mike Cohn mentioned product owner, ScrumMaster, and even functional manager, as examples of leaders who can influence the direction and success of a Scrum project, and we wholeheartedly agree with him. See his blog at http://blog.mountaingoatsoftware.com/the-role-of-leaders-on-a-self-organizing-team.

Figure 11.1
Management and leadership as two halves of a round circle.

But to paraphrase what Mike Cohn wrote on his blog, there is more to leading a self-organizing team than buying food or letting the team do what they want. Leaders on a Scrum project should influence teams in an indirect way, and that is what we address in this chapter.

Last but not least, people often compare management with leadership as if they were opposing one another. We think they complete one another rather than oppose, and this is why we think of them as being two halves of a round circle, as illustrated in Figure 11.1. No side is better than the other, and they are often intertwined.

Like Peter Ducker, the late management guru, said, "strategy without execution is only a vision." We would say leadership without management is like having a strategy without being able to execute it.

Applied to Scrum, this means that the ScrumMaster and the product owner should not hesitate, even with a self-organizing team, to exercise their leadership and management skills in talking to the development team, should they feel that the project is not progressing as it should or the team is not performing as it should.

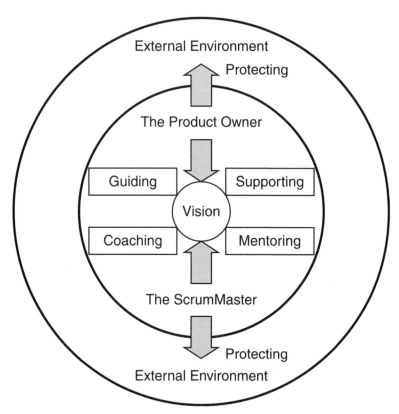

Figure 11.2
The two sides of management and leadership

Things become more interesting when you realize that they have to exercise these skills with subtlety, and indirectly, both with the team and with people outside of the team, but who can influence the team's performance (Figure 11.2).

What Figure 11.2 conveys is that there are two sides to the product owner and the ScrumMaster's project management and team leadership roles: one facing internally toward the team and the other facing the external world.

Traditionally, people took the position that the ScrumMaster should protect the team from disturbances coming from outside of the team, including from the product owner who may come to the team, during the sprint, to ask them to take care of some new requests.

However, with practice, it has become clear that there are instances where the product owner is not the business manager of a business unit but someone who has to work with different business units and who has to resolve sometimes conflicting priority between these units.

This is to say that the product owner may need, in some cases, to push back the different business units, in order to protect the team, when it comes to new requests these business units may want to introduce in the middle of a sprint. This is when the product owner truly acts as a servant-leader, assisted in this role by the ScrumMaster, trying to protect the team from outside disturbances.

Even though our discussion that follows is somewhat different from the CDE (Container, Difference, Exchange) discussion on how to lead a self-organizing team in Mike Cohn's excellent book, "Succeeding with Agile Using Scrum" it does share a common premise with Mike Cohn's book in that the Scrum project team requires quite a bit of management and leadership to work, contrary to popular beliefs.

To better understand the management and leadership role of both the product owner and the ScrumMaster, let's review the internally facing side, as shown in the quadrant of servant-leadership in Figure 11.3, and see what their different aspects are and what the product owner and ScrumMaster could or should do to help improve the team's progress toward the project goals.

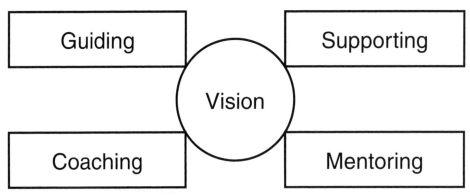

Figure 11.3
The CSM/PO internal servant-leadership quadrant.

Vision: This is what the product owner role is most known for—being responsible for the product vision, goals, and business requirements. By asking probing questions, the ScrumMaster can help the product owner formulate his or her vision and identify the product goals more clearly. Having a clear product vision will help the product owner answer any questions the team may have regarding business requirements and the product direction.

Supporting: This is something both the product owner and the ScrumMaster are there to provide. Normally, the ScrumMaster's most known role is to help remove impediments and assist the team in understanding the Scrum process, but removing impediments is something the product owner could and should also help with when it comes, for example as indicated above, in resisting business people's pressure to have team members work on a new item that was not planned for the current sprint.

Guiding: By this, we mean the ability for the ScrumMaster and the product owner, two of the three types of leaders Mike Cohn referred to in his book, to exert a positive influence on the team, either to promote more collaboration or a better performance.

Mentoring: Whenever possible, the ScrumMaster and the product owner should not hesitate to share with the team what they know in order to help team members become even better at what they do, especially when the product owner and ScrumMaster happen to be experts themselves in those areas.

Coaching: One of the least practiced aspects of management and leadership in the traditional command and control environment, coaching is a technique the product owner or ScrumMaster could and should often use to unleash a team member's potential.

Now that we have reviewed the different aspects of the internally facing side of team leadership, let's turn our attention to the externally facing responsibility of the ScrumMaster and the product owner and see what they should and could do to help the team with the external environment, namely with the team's direct management and with other outside stakeholders. On top of what the product owner and the ScrumMaster can do to support, guide, and coach the team, there is something else, which is as important or even more important, they should do to provide the team with the most critical condition for great teamwork: namely, the job safety factor as mentioned in Chapter 10.

Figure 11.4 captures this kind of intervention the ScrumMaster and the product owner should do, for instance, with the team members' functional managers by explaining to them what Scrum is and why team members should not be punished for refusing to work on any ad hoc issues that could interfere with their sprint work.

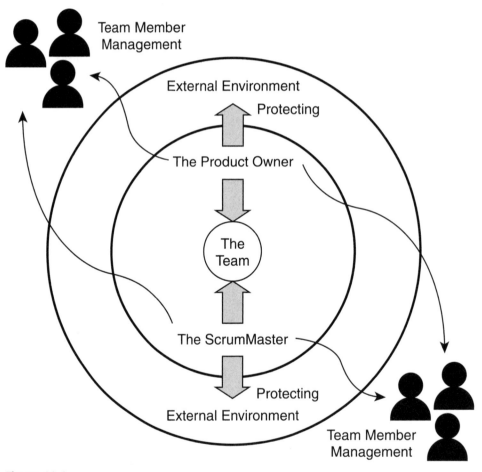

Figure 11.4
Outside intervention in team members' favor.

COACHING FOR SUPERIOR PERFORMANCE: THE GROW MODEL

A well-known technique for coaching, one of the preferred techniques used by servant-leaders to enhance a team member's performance, is known as the GROW model (which stands for Goal, Reality, Options, and Will). This technique can be used by anyone and requires no special training. It is known to provide a very structured and effective approach for employees and managers to establish goals and identify ways to work toward achieving them.

Every coach has his own way to coach but what follows is an example of how a coaching session can be structured using the GROW model, which we extended with a new stage (Results) in order to provide an opportunity for continuous improvement.

1. **Goal Establishing:** First, help your team member define his goals. To do this, you can use the same SMART technique that was discussed in Chapter 4, "A Visual Requirements Gathering for the Product Backlog." With SMART (Specific, Measurable, Achievable, Realistic, and Time-based) the goal can be achieved within a given timeframe.

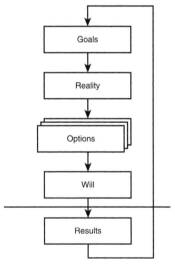

Figure 11.5
The extended GROW technique.

2. **Examine (Current) Reality:** Next, ask your team member to describe his Reality, meaning the current reality he lives in. This is an important step. Too often people try to solve a problem without fully considering their starting point, and, therefore, often miss some of the information they need to solve the problem effectively. As the Chinese proverb goes, if you do not know where you are, no map can ever help you know how to get to where you want to go. As your team member tells you about his Current Reality, the solution to his problem will begin to emerge.

3. **Explore the Options:** Once you and your team member have established the Goals and explored the (Current) Reality, it's time to explore what is possible—meaning, all the possible options you have for solving the problem. Resist the temptation to do this by yourself. Instead, help your team member generate on his own as many good options as possible, and discuss them with your team.

   Let your team member do most of the talking and offer ideas first. Then suggest your ideas.

4. **Establish the Will:** By examining the current Reality and exploring the Options, your team member will now have a good idea of how he can achieve his Goal.

   That's great but it may not be enough, so your final step as coach is to get your team member to commit to some specific actions. In so doing, you will help the team member establish his or her will and motivation to improve.

5. **Review Results** (extended by us): By reviewing the results he achieves against the established goals, you and your team member will be able to identify gaps and what needs to be done to improve his performance.

For a useful example of the GROW model, imagine that you plan to make a trip.

First, you start with a map to visualize where your team wants to go (Goals) and identify where your team currently is (Current Reality). Then you explore various ways (Options) your team can make the trip. Finally, you will help ensure that your team is committed to making the trip (Wills) and is prepared for all the conditions and obstacles they may encounter on their way. As they progress on their road toward the destination (the established goals), you should remember to review their achievements (Results) regularly in order to identify gaps and actions they may need to take to put themselves back on the right track until they reach the final destination (Goals).

Traits of a Caring Leader and Manager

Before moving further ahead, let's say that in order to be a good leader or a true manager, we think you should be:

1. **Honest:** Honest means that you should say what you do and do what you say. This also means that when you make a mistake, you will not hesitate to admit it. Because no one is perfect, people will not hold a grudge against if you sincerely admit your mistakes; on the contrary, they will respect you more for your honesty. And if people respect you, they will be more likely to follow you than someone they do not respect.

2. **Open:** One of the most important character traits of a leader is to be open to people's ideas and opinions. Do not shut down any suggestion coming from the team or from people around you without first reviewing its merits.

3. **Authentic:** This means that you should not try to behave in a way that is not true to your values and beliefs. In other words, you do not try to play games by pretending to be someone you are not.

4. **Available:** We are all busy in corporate environments, but as a leader people expect you to be available to give them advice, listen to their concerns, and to give them feedback or clarification about something they do not understand well. So, adjust your calendar if you have to, but try to make yourself available to sit down with team members for at least a short talk before you find out if their issues or concerns would warrant any further clarification or meeting. As a servant-leader, you should keep your door open as much as possible to signal that even though you may be busy as a leader, you are always available to support the team.

5. **Caring about others:** In a society where success and promotion are key words, it may be hard to ask you to care about others. But when you think about it, it is ultimately your success that you are taking care of when you help your team members succeed at what they do. So, when

worse comes to worst, do try to think of taking care of the people you work with. That can only help you become even more successful. But if you are also a true servant leader who cares about people without always thinking about your own benefits, then that can enhance your image as a leader and a good human being.

Summary

The fact that the Scrum development team is self-organizing does not mean that there is no project management or leadership on a Scrum project, as is often the misconception.

Unlike the traditional command and control environment, the management responsibility is now split among the three components of the Scrum team: the ScrumMaster, the development team, and the product owner.

As far as leadership goes, anyone can be a leader as long as she has some influence over the team, but the people who we think can exert a lot of positive leadership over the team are mainly the product owner and the ScrumMaster, two of the three main types of what Mike Cohn referred to as leaders in his book, *Succeeding with Agile using Scrum*.

In order to sum up the different aspects of leadership along with techniques, which the product owner and the ScrumMaster could use, a quadrant of servant-leadership was presented, which has five components, namely vision, support, guide, mentoring, and coaching.

While most of these leadership aspects are somewhat well known, coaching is still relatively new, at least in software development. This is the reason we went into more detail on coaching in this chapter and, in particular, on the GROW model, which we extended with a new stage (Results) to provide an opportunity for continuous improvement as a support for the idea of continuous improvement in Agile.

To round out our discussion on management and leadership, you were also reminded in this chapter that the product owner and ScrumMaster should possess the following qualities to be good leaders and managers: (1) honesty, (2) openness, (3) authenticity, (4) availability, and (5) caring (about others).

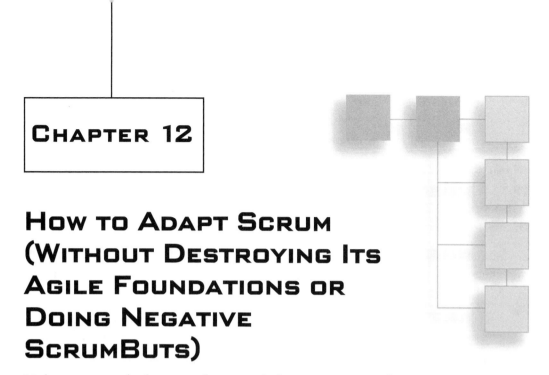

CHAPTER 12

HOW TO ADAPT SCRUM (WITHOUT DESTROYING ITS AGILE FOUNDATIONS OR DOING NEGATIVE SCRUMBUTS)

Unless you are lucky enough to work for a company where top management supports Scrum, middle management also supports Scrum, and the whole company or IT department has been completely reorganized for Scrum, your project or company environment may not be as perfect as Scrum prescribes.

Usually, you will find yourself in a company where management may have heard about Scrum or may even have tried it on a few projects, but they have not fired all the specialists and hired generalists or let go of all their project managers to replace them with only ScrumMasters. With the exception of some commercial software companies, most of corporate America, which represents around 99% of all companies, is still organized the old way, meaning with many separate functions within the IT departments. To see the truth of this statement, go to the Career page on the website of Capital One, one of the companies often cited as having adopted Scrum, and see how many business analysts, business systems analysts, and project managers they are still hiring. The same observation is true of the other large companies known for having moved into Agile or Scrum, such as Verizon, Sabre, NBC Universal, General Dynamics, Texas Instruments, and American Airlines, just to mention a few.

Because of this, you and your Scrum team will normally have to do a lot of education and negotiation to make things happen. All in all what we are saying is that you will need to adapt Scrum (without destroying its Agile roots) to make it work in your current company as it is currently set up. Scrum is, after all, only a means to an end, and for this reason, you should be, not dogmatic as some experts tend to be, but pragmatic as a practitioner should be.

If you need further convincing that you can and must adapt Scrum to your environment, refer to the article, "Scrum in the Church," by Jeff Sutherland, one of the original creators of Scrum, and Arline C. Sutherland, his spouse, in which they considered that adaptations were necessary as environments changed.

In that same article, Arline mentioned that, rather than every day, her church volunteers had their daily stand up only once every Friday when they came to church because they did not come to the church every day.

So, if you are convinced that we can adapt Scrum to our environments if we have to, the question now is how we can adapt Scrum without destroying its Agile foundations, or doing what is known as negative ScrumButs.

How to Adapt Scrum Without Doing Negative "ScrumButs" with Excuses

We asked ourselves this question some time ago while feeling completely lost when we first started to use Scrum. Luckily, after a few years, things started to sink in and we began to understand more about how we can adapt Scrum without betraying its Agile principles.

Things happen as if there were two kinds of "ScrumButs": the good ones and the bad ones.

The bad ones are more like what Ken Schwaber called "ScrumButs," or bad excuses, or wrong application of Scrum.

One example of negative "ScrumButs" would be: "We do Scrum, but we do not have anyone available to serve as a product owner."

The good ones would be more like the ones Jurgen Appelo, a CIO and well known Agile blogger, wrote about on his blog ("Scrumbuts are the best part of Scrum") back in 2009 where he gave some examples of positive "ScrumButs," which he called, like us, Scrum adaptations.

He went on to say that this is the best part of what teams can learn from Scrum Retrospectives, and we agree with him. On that same page of Jurgen Appelo's blog, Mike Cottmeyer, founder of the APLN in Atlanta, also agreed that the dogmatism of many Scrum practitioners was quite counter-productive. He believed, like us, that making adaptations should be encouraged unless it is to hide legitimate impediments.

We believe the subtle difference between these two types of ScrumButs is mainly based on whether the reason you have for not doing something as Scrum would normally require is good or bad. How to know if it is a positive or negative "ScrumBut" will take a lot of practice and especially a good understanding of the Agile spirit that we shared with you in Chapter 1, "It Is All About Agile and Scrum—Setting the Stage."

EXAMPLES OF SITUATIONAL SCRUM ADAPTATIONS

Without pretending to be exhaustive, below are some examples of situations where we have seen Scrum somewhat modified or even have suggested to teams to use Scrum somewhat differently from what it should be so that we can still use it despite the fact that some of the Scrum conditions were not present.

Organization Dimension

What if your organization still requires that your project status be reported in a PMO weekly meeting, using another template instead of the Burndown chart?

Besides the need to adapt to the request, mention should also be made with regard to the validity of the Burndown chart as a way to report the project team progress.

We have to admit to seasoned project managers, PMP or not, Burndown charts can be good quality, but what kind of progress do you think this chart really shows to a seasoned manager? Some but not much, but because the sprint is relatively short (around 30 days), it is somewhat acceptable.

When you take the time to think about it, you can easily see that knowing how many hours remain to perform does not really tell you any detail as to what has been done.

The remaining hours may sound a little more realistic than the traditional percentage of completion but not really much.

Because Scrum relies on transparency, we think a better measurement would be to report on the progress of the user stories, as shown in Figures 12.1 and 12.2, respectively, the story bar chart and its update.

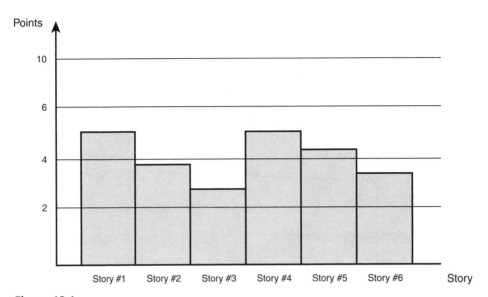

Figure 12.1
Burndown chart as story bar.

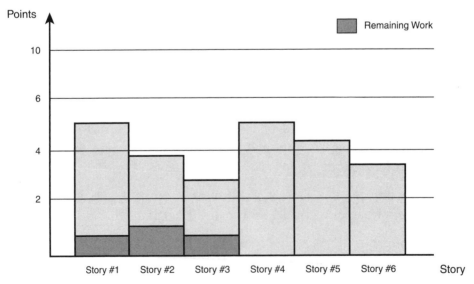

Figure 12.2
Story bar update.

What if management wants to see how much money has been spent on your Scrum project?

We have not found much in the general Scrum literature that addresses this legitimate question, and this is why we talked about the earned Value Analysis in Chapter 2, "Finance Speak."

If Scrum experts do not show enough interest in business management concerns with regard to financial project analysis, we are afraid that Scrum will not be part of the project management mainstream for a long time to come.

What if your organization still requires that someone be designated as the project manager on your Scrum project?

In this case, you should try to make it clear to management that one of the tenets of Scrum principles is team self-organization and the impact this would have in terms of project management.

As a matter of fact, being an Agile project manager would not mean directing people's work anymore but motivating and removing impediments to protect the teamwork during its sprint. Does that mean that the project manager can no longer suggest to the team what they should do to reach a high-level performance? Probably yes, but indirectly though.

What if no one is available or experienced enough to take on the role of the ScrumMaster?

There are two possible scenarios here:

First, if the team is new to Scrum, you may be in trouble unless you find out that someone from the team is quite versed in Scrum and ask her to play that role.

Second, if the team has had some experience working together with Scrum, the solution to this may be that you can just forgo the ScrumMaster role. If this is the case, just share the duties of the ScrumMaster among yourselves, as Jurgen Appelo also wrote about in his above mentioned blog.

What if management insists that one of the functional managers takes on the role of ScrumMaster?

Believe it or not, we have seen this before. The danger with this is that the manager is still used to the old style of command-and-control management philosophy and not Scrum. You simply cannot be a ScrumMaster if you have not made the transition from command and control to servant leadership and, especially, if you do not know and understand the servant-leadership foundation of Scrum. Among all other scenarios we have gone through so far, this may be the most potentially damaging situation.

So, before things get out of hand, you should have plenty to talk about with the manager regarding the changes in project management responsibilities with Scrum. Rather than saying no, you should say yes to give everyone a chance to transition into a new role, but if you are their coach, there will be a lot of education and hand holding that you will need to do. But that is what a coach is for, right?

What if team members are not able to meet physically or hold their daily stand-ups every day?

It can be okay if you can neither meet physically nor hold the daily standups every day. The only thing to remember in this situation is to be creative in finding a way to keep team members abreast of their progress towards the sprint goals. Skype and/or an electronic task board will be helpful.

Should you feel the need to be convinced by a higher authority about the fact that you cannot do daily Standup, find a copy of "Scrum in Church," an article co-written by Arline Conan Sutherland and her husband, Dr. Jeff Sutherland, one of the creators of Scrum, for Agile 2009. By reading that article, you will find out that this is exactly what Dr. Sutherland's wife went through herself in trying to implement Scrum daily Standup in her church environment.

What if the company management gives you a big team, larger than nine or ten people, to get the job done?

As long as management does not require that you keep a team this big, split the team into two to reach for an optimum team size between seven and nine people. Next, divide their work around the common-data element concept as we explained in Chapter 6, "The Influence of Architecture Vision on Team Velocity and Software Quality." This will help you organize the project teamwork around the feature team concept, which should allow small teams to operate, as independently as possible, while integrating as smoothly as possible their work into the larger product architecture.

Infrastructure Dimension

What if the needed testing infrastructure is not in place to help the team do automated, regression, or integration testing?

This could be a problem because automated testing and continuous integration are critical to Scrum success. One thing you can do in this case is either (1) try to talk with the QA department to get their help with this as soon as you can, or (2) try to do it on your own by having your team safely download some open-source automated testing and continuous integration software, even in your own development space, as suggested in Chapter 9, "The Importance of Automated Testing, and Continuous Integration."

What if your development team does not want to practice TDD (Test-Driven Development)?

Just in case you may be not familiar with TDD, let's say that it is an engineering practice by which your developers are asked to write unit test cases first (trying to make them fail) before they write your code (trying to make these same tests successful).

We know that many Scrum experts have come out in favor of TDD, and we think that it can be great. But if your team does not know, or want to do, TDD, you may still be okay (as long as you get your users do a lot of acceptance tests).

We say this because we have had the opportunity to work with excellent developers who did not do TDD but still delivered excellent code that worked the first time every time.

We still strongly recommend, if you have time and money, that you get your team to learn and practice TDD because it has proven to be a very effective engineering practice.

What if the testing team does not have anyone available to assign to work on your new Scrum project?

This will be a problem since early and continuous testing is a key part of being Agile. So, the first thing to do is to get some BA's (Business Analysts) or developers who can jump in to play this role. Your team velocity may take a hit at the beginning while the new guys try to get used to the tasks, but everything will likely work out as soon as you take action early on.

Team Dimension

What if most of your team members are new to Scrum and you do not have a ScrumMaster available to guide them?

This could be a problem unless you have someone on the team who is experienced with Scrum. If this is the case, ask him or her to serve as the ScrumMaster for the rest of the team and move forward.

If you do not have anyone on the team who knows enough about Scrum, this may be the time to ask for a coach.

What if they think that both the product owner and ScrumMaster should be combined into one due to budget constraints?

We do not think that this is optimal, but it is a scenario that has worked for us, although with some risks. Even though some experts have said that this should not be allowed, we still think that you go for it if this is the only way to try your hand at Scrum. But take precaution to ensure that this person is fully committed to do whatever it takes to get this new and combined role to work. By commitment, what we mean is that:

1. He should be committed to clearly let the team know when he is acting as a ScrumMaster and when he is acting as the product owner.

2. He should never take advantage of the situation to flip flop between the two for his own benefit.

All in all, this may be one of riskiest "ScrumButs" situations, but if this is the only option you are given to try Scrum, then go for it, while watching for the first opportunity, whenever you can, to get the roles to be split up.

Technology Dimension

What if the team is new to some supporting technology or infrastructure (such as automated or continuous integration tools), but no training in the technology will be provided?

As far as we can tell, this is going to be a problem that, sooner or later, will hit the team very hard because of their lack of knowledge of the tools they are supposed to use to help with their work. So, even if you are in a hurry to try Scrum, make sure to include some training money in your budget to ensure that your people are properly trained before you deploy them.

Process Dimension

What if teams do not define what they mean by *done*?

Even when one team works by itself, it is important to define what we mean by *done* since so many activities will depend on that. But when you have two or more Scrum teams working together, and no one wants to define done, then you are headed for problems. You have to define done whether you like it or not.

What if management suggests that you get some specialized phases organized in Scrum to take care of some of the activities that the team would not have time to take care of?

One of the Scrum principles is that everything should be done within the sprint. This is to say that you should never really need specialized Scrum phases, such as a testing iteration or a requirements phase.

Avoid this specialization phasing as much as you can, because it will bring you back to the waterfall model before you realize it.

What if someone suggests that a sprint should be longer than 30 days?

You have to be careful in dealing with this even though you do have some leeway to decide whether the sprint length should be more than 30 days.

While we have heard of six-week sprints, we really think that there is no reason not to stay with four-week sprints if you do Scrum. We recommend that you stay with four-week sprints and reduce the number of points to deliver, but do not extend the sprint length only because you think your product is a rather complex one and, therefore, your team will need more time to design code.

What if your company says that they still want requirements to be gathered as much as possible at the beginning of the project?

Believe it or not, this is something we still see happen too often in too many companies, especially the ones that are not readily set up for Scrum. But, doing this will defeat the very purpose of Agile and Scrum, which both talk about daily (or at least regular) interaction with the business end users to help ensure that their requirements be understood. So, do not do this and try to start on the right footing by gathering only high-level requirements for release planning and then gather some more by keeping the conversation going with the business users throughout the process.

What if management still insists that you use Scrum within your company's current Software Development Life Cycle (SDLC)?

If your company SDLC is a waterfall life cycle, then it is going to be impossible because Scrum is based on an incremental framework. So, go back to your management and explain to them that Agile is not waterfall but incremental and iterative.

What if the QA or infrastructure team tells you that they do not have a good foundation for continuous integration or daily build?

Dangerous situation for sure since this is the very foundation of Agile and Scrum. Do not start your Scrum project unless something like this exists first and you will not regret it.

Business Dimension

What if business management does not have any product owner?

In this case, ask if you could have access to someone such as a business manager or, at least, a knowledgeable and respectable business analyst, who could take on this role. This person should have the needed empowerment and support from their business management to make all the decisions for them.

We know we have not covered all the situations in this chapter you may encounter in the real life world. The intent here was only to give you an idea how you can adapt Scrum to your real world situations while keeping your adaptations fully in line with the Agile and, therefore, Scrum, spirit.

Summary

We all have, at one time or another in our software professional life, wished that we could discover some process or methodology that we could apply to every project, and that it would ensure that things just work out for the best.

Unfortunately, work life is not that simple, and for those of us who have been looking for a long time, no such process or methodology has ever existed nor will it. This is also true for Scrum.

Without giving way to what some experts call negative "ScrumButs," we have reviewed in this chapter some examples of situations where you may need to adapt Scrum while trying not to destroy its Agile spirit. This is the reason we started our book with a discussion on the Agile Manifesto in Chapter 1.

Others, such as Rev. Arline Conan Sutherland, Dr. Jeff Sutherland's spouse, and Jurgen Appelo, have written about their experience with Scrum adaptations, which Jurgen considers to be the best of Scrum retrospectives.

In following their example, we have also related some of our experience with the positive "ScrumButs" in this chapter for you to take inspiration from. We are sure that you will have your own adaptation to write about sometime in the near future.

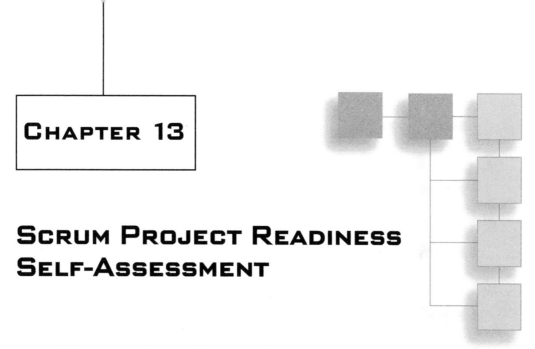

CHAPTER 13

SCRUM PROJECT READINESS SELF-ASSESSMENT

It would be great to know what your chance of success is before you start your Scrum journey so that you can know where you should put your focus to improve your odds. In this chapter you will learn how to do a straightforward self-assessment of your project so that you can predict your chances of success before you begin.

A SIMPLE TOOL FOR YOUR SCRUM READINESS ASSESSMENT

In Figure 13.1, you can see that the assessment is based on a scoring of six dimensions, which we have seen throughout the book.

1. **Organization Dimension**

   This is mainly to assess if your different departments and teams are familiar with Scrum values and practices or not. The more they are, the better your experience will be.

2. **Infrastructure Dimension**

   This is mainly to assess if your testing infrastructure is in place to allow your team to perform all the needed tests, which we mentioned in Chapter 6, "The Influence of Architecture Vision on Team Velocity and Software Quality."

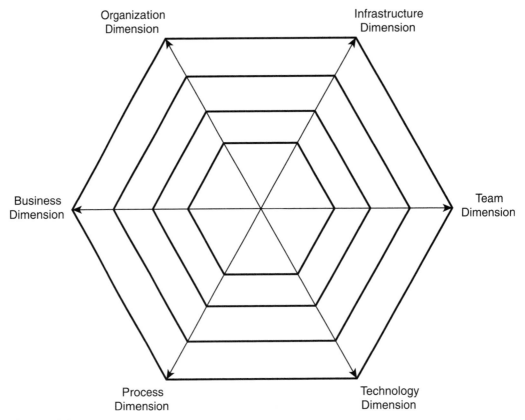

Figure 13.1
The Scrum self-assessment readiness matrix.

3. **Team Dimension**

This is mainly to assess the level of relationship between your project team members, a key ingredient to a good teamwork.

4. **Technology Dimension**

This is mainly to assess whether your team is knowledgeable about the technology to be used. While not being a problem per se on a Scrum project, this is to help you know where your team stands on this so you can factor it into your estimate.

5. **Process Dimension**

This is mainly to assess if your company has already had good knowledge or practical experience with Scrum or not.

6. **Business Dimension**

This is mainly to assess whether your business partner is quite aware of or familiar with Scrum requirements and practices. As you can guess, the more they are aware, the better you will be. Among the first benefit of the business knowing about Scrum is that you will likely get a product owner who is empowered, fully engaged, and knowledgeable.

Depending on the answers and scores you get for these, they will either help you or make your Scrum journey a rather difficult one.

The way the questionnaire works, the more your answer to a question is good or positive, the higher your score will be; the maximum (best) is +2 while the minimum (worst) is 0.

When you total up all your responses, you will get a score somewhere between 0 and 36.

If you get a total of 0 (minimum), it means that your project environment is such that you are going to have a hard time delivering on your project promises.

If you get a total of 36 (maximum), it means that your project environment is such that you have a maximum chance of being successful at delivering on your project promises.

If your score is over 18 (with +18 being the average), you are above average and can be very successful with Scrum, but it looks as if you have some issues to work on to improve your team's ability to deliver. This could be to help the project team members work well together if they are new to one another or if they have had some bad experience on a previous project.

If you get a total of less than 18, this means that your chance of success is far less than average. You can still be successful, though, if you try hard to improve some issues in your project's surrounding environment, thereby increasing your team's ability to deliver.

Print out this questionnaire in Figures 13.2–13.7 and complete it to the best of your ability, and soon you will be on your way towards becoming a Scrum practitioner.

Organization Dimension

Factor	Value Range (0/+3)
1. Have different departments worked successfully together on a Scrum projects previously?	
2. Does some strong resistance within the organization exist with regard to Scrum?	
3. Does a great support for Scrum between different departments exist within the company?	

Figure 13.2
Organization dimension.

Infrastructure Dimension

Factor	Value Range (0/+3)
1. Is automatic testing already in place and a common practice?	
2. Is continuous integration testing already in place and a common practice?	
3. Is daily build environment already in place and a common practice?	

Figure 13.3
Infrastructure dimension.

Team Dimension

Factor	Value Range (0/+3)
1. Is the team completely new to Scrum?	
2. Have the team members successfully worked together before?	
3. Do team members know well and appreciate one another?	

Figure 13.4
Team dimension.

Technology Dimension

Factor	Value Range (0/+3)
1. Is the development team very experienced in the programming language?	
2. Are development team members very experienced in the technology to be employed?	
3. Is a Scrum production environment already ready?	

Figure 13.5
Technology dimension.

Process Dimension

Factor	Value Range (0/+3)
1. Is Scrum the company's adopted process framework?	
2. Is there a good support for Scrum within the company?	
3. Is there strong resistance against Scrum within the company?	

Figure 13.6
Process dimension.

Business Dimension

Factor	Value Range (0/+3)
1. Is there a Product Owner fully available and completely engaged with the team?	
2. Is the Product Owner familiar with Scrum but has no practical experience?	
3. Has the Product Owner successfully used Scrum before?	

Figure 13.7
Business dimension.

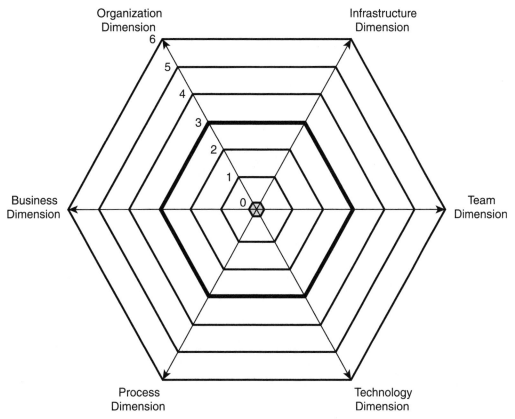

Figure 13.8
A minimum score on the Scrum self-assessment readiness matrix.

Here you are at the end of the questionnaire.

Depending on all the answers you get, you may get a minimum of 0, represented by a small dot in the middle of Figure 13.8.

However, if you are really lucky, you may get a maximum of 36, which covers the whole of Figure 13.9, with the second ring representing the average value.

If you are like some teams and companies, you may get a total value that averages around 18, with some high and some low scores on the different dimensions. Figure 13.10 illustrates this case.

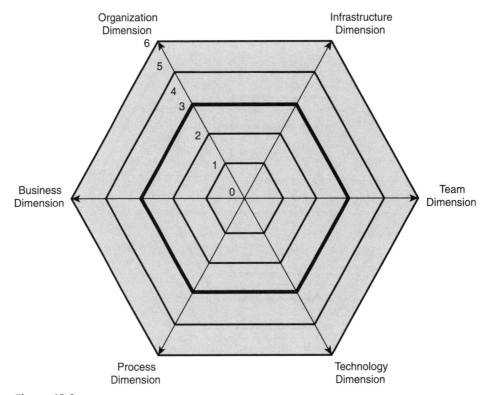

Figure 13.9
A maximum score (36) on the Scrum self-assessment readiness matrix.

If this is the case, it will be your responsibility to try to get the lower score to become higher as you go (or before you go) in order to improve on your project team's chance of being successful with Scrum.

EXAMPLE

For illustration purposes, let's go through the six dimensions and see how we scored when we first started to use Scrum in our business a few years ago (Figures 13.11–13.15).

Take a look at the score for each dimension in Figure 13.16. You will notice that while we were doing quite well with our organization, business, technology, team, and process dimensions, we need to make an effort to improve on our (testing) infrastructure dimension, which only got a score of 1.

Example   165

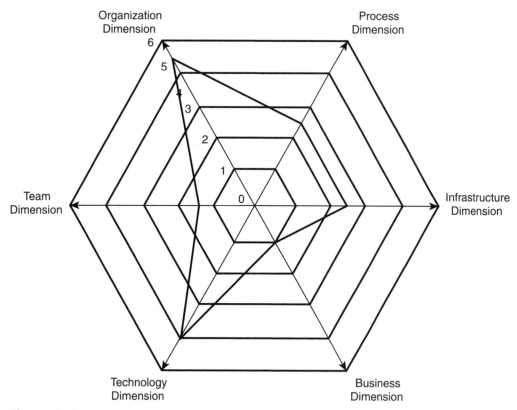

Figure 13.10
An average score (18) on the Scrum self-assessment matrix.

Factor	Value Range (-2/+2)
1. Have different departments worked successfully together on a Scrum project previously?	-2
2. Does some strong resistance within the organization exist with regard to Scrum?	+1
3. Does a great support for Scrum between different departments exist within the company?	+1

Figure 13.11
Organization dimension.

Factor	Value Range (-2/+2)
1. Is automatic testing already in place a common practice?	-2
2. Is continuous integration testing already in place and a common practice?	-2
3. Is daily build environment already in place and a common practice?	-2

Figure 13.12
Development infrastructure dimension.

Factor	Value Range (-2/+2)
1. Is the team completely new to Scrum?	+1
2. Have the team members successfully worked together before?	+1
3. Do team members know well and appreciate one another?	+2

Figure 13.13
Team dimension.

Add the scores for the six environment dimensions to determine the total value we obtained for the self-assessment. In this case, the total is 20 (3+1+4+4+3+5). What this means to us is (1) that the environment makes our project team job neither difficult nor easy, and (2) therefore, the coefficient of multiplication we should use to do the story estimation is 1.

Example   167

Factor	Value Range (-2/+2)
1. Is the development team very experienced in the programming language?	+2
2. Are development team members very experienced in the technology to be employed?	+2
3. Is a Scrum production environment already ready?	0

Figure 13.14
Technology dimension.

Factor	Value Range (-2/+2)
1. Is Scrum the company's adopted process framework?	+1
2. Is there a good support for Scrum within the company?	+1
3. Is there strong resistance against Scrum within the company?	+1

Figure 13.15
Process dimension.

With this in mind and with our first sprint planning meeting under way, we were able to calculate our story point and obtain the table in Figure 13.17 for the first three stories, which had an UP (Unadjusted Point) of 7, 7, and 8.

As a result of our effort to improve on our testing infrastructure, we were able to improve our score on the testing dimension and obtain a total value of 25 for the self-assessment as can be seen in Figure 13.18.

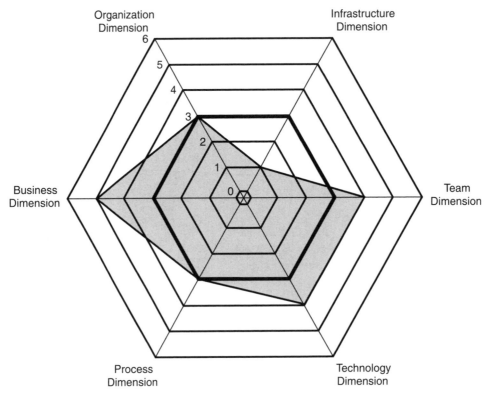

Figure 13.16
The scoring of a start-up company when it starts its first Scrum project.

	Characteristics				Total UP (Unadjusted Points)	Coefficient	AP (Adjusted Points)	ED (Environment Dimension)	PPS (=(AP*ED)/36)
PBIs (Story)	Interaction Type	Business Rules	Entities	Data Manipulation Type					
Sprint 1									
Sign Up	3	1	1	2	7	1	14	20	8
Sign In	3	1	1	2	7	1	7	20	4
Logout	3	1	1	1	6	1	6	20	3
Add Room	3	1	1	2	7	1	7	20	4
Total									19

Figure 13.17
Estimation matrix for sprint 1. Legend: Remember that AP (Adjusted Points) = UP (Unadjusted Points) × C (Coefficient) and PPS (Points Per Story) = (AP × ED)/36.

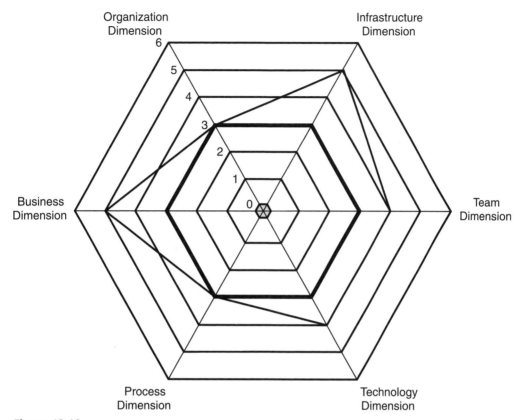

Figure 13.18
The scoring after testing infrastructure was improved.

With this result, we knew that we were able to improve on our coefficient of multiplication and, therefore, should use 0.5 (instead of 1 during sprint 1), which yields the table in Figure 13.19, knowing that the UP (Unadjusted Points) for the four new stories were all equal to 8.

PUTTING IT TOGETHER

The idea behind this assessment is that once you know where you land, you can then try to improve your score from that dimension until it reaches a certain value, like 4, which should give you a better hope to be more successful with Scrum.

	Characteristics				Total UP (Unadjusted Points)	Coefficient	AP (Adjusted Points)	ED (Environment Dimension)	PPS (=(AP*ED)/36)
Sprint 3	Interaction Type	Business Rules	Entities	Data Manipulation Type					
Edit Profile	3	1	1	3	8	0.5	4	24	3
Cancel Account	3	1	1	1	6	0.5	3	24	2
Delete Room	3	1	1	1	6	0.5	3	24	2
Browse Rooms	3	1	1	1	6	0.5	3	24	2
Browse Recordings	3	1	1	1	6	0.5	12	24	8
Total									17

Figure 13.19
Estimation matrix for sprint 2 after testing infrastructure is improved. Legend: Remember that AP (Adjusted Points) = UP (Unadjusted Points) × C (Coefficient) and PPS (Points Per Story) = (AP × ED)/36.

All in all, your goal will be to get closer and stay close to the following targets:

1. Frequent software delivery.

2. Regular collaboration between the business and the software team.

3. Time-boxing everything or every meeting to avoid having things drag out too long.

4. Frequent inspect and adapt cycle.

5. Team self-management and empowerment.

6. And everything, at a sustainable pace (for team not to be burned out).

SUMMARY

One of the ways to know what your chance of success is with Scrum is to perform an honest self-assessment of where you stand using some sort of Scrum project readiness matrix. In this chapter we provided you with an easy to use and straightforward matrix, comprising six dimensions.

1. Organization Dimension

2. Infrastructure Dimension

3. Team Dimension

4. Technology Dimension

5. Process Dimension

6. Business Dimension

Your answers and the scores you get for these dimensions will help or hinder your Scrum journey.

If you get a total of 36 (maximum), this means that your project environment is such that you have a maximum chance of being successful.

If you get a total of more than 18 (with 18 being the average), this means that your chances of success are above average, and although there are some issues, you can be very successful with Scrum.

If your total is less than 18, this means that your chance of success is below average.

If you get a total of 0 (minimum), this means that your project environment is such that you are going to have a hard time delivering on your project promises.

For illustration purposes, an example was given in this chapter of the scores of a start-up company when it started its first Scrum project for the six environmental dimensions. The company's total was 20.

We also provided some suggestions in this chapter on how to improve your odds for success.

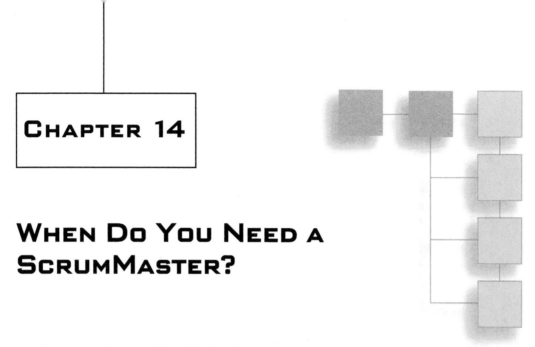

CHAPTER 14

WHEN DO YOU NEED A SCRUMMASTER?

We have not discussed in depth the ScrumMaster until now because, in a way, this book should serve as your ScrumMaster. However, in order to complete the description of the role of the ScrumMaster we will describe, in this chapter, the qualities you should look for in a human ScrumMaster.

Experience has taught us that a ScrumMaster should, first and foremost, possess seven qualities and skills, shown in Figure 14.1.

The seven qualities a ScrumMaster should have are:

1. In depth theoretical and practical knowledge of Scrum
2. Great servant-leadership ability
3. Strong organizational skills
4. Great communication skills
5. Excellent presentation skills
6. Conflict resolution skills
7. Excellent human development skills

Let's review these qualities, one by one:

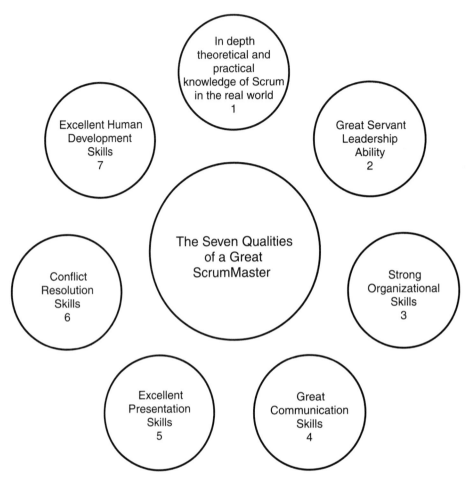

Figure 14.1
The seven qualities of a ScrumMaster.

IN DEPTH THEORETICAL AND PRACTICAL KNOWLEDGE OF SCRUM

Among the seven qualities of a ScrumMaster, it is quite understandable that knowledge of Scrum should rank first.

More than a theoretical knowledge of Scrum, even if that knowledge is confirmed by certification, a practical knowledge of Scrum earned from experience is what will serve you best in a ScrumMaster.

As you know by now, although Scrum looks simple in theory, implementing Scrum in the real world is quite challenging, especially if the company in which you work has not reorganized its operations around Scrum. This is why we covered early in this book how to approach the other teams to get their buy-in and collaboration.

GREAT SERVANT-LEADERSHIP ABILITY

Because Scrum is part of the Agile movement and is based on the idea that a team will be more effective if its members are allowed to be self-organized and empowered to do their job as they see fit, it is important that the ScrumMaster should be someone who understands and believes in servant-leadership.

In other words, one of the most critical roles of the ScrumMaster is to serve the team during sprints by removing as many impediments as possible and to protect the team as much as possible from external disturbances.

STRONG ORGANIZATIONAL SKILLS

If the team and the product owner are new to Scrum (or even when they are familiar with Scrum), they will rely on the ScrumMaster to help organize quite a few meetings as required by Scrum to reap the benefits of Scrum and to carry out their work.

From release planning to sprint planning meetings to the daily Scrum to Scrum review and retrospective, it is clear that there are quite a few meetings that the ScrumMaster should help organize.

Without the ScrumMaster's help, the team and the product owner will have difficulty coping with all the meetings while trying to move forward with their work.

GREAT COMMUNICATION SKILLS

With the ScrumMaster being the person who is supposed to know the most about Scrum, there is no doubt that communication skills should be high on her list of skills and qualities.

Why? It is because the project's ScrumMaster will be expected to communicate with a lot of people, including team members, other teams, technical and business management, and the product owner to help them understand the benefits and requirements of Scrum.

A less well known aspect of the ScrumMaster's role is to help the product owner prepare for and attend management reporting meetings, which, obviously, requires that the ScrumMaster be well versed in communication.

Excellent Presentation Skills

Because communication is one of the most crucial aspects of a ScrumMaster's role, the ability to do presentations is another skill the ScrumMaster should have to be successful. Whether by using PowerPoint or any other tool for presentation to communicate with the rest of the organization, it is key that the ScrumMaster hone as much as possible his presentation skills.

Conflict Resolution Skills

Unless you are lucky enough to work in a company where everyone loves everyone else or where Scrum has proven to be so successful that no one is in conflict with anyone else, your team is likely to experience conflict. One of the skills the ScrumMaster should absolutely master is knowing how to help team members resolve conflict in case their conflict ends up affecting the team's ability to deliver. This is another lesser known aspect of the ScrumMaster's leadership role. It isn't often discussed in a classroom setting, but it is, in practice, something the ScrumMaster is expected to help with in order to keep the team moving forward.

Great Human Development Skills

This is another skill the ScrumMaster should have to help guide and develop the team into a high performance team. This can be accomplished mostly by way of indirect challenge and encouragement.

Summary

One of the most critical roles on a Scrum project, the ScrumMaster is, whether one likes it or not, someone who should be expected not only to help remove impediments but also to help resolve conflict and help turn the team into a high performance team. For this, he should have at least seven qualities, which we reviewed in this chapter.

CHAPTER 15

PARTING THOUGHTS

Here you are at the end of our book. Thank you and congratulations! Rather than just let you move ahead alone, here are some parting words as to how to apply the book to your real-world project situations.

The first assumption we make is that you read Chapter 1 first, either as your introduction to Agile and Scrum or as a refreshment of the Scrum class you just took with the team. Even if you may have read other books or whitepapers on Agile or Scrum, Chapter 1 will help you be on the same page as us and help you successfully adapt Scrum to your environment in case you have constraints that will not let you use Scrum "out of the box," as is the case in most of the project situations we have seen.

In order to benefit the most from what you have learned in this book, you should:

- Use or customize the questionnaires in Chapter 13 to do a Scrum readiness self-assessment of your project environment as soon as you can in order to have an idea of your chance of being able to deliver with Scrum. Do this preferably before you begin your project journey or as soon as you get management's green light to move forward. Try to be honest in answering the questions.

- Because the focus of business executives is on the financial side, try to temper your excitement for Agile or Scrum by talking less about how much you are going to be able to deliver better software faster and more about financial returns. Quantify what you think management will get from your project in terms of financial returns and costs, and management will be more likely to listen to your ideas. This is what we deal with in Chapter 2.

■ Although it is important to have support from your executives and top management, remember to seek good buy-in and collaboration from middle management; it is during their interaction with Scrum teams that the rubber meets the road for your project. As we said in Chapter 3, this relationship with middle management will make or break your project, regardless of the support you may have from top business management.

■ Believe it or not, we have seen more Scrum projects lag in performance or simply fail due to a lack of good, properly written, requirements for Scrum rather than a lack of funding or technical know-how. So unless you are an expert in requirements gathering for Agile or Scrum, Chapter 4 should be something you want to read in order to investigate a technique that is useful to everyone. The way requirements are written also has an impact on how successful you will be with your project release and sprint planning, and we show you how to write effective Agile requirements.

■ As Agile and Scrum become more widespread, one of the impediments to their implementation across the enterprise is the fact that team velocity, or the number of user story points that the team can deliver per iteration or sprint, is not comparable between different teams. So, if you want to know how to estimate story points so that they can be easily explained and comparable between different teams, you should make it a point to try the technique in Chapter 5.

■ Despite the fact that some of us may wish that we no longer have anything to do with software architecture altogether, in the same way that architecture is essential to the stability and scalability of a building, software architecture is critical to our software quality and, therefore, project success. Given the Agile nature of our project, the key here is to learn how to identify it or at least its intent without spending all our time fleshing it out first, and to use it to improve team velocity and software quality. This is the main subject of Chapter 6.

- The benefits of a good architecture vision are expanded upon in Chapter 7. You should leverage the developments in Chapter 7 to understand how to use architecture vision to come up with release plans that can deliver the most business value yet avoid having user stories drive a fractional, and ultimately incoherent, system design.

- Everyone is important on a Scrum project, but the product owner is without a doubt the one person who could make the business love or hate your team. You may want to refer to Chapter 8 often to see what personal and professional qualities a product owner should have to make sure that your product owner has what it takes. If, for some reason, your product owner happens not to be like the person we describe in Chapter 8, then you have your work cut out for you.

- Among all the important things you should verify is whether your project testing environment is ready for your delivery. As we guess that you do not have an unlimited timeline or budget, we will recommend that you do the three most important tests: automatic, regression, and continuous integration tests. Review this in Chapter 9 to know how you should organize your testing infrastructure.

- Even though budget, requirements, and testing infrastructure, among other things, are important items for you to take care of, we strongly recommend that you pay attention to the dynamics between all the team members who have been lined up on your project. For all the projects we have been involved with, it is always teamwork that either makes or breaks the project. This is something Patrick Lencioni discusses in his book, *Five Dysfunctions of Teams*. Refer to Chapter 10 as often as you need because teamwork is key to your success.

- Believe it or not, the fact that the team is self-managed on a Scrum project does not make project management and team leadership easier, just different. In some ways, the leadership and project management challenges can become even more complex.

- So, as we recommend that you look into your team dynamics as early as possible, we will make you the same recommendation that you look into the soft side of project management and team leadership as soon as you can. You will find guidance for this in Chapter 11.

- As soon as you finish the self-assessment for your Scrum project readiness, you should look at the results and see how you can gain inspiration from Chapter 12 to see what aspect of Scrum you should modify in order to get it to work in your environment. The sooner you take care of this, the more time you will have to find out whether your adaptation is working or not and eventually make another round of adaptations, as needed.

- Last but not least, Chapter 14 will give you a summary of the human qualities that each ScrumMaster should have to be successful.

Good luck to you in your Agile/Scrum journey!

Andrew Pham

Phuong-Van Pham

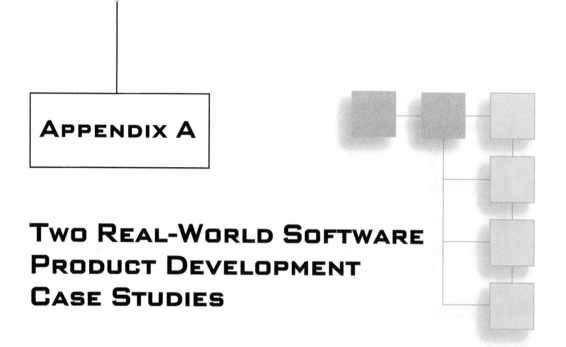

Appendix A

Two Real-World Software Product Development Case Studies

Introduction

In this appendix, we will lead you through two examples of how the advice given in this book has been successfully used to build and deploy two software products, with Scrum teams as small as five people and Sprints as short as one week.

Ruby and Ruby on Rails (RoR)

In order to better understand the examples, which are a subset of the actual applications, it is recommended that you know a bit of Ruby on Rails. If you have no previous experience with Ruby on Rails but have used other web frameworks, like Django or CakePHP, feel free to skip on to the case studies. If you have no experience, no problem! We will explain Ruby, Ruby on Rails, and all the code examples as we present them.

Ruby, the Language

In order to provide you with some knowledge about Ruby if you happen not to be a Ruby developer, we are going to review the fundamental Ruby syntax in the following pages. While it is by no means a complete introduction, it will help you understand the examples written in Ruby later in this appendix.

Syntax and Constructs

Ruby syntax is extremely simple yet versatile—meant to be adopted by the programmer in the way she prefers. For example, while in other languages you would always have semicolons to terminate a statement, Ruby lets you leave them off. However, if you want, Ruby lets you terminate each line with a semicolon. It all depends on your personal programming style. We will go through syntax and constructs simultaneously because they are not mutually exclusive topics.

Since Ruby is primarily an object-oriented programming language, we will delve into the topic of objects and how to create them in Ruby. Object-oriented languages allow us to structure our programs in terms of real-world objects, which many argue makes it easier to organize code and develop in general.

Classes and Objects

First, it is important to understand the relationship between classes and objects in all object-oriented languages, not just Ruby. A class acts as a blueprint from which an object is created. An often-used analogy is that a class is a blueprint for a house, and each object is an actual house created from that blueprint. Classes are important because they allow us to set up the state (attributes) and behavior of each object instantiated (created) from it.

So as an example, let us create an empty class that will model a person, and we will fill in as we go along in the chapter.

```
class  Person
end
```

That's it! Now we have a class Person that we can fill in to truly model a person with its attributes and behaviors. If we wanted to create an actual object from this class, it would be simple in Ruby. All you have to do is use the new method like so:

```
Person.new
```

Now, we can begin to fill in the attributes of a person. In order to do so, however, we need to first learn about variables in Ruby.

Variables

Variables are ways for programs to hold data and manipulate it throughout the program's life. However, variables in Ruby are different from typed languages such as Java because you do not need to explicitly state the kind of data you expect it to hold beforehand. For example, to create a variable in Java that will hold a number, you must do this:

```
int variableInJava = 10;
String variableInJava = "This is a string";
Array variableInJava = {1, 2, 3, 4, 5};
```

In Ruby, all you have to do is this:

```
variableInRuby = 10;
variableInRuby = "This is a string"
variableInRuby = [1, 2, 3, 4, 5];
```

Although this is an extremely simple example, this ability lets you create or change variables easily during runtime (when a program is running) which is very useful as your programs increase in complexity.

Now, let's add some attributes to the Person class.

```
class Person
    # This is a comment - this line is ignored by the interpreter.
    attr_accessor :name, :age, :weight, :height
end
```

Now the Person class has the ability to create Person objects, each with a name, age, weight, and height. There are a couple of new things introduced in the previous example, namely, the attr_accessor method (and methods for that matter) and the strange ':' syntax.

attr_accessor is a method (we'll explain more about what methods are later) that essentially creates instance variables with names corresponding to the list of names we give it (in this case, we gave them the names name, age, weight, and height). Because our class has this declaration, each instance (object) of our class will have those instance variables available. The ':' is a literal constructor of Ruby's Symbol class. It is essentially a way of identifying something immutably. With that in mind, let's go on to talk about data types in Ruby.

Data Types

Ruby has many different data types represented by the classes String, Array, Hash, Fixnum, Symbol, and more.

Strings are essentially ways for Ruby to represent letters, words, sentences, or anything similar. To create a string in Ruby, you can do this:

```
@string = "This is a string"
```

This will create an instance variable that holds the string "This is a string."

Arrays are used to hold collections of objects in Ruby. For example, this would be similar to the concept of a family—a family is merely a collection of people related to one another. To create an array in Ruby, you can do this:

```
@family = ['John', 'Mary', 'Adam', 'Susan']
```

To get 'John' from the array, you use an index like so:

```
@family[0] # This will give you 'John'
```

Hashes are similar to arrays except you can identify each value with a unique key for retrieval later. For example, going back to the previous example, instead of having to use a number-based index to get 'John', you could create a hash like this:

```
@family = {'Dad' => 'John', 'Mom' => 'Mary', 'Son' => 'Adam', 'Daughter' => 'Susan' }
```

And then you could get 'John' from the hash by doing this:

```
@family['Dad']
```

Whole numbers in Ruby are commonly represented by Fixnums. Creating a whole number is simple; all you have to do is this:

```
@number = 1
```

This will give you an instance variable with a value of 1.

Symbols are similar to strings but are usually used to identify other things—just like the definition of symbol itself. They are commonly used in hashes to act as a key for a value. So like the example before, you could create a hash for a family like this:

```
@family = { :dad => 'John', :mom => 'Mary', :son => 'Adam', :daughter => 'Susan' }
```

Methods

Methods are ways of introducing behavior into programs. Typically, you would call a method in an object in order to make it do something. For example, let's add a greet method to the Person class.

```
class Person
    # This is a comment - this line is ignored by the interpreter.
    attr_accessor :name, :age, :weight, :height

    def greet
        puts "Hello, my name is #{self.name}."
end
end
```

If we create a new Person and give him the name 'John', and then call greet, this will happen:

```
@person = Person.new
@person.name = "John"
@person.greet
=> Hello, my name is John.
```

As you can see from the introduction above, Ruby stresses simplicity and ease; therefore, many programs written in Ruby can usually be read and understood by non-programmers, since the syntax is meant to reflect natural language as much as possible. While it is often considered simple, Ruby is also a very versatile language with the ability to combine many simple constructs to create programs that accomplish extremely complex goals.

Let's now examine the Ruby on Rails framework while simultaneously explaining the Ruby code used within each example.

Ruby on Rails (RoR), the Web Framework

Ruby on Rails is a web framework used in conjunction with Ruby by David Heinemeier Hansson. The term "web framework" in the real-world usually refers to software that enables you to write better programs by giving you specific or recommended ways of organizing your code. It also gives you much reusable code, which prevents you from wasting development time re-creating the wheel.

Two oft-stated principles of Ruby on Rails are don't repeat yourself and convention over configuration. Don't repeat yourself simply means that you should structure your program in such a way that you can reuse code as much as possible, not wasting time coding the same thing over and over again. Convention over configuration means that Ruby on Rails comes with a predefined configuration that is often well-suited for the creation of most web applications. You won't have to waste time tweaking the software to match your need. Of course, if you absolutely have to, you still have the option of tweaking the software. These principles make Ruby on Rails a good candidate as a web framework for Scrum teams hoping to create a web application.

MVC

One of the biggest advantages of Ruby on Rails comes in the form of how it recommends (essentially forces) you to organize your code. This three-tiered structure is typically referred to as MVC or Model-View-Controller. Three-tiered simply means that there are three different related layers of code that work together to produce a desired effect in an application. In the following sections, we will explain what each part of the MVC architecture does, but in a different order than is often shown in different books.

View   The View is what the user sees. When you go to a website, the page that shows up on your screen is called the View. It usually comprises HTML, CSS, and embedded Ruby, which structure, style, and populate the View, respectively.

What is typically shown in the View? Data that is most relevant to the user—but where does that come from? Here's where the model comes in. . . .

Model   The Model is the way data in your application is stored, retrieved, and manipulated. Often, the Model is described as the part that contains business logic and data.

In Rails, the Model is a class that typically uses ActiveRecord to access data in the database. The use of ActiveRecord is what creates an object-relational mapping between your objects and database-backed data. What that means is that each row in the database has the potential to be interacted with as an object (instead of long, complex SQL statements), leading to more simplistic and comprehensible data manipulation within your application. As an example, say you have a Computer model. The Computer model has a few properties such as speed, memory, and hard drive. With ActiveRecord, you would have a table in your database called Computers with columns labeled Speed, Memory, and Hard drive. Now, when you want to add a row to the Computers table, you would declare and instantiate a new computer somewhere in your application (usually in the controller or model) with the following code:

```
@computer = Computer.new
```

Then you would define the properties of the computer to your liking (see how ActiveRecord automatically maps these property names to columns in your database without you having to ever declare it?):

```
@computer.speed = "2"
@computer.memory = "1024"
@computer.hard_drive = "320"
```

This is where the beauty of the ActiveRecord component in Rails comes in—if you want to save this new computer object to the database, all you have to do is:

```
@computer.save
```

That's it! Now your computer is saved to the database. But what if you want to retrieve it later to inspect its properties? All you have to do is (assuming this computer is the first computer in the Computers table):

```
@computer = Computer.find(1)
```

Now, you can inspect its properties with:

```
# This is a comment
# puts simply prints out whatever you ask it to, to the console - in this case,
# "speed", "memory", and "hard_drive"
puts @computer.speed
puts @computer.memory
puts @computer.hard_drive
```

In case you ever want to delete a computer, all you have to do is (if you know the ID of the computer in the database):

```
@computer.destroy
```

ActiveRecord certainly makes developers' lives easier when it comes to accessing, manipulating, or deleting data in a database by acting as a more intelligent layer between your classes and the database.

The last question is, how does the application know what View to show and, correspondingly, what data to retrieve, from the Model to show in the View?

Controller   The controller acts like a middleman between the view and model. When you type a URL in your browser, you are sending a request to the servers the website is located or hosted on. There is a controller-like structure that receives that request and sends the view you want back to you while also retrieving the data from the model to be shown in the view.

A summary of how RoR will fit into an MVC framework is presented in Figure A.1 below, taken mainly from what you saw in Chapters 6 and 7.

So Why Is MVC Good?   The MVC architecture allows you to organize your code in such a way that, for example, changing how parts of it look to users only requires you to modify a certain part of the application as opposed to having to dig through the entire application to find different parts to change, which often takes hours or days.

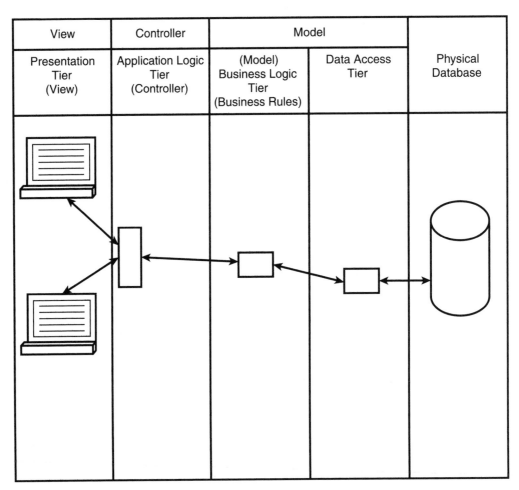

Figure A.1
Diagram of the MVC Framework.

This means that under real-world constraints and conditions in which change is imminent and inevitable, you can easily be flexible and move with the flow without incurring large development costs.

VERSION CONTROL AND TESTING FOR WEB DEVELOPMENT WITH RoR

To develop the case studies which are presented in this appendix, we used Ruby on Rails in conjunction with Git for version control, and Test::Unit for testing, both of which helped create an environment very conducive to better development for reasons we will soon be explaining.

Git—Version Control

Git is an open-source and free version control system that was created as an alternative to Subversion, Mercurial, and CVS. A version control system allows you to essentially store all of your code into one central place in the form of snapshots. This means, if you begin working on a part of the application and you realize that you just messed up the entire application, you can easily get the last working code you stored in the version control system and start over on a clean slate.

However, the real benefits of a version control system such as Git are the collaboration capabilities. Since all the code is stored in a central location, this means that several developers can work together in parallel on different or the same parts of the application (an important tenet of this book) and "push" the code they worked on back into the repository while Git merges all of the code together to produce a copy of code that integrates all of the changes made in parallel by the different developers (another important tenet of this book).

While the decision of which version control system to use depends on the needs of your application, we decided to use Git because it is easy-to-use, simple to set up, and free (because it is open-source software).

Testing and Testing Framework

Testing is important not only in that it ensures that your application functions as expected without much effort (and therefore allows for more flexibility in development because changing the application has a lower cost since you have tests to ensure it still works), but also in that it ensures that the application fulfills the needs of the client, specifically with user acceptance tests.

Test::Unit is a testing framework for Ruby and Ruby on Rails that, despite its name, can do unit, functional, and integration testing. It is a very straightforward and simple testing framework with much of the testing done through assertions—which are programmatic ways of saying, "The result this code produces should match this expected outcome."

There are three major types of tests that you can run using an automated testing tool such as Test::Unit on a RoR project:

1. **Unit tests:** Testing individual, atomic parts (can no longer be broken down into a smaller part) of your application—usually for errors in logic with strict inputs and outputs.

2. **Functional tests:** Testing the coordination of individual, atomic parts of your application without the interface (which is often the view).

3. **Integration tests:** Testing the coordination of individual, atomic parts of your application along with the interface (which is often the view).

Automated Testing

As we explained in Chapter 9, automated testing differs from manual testing in that a software program runs all your code tests, instead of requiring you to go through and manually test each part of the code yourself, which could take hours, even days, depending on your code base. But in order to do automated testing, you must do a little more work and create tests using one of the testing frameworks available, such as Test::Unit, which we used and which we will be demonstrating in our case studies later on. However, the payoff in doing a little extra work allows you to greatly minimize the cost of changing your code and adding features since, if you're ever worried about breaking another part of your application after changing a part of it, you can simply run a command and have all of your tests run to ensure nothing is broken.

Regression Testing

Regression testing seeks to ensure that with every change to the code, no other parts of the code are broken, which could lead to the loss of functionalities.

Regression testing can easily be done by doing automated testing, which can run all the tests automatically. Having good automated testing (meaning that it tests all of your code in different scenarios) is the same as having good regression testing. This is very important to have since it reduces the cost of changing already coded parts of an application—which will inevitably happen. The reason it reduces the cost of changing already coded parts is because if you change a part of an application, you can simply run the automated tests to ensure that nothing was broken. Therefore, you will have fewer reservations about changing parts of your application since all of the uncertainty of new code is taken out.

User Acceptance Testing

User acceptance testing is one of the most important processes that is usually performed at the finish of a project. It involves designating a person, other than the person who created the automated tests, to design scenarios to be performed in reality by your client. Doing this allows you to ensure that the application meets the needs of the client and satisfies them. User acceptance testing is very crucial since, while the application may function as expected, it may not necessarily fulfill the user's needs. Doing user acceptance testing makes sure that it does.

Test::Unit—A Testing Framework

Test::Unit is a testing framework for Ruby and Ruby on Rails that, despite its name, can do unit, functional, and integration testing. It is a very straightforward and simple testing framework with much of the testing done through assertions—which are programmatic ways of saying, "The result this code produces should match this expected outcome."

CASE STUDY 1 (NOSHSTER)

Noshster is a worldwide social network for foodies to blog about the dishes they've eaten and share and review the restaurants where they ate them.

Product Vision and Goal

The product vision of Noshster is to create a social network for foodies that can be simply and intuitively used to track the dishes they've eaten, discover new foods by following other Noshster members they find interesting, and share reviews of the restaurants where they've eaten different dishes.

The overall goal of Noshster is to give the user the ability to satisfy a craving by helping them find the best restaurant that serves a particular dish.

Using the approach we recommended in Chapter 8 for the Product Owner to identify product vision, Noshster's vision can be summarized as follows:

- **Who**: Foodies
- **Why**: Find the best dishes around the world
- **What**: Dishes rated, rather than restaurants
- **Where**: Best food by looking at rating of dishes in all regions of the world
- **When**: 24×7

Requirements Gathering Using the Book's Visual Technique

Using the visual requirements gathering technique in Chapter 4, the team was able to identify the following requirements using the tree and forest analogy (Figure A.2).

Architecture Vision and Release/Sprint Planning

With Noshster, as an example for this book, we decided to vertically slice the application. That is, instead of working on the same "tree" of features in different Sprints, we worked on and finished the same tree within one Sprint. We will go through an example where we horizontally slice the application in the next case study.

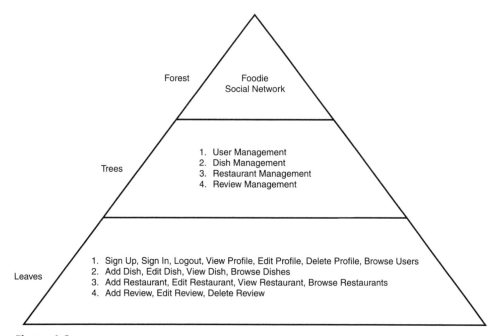

Figure A.2
The tree and forest requirements pyramid for the social food network Noshster.

Whether you vertically slice or horizontally slice the application depends on several factors such as:

1. What foundation of features do you need in order to develop the rest of the application efficiently without having to redesign? Do you need to have each "tree" of features completely developed before moving on to the next, or do you only need a subset?

2. Which organization of features allows you to provide the most business value to the product owner or the business as you progress through development?

But first let's get back to the process and see how we were able to see things more clearly using the recommendations that were given in this book. At first, we were presented with several requirements, which, when thrown together, looked quite overwhelming as in Figure A.3 below.

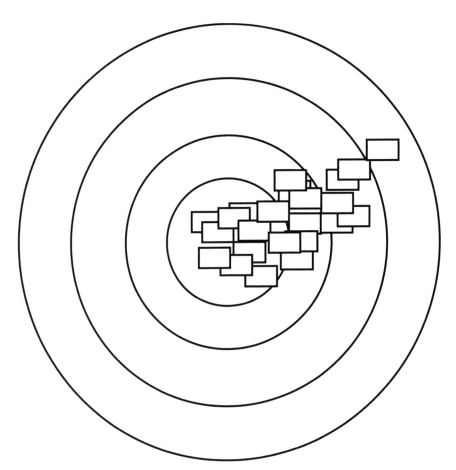

Figure A.3
When the requirements list was thrown at us at first sight.

Architecture Vision

Using the approach we learned in Chapter 6, we were able to quickly see more clearly, as in Figure A.4 below.

In discussions with the CEO, the Scrum team suggested and got the CEO to agree to get the team to focus on the user concept first to make sure that all different types of users around the world were identified as part of the foundation for this worldwide application. After that, they will get to the dish,

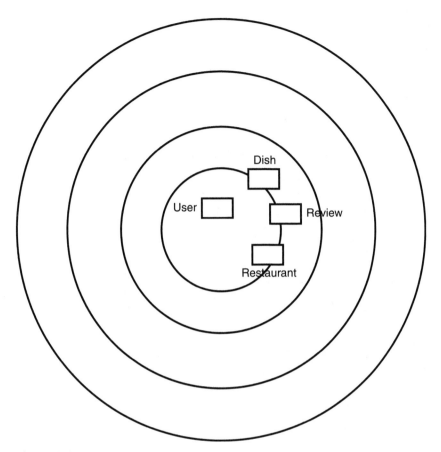

Figure A.4
See the forest for the trees.

then to the restaurant, and finally, to the review. In other words, they were building the software by working vertically around its common data elements. They did this because having all of the user characteristics first would allow the company to ensure that the software be really worldwide. This is to say that their architecture vision looked like that shown in Figure A.5.

By looking at the business data elements, the team envisions that the application data architecture will look like that shown in Figure A.6, at least at a high level.

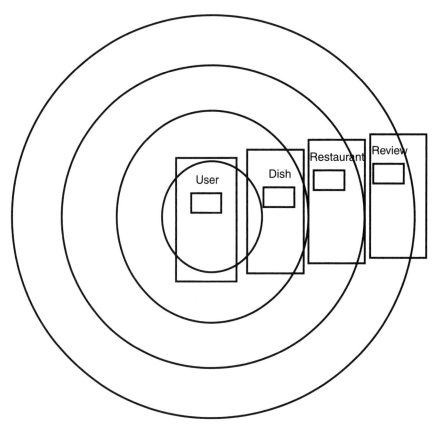

Figure A.5
Slicing Noshster vertically.

Noshster Release and Sprint Planning				
Forest			**Trees**	**Leaves**
Social Foodie Network				
	Release 1			
		Sprint 1		
			User Management	Sign up, Sign in, Logout, View Profile, Edit Profile, Delete Profile, Browse Users
		Sprint 2		
			Dish Management	Add Dish, Edit Dish, View Dish, Browse Dishes

Forest		Trees	Leaves
(Continued)			
Release 2			
	Sprint 3		
		Restaurant Management	Add Restaurant, Edit Restaurant, View Restaurant, Browse Restaurants
	Sprint 4		
		Review Management	Add Review, Edit Review, Delete Review

Project Estimation Using the Objective Criteria Technique

The chart below is a summary of the points estimated for each story within each Sprint using the objective criteria technique presented earlier in the book. You can find the formulas used to calculate each column in Chapter 5.

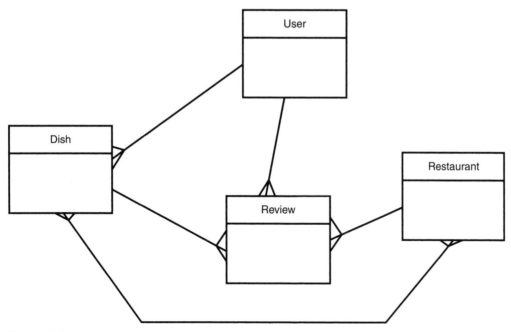

Figure A.6
Noshster high level data model.

| PBIs (Story) | Characteristics | | | | Total UP (Unadjusted Points) | Coeffi- cient | AP (Adjusted Points) | ED (Envi- ronment Dimensi- ons) | PPS (=(AP* ED)/36) |
	Interac- tion Type	Busi- ness Rules	Enti ties	Data Manipul- ation Type					
Release 1									
Sprint 1									
Sign up	3	1	1	2	7	1	7	18	3.5
Sign in	3	1	1	2	7	1	7	18	3.5
Logout	3	1	1	1	6	1	6	18	3
View Profile	3	1	1	1	6	1	6	18	3
Edit Profile	3	1	1	3	8	1	8	18	4
Delete Profile	3	1	1	1	6	1	6	18	3
Browse Users	3	1	1	1	6	1	6	18	3
Sprint 2									
Add Dish	3	1	1	2	7	1	7	18	3.5
Edit Dish	3	1	1	3	8	1	8	18	4
View Dish	3	1	1	1	6	1	6	18	3
Browse Dishes	3	1	1	1	6	1	6	18	3
Release 2									
Sprint 3									
Add Restaurant	3	1	1	2	7	1	7	18	3.5
Edit Restaurant	3	1	1	3	8	1	8	18	4
View Restaurant	3	1	1	1	6	1	6	18	3
Browse Restaurants	3	1	1	1	6	1	6	18	3
Sprint 4									
Add Review	3	1	1	2	7	1	7	18	3.5
Edit Review	3	1	1	3	8	1	8	18	4
Delete Review	3	1	1	1	6	1	6	18	3

Noshster Development

Now, we will begin going through the code that makes up each Sprint in each release for the example application and show how we integrated them.

Noshster Release 1—Sprint 1

The goal of the first Sprint of release 1 was to create a solid foundation of user management features upon which the second Sprint will be built.

Stories (Release 1—Sprint 1)   The stories that will be developed during release 1—Sprint 1 are:

1. Sign up

2. Sign in

3. Logout

4. View profile

5. Edit profile

6. Delete profile

7. Browse users

In Figure A.7, you will find the organization of data models for Release 1— Sprint 1.

In Figure A.8, you will find a more detailed description of the data models for Release 1—Sprint 1.

Models The User model enables the Noshster application to store user registration information. It uses the Authlogic plugin and specifies that a potential user does not need to type in a password confirmation (only a username, password, email, etc.) to sign up. The Authlogic plugin is a great user management plugin that adds user registration and authentication capabilities to an application. It abstracts away some details so that you don't have to worry about coding this often-used and often-constant part of an application. Some of the details that it abstracts away are the user validation (ensuring the user provides input for certain fields like a username, password, or email) and password encryption (manipulating the password so that it is stored in the database in such a manner that if the database were hacked, no one would be able to sign in with your password because it's encrypted).

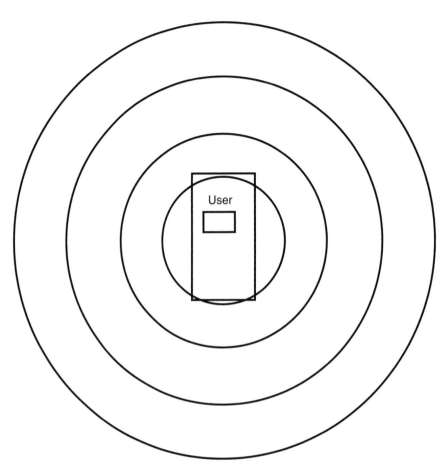

Figure A.7
Focusing development on the user business concept.

User
First Name
Last Name
Address
Location
Referred By

Figure A.8
Data model in progress (Release 1—Sprint 1).

```
class User < ActiveRecord::Base
  acts_as_authentic do |c|
    c.require_password_confirmation = false
  end
end
```

The UserSession model enables the Noshster application to authenticate user sign-ins against user registration information stored in the database. Therefore, when a user tries to sign in with invalid credentials that don't match what is in the database, the application puts out a friendly error. Otherwise, it lets the user go into what is normally a restricted area. This model abstracts a lot of details out and that's okay in this case because signing in to an application is typically the same across all applications and doesn't require much customization. It allows you to worry about the parts of your application that can actually provide unique value.

```
class UserSession < Authlogic::Session::Base
  def to_key
    new_record? ? nil : [ self.send(self.class.primary_key) ]
  end
end
```

Views
Sign up

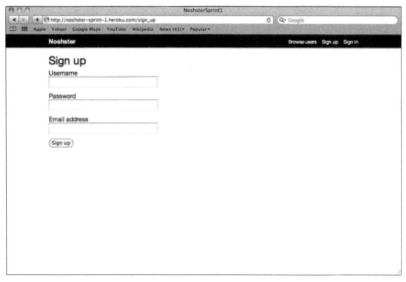

Figure A.9
Sign up page.

This view takes the above sign up form and adds extra information like a title, etc.

```
<h1>Sign up</h1>
<%= form_for @user do |f| %>
    <%= f.error_messages %>
    <%= render :partial => 'form', :object => f%>
    <%= f.submit 'Sign up' %>
<% end %>
```

Form partial (a form used in both sign up and edit profile pages)

This is a reusable form that shows the user a sign up form, which they can then use to fill in their user registration information. It is used on the line <%= render :partial => 'form', :object => f %> in the Sign up code.

```
<p>
    <%= form.label :username %><br/>
    <%= form.text_field :username %>
</p>
<p>
    <%= form.label :password %><br/>
    <%= form.password_field :password %>
</p>
<p>
    <%= form.label :email_address %><br/>
    <%= form.text_field :email_address %>
</p>
```

Sign in

Figure A.10
Sign in page.

This view takes the sign up form, but gears it towards allowing users to use the form to sign in to the web application.

```
<h1>Sign in</h1>
<%= form_for @user_session do |f| %>
    <%= f.error_messages %>
    <p>
        <%= f.label :username %><br/>
        <%= f.text_field :username %>
    </p>
    <p>
        <%= f.label :password %><br/>
        <%= f.password_field :password %>
    </p>
    <%= f.submit 'Sign in' %>
<% end %>
```

Logout page

Figure A.11
Logout page.

View/delete profile

Figure A.12
View/delete profile page.

This view shows the user pertinent profile information and presents a button that allows users to delete their accounts.

```
<h1><%= @user.email_address %></h1>
<% if @user == current_user %>
    <%= button_to 'Delete profile', @user, :method => :delete %>
<% end %>
```

Edit profile

This view presents an edit user form so that the user can update his profile.

```
<h1>Edit Profile</h1>
<%= form_for @user do |f| %>
    <%= f.error_messages %>
    <%= render :partial => 'form', :object => f %>
    <%= f.submit 'Update profile' %>
<% end %>
```

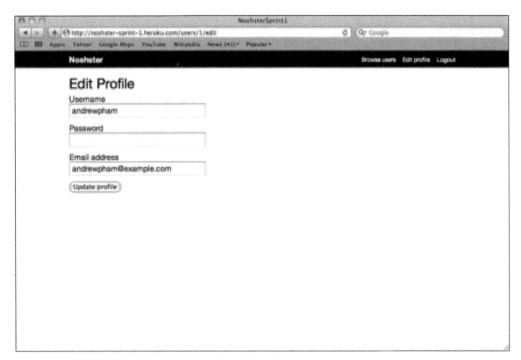

Figure A.13
Edit profile page.

Form partial (a form used in both sign up and edit profile pages)

This is a reusable form that shows the user a sign up form, which he can then use to fill in his user registration information. It is used on the line <%= render : partial => 'form', :object => f %> in the Edit Profile code.

```
<p>
    <%= form.label :username %><br/>
    <%= form.text_field :username %>
</p>
<p>
    <%= form.label :password %><br/>
    <%= form.password_field :password %>
</p>
<p>
    <%= form.label :email_address %><br/>
    <%= form.text_field :email_address %>
</p>
```

Delete profile

Figure A.14
Delete profile page.

This view shows the user pertinent profile information and presents a button that allows her to delete her account.

```
<h1><%= @user.email_address %></h1>
<% if @user == current_user %>
    <%= button_to 'Delete profile', @user, :method => :delete %>
<% end %>
```

Browse users

This view takes all of the users returned from the database in the controller and displays them.

```
<h1>Browse users</h1>
<%= render @users %>
```

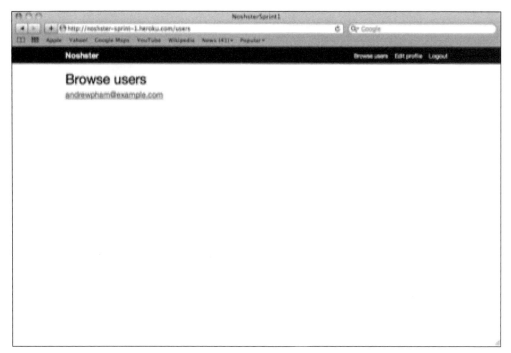

Figure A.15
Browse user's page.

User partial (to reuse showing user details on browse user's page)

This is the reusable view partial that is used in the above page on the line <%= render @users %> to display user information in a specific way.

```
<div class="user">
    <%= link_to user.email_address, user %>
</div>
```

Controllers

The UserController controller takes in the request from the browser and returns the proper view and necessary data. For example, if a user goes to the sign up page, the UserController controller returns the sign up page along with an empty User object to be filled in later. In another example, when a user actually clicks the sign up button, the controller receives the information typed into the form, puts it into the empty User object, and tells the object to save itself (this is when the model takes over and validates the data).

```
class UsersController < ApplicationController
  before_filter :require_no_user, :only => [:new, :create]
  before_filter :require_user, :only => [:edit, :update]

  # the index action asks the User model to query the "users" table in the
database and get all the users in order of alphabetical email addresses.
  def index
    @users = User.order('email_address ASC').all
  end

  # the new action instantiates a new User object, but it isn't created and saved
to the database just yet.
  def new
    @user = User.new
  end

  # the create action instantiates a new User object, populates it with user in-
putted values (params[:user]), and then attempts to save it. This may fail if the
user did not provide all the values required by the model in its validations or
provided incorrect data. If it saves successfully, then it creates a notice that
will be displayed to the user and redirects them to a new page. If not, it will
render the new action, which is typically a page a form, so that they can retry.
  def create
    @user = User.new(params[:user])
    if @user.save
      flash[:notice] = 'Sign up successful!'
      redirect_to @user
    else
      render :new
    end
  end

  # the show action asks the User model to query the database for a specific user so
that in the view, it can display a user's details.
  def show
    @user = User.find(params[:id])
  end

  # the edit action uses some of the functionality provided by the Authlogic
plugin which stores the currently signed-in user in the @current_user object.
Then it creates a new variable to hold that user. The view for the edit action
```

typically contains a form with the user's details already filled in, for easier
updating.

```
def edit
  @user = @current_user
end
```

the update action takes in the form values (params[:user]) and then attempts
to update the current user's details in the database. This may fail if the user did
not provide all the values required by the model in its validations or provided
incorrect data. If it succeeds, then a notice is created that will be shown to the
user and then it will redirect the user to another page. If it fails, the user will
be shown a form to retry.

```
def update
  @user = @current_user
  if @user.update_attributes(params[:user])
    flash[:notice] = 'Profile updated!'
    redirect_to @user
  else
    render :edit
  end
end
```

the destroy action takes the current user and deletes their information from
the database - therefore making them no longer a user.

```
def destroy
  @user = @current_user
  current_user_session.destroy
  @user.destroy
  redirect_to root_path
end
end
```

The UserSessionsController controller takes in credentials provided by the user in
the sign in form, puts it into an empty UserSession object, and then tells it to save
itself. It will then take the necessary action depending on whether the model object
was able to save itself (meaning it was authenticated successfully). It also has the
capability to log users out of the system and return them to the homepage.

```
class UserSessionsController < ApplicationController
  before_filter :require_no_user, :only => [:new, :create]
  before_filter :require_user, :only => :destroy
```

```
# the new action instantiates a new UserSession object
def new
  @user_session = UserSession.new
end
```

the create action instantiates a new UserSession object and fills it with input from the user (params[:user_session]). It then tries to save it, which will authenticate the credentials provided by the user and try to match it to the values stored in the database. If this succeeds, it will create a notice to show the user and redirect them to their user page. If it fails, it will show a page with a form so that they may retry.

```
def create
  @user_session = UserSession.new(params[:user_session])
  if @user_session.save
    flash[:notice] = 'Sign in successful!'
    redirect_back_or_default @user_session.user
  else
    render :new
  end
end
```

the destroy method takes the current user session and deletes it from stored values, essentially logging out the currently signed in user.

```
def destroy
  current_user_session.destroy
  flash[:notice] = 'Logout successful!'
  redirect_to root_path
end
end
```

Noshster Release 1—Sprint 2

The goal of the second Sprint of release 1 is to build the dish management features on top of the user management foundation of features developed in the preceding Sprint.

Stories (Release 1—Sprint 2)   The stories that will be developed during this Sprint are:

1. Add dish

2. Edit dish

3. View dish

4. Browse dishes

As mentioned in the book, one of the benefits of organizing development work around common core business data elements is to allow teams to work in parallel, as we also did here with Noshster, in splitting the developers into three separate groups to work concurrently on the view dish and edit dish after we were almost done with implementing the add dish user story.

In Figure A.16, you will find the organization of data models for Release 1—Sprint 2.

In Figure A.17, you will find the relationship of the data models for Release 1—Sprint 2.

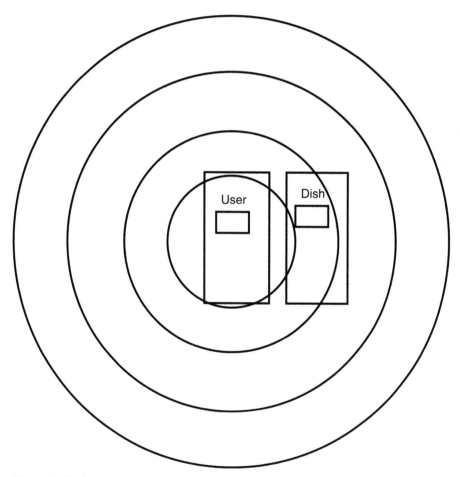

Figure A.16
Extension to the first data ring.

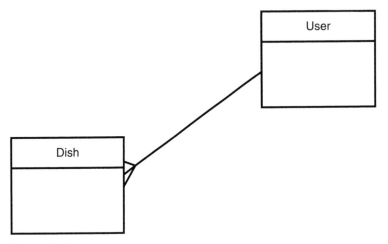

Figure A.17
Noshster's high level data model for the second Sprint.

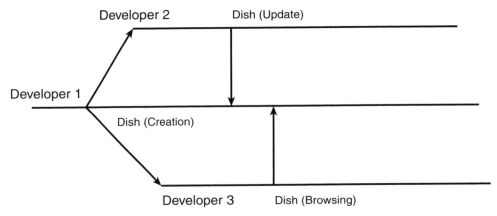

Figure A.18
Noshster's parallel software development.

Noshster Parallel (Concurrent) Software Development(Release 1—Sprint 2)
As indicated in Chapters 6 and 7, one of the numerous advantages of designing
and developing software around common data elements is the fact that after the
entity is created, we can have two or more teams work in parallel (concurrent)
with one another. And that was done for Noshster Sprint #2, as can be seen in
Figure A.18. Parallel software development is made very easy with the use of
a version control system, such as Git, since developers can simply work on

different parts of an application and have them be automatically merged together when they put them in the version control system.

Noshster Model—View—Controller (Release 1—Sprint 2)   The Dish model allows the Noshster web application to store dish information that is provided by the user. It ensures that a dish name and description is provided and that the dish name is unique. It also accepts a file and stores it onto Amazon S3 while connecting it to the dish record in the database so that it can be retrieved later.

```
class Dish < ActiveRecord::Base
  validates :name, :presence => true, :uniqueness => true
  validates :description, :presence => true

  has_attached_file :picture, :styles => { :medium => '350x350#', :small =>
'150x150#', :thumb => '75x75#' }, :storage => :s3, :s3_credentials =>
"#{Rails.root}/config/s3.yml", :path => ":attachment/:id/:style.:extension"

  validates_attachment_presence :picture
end
```

Views
Add dish

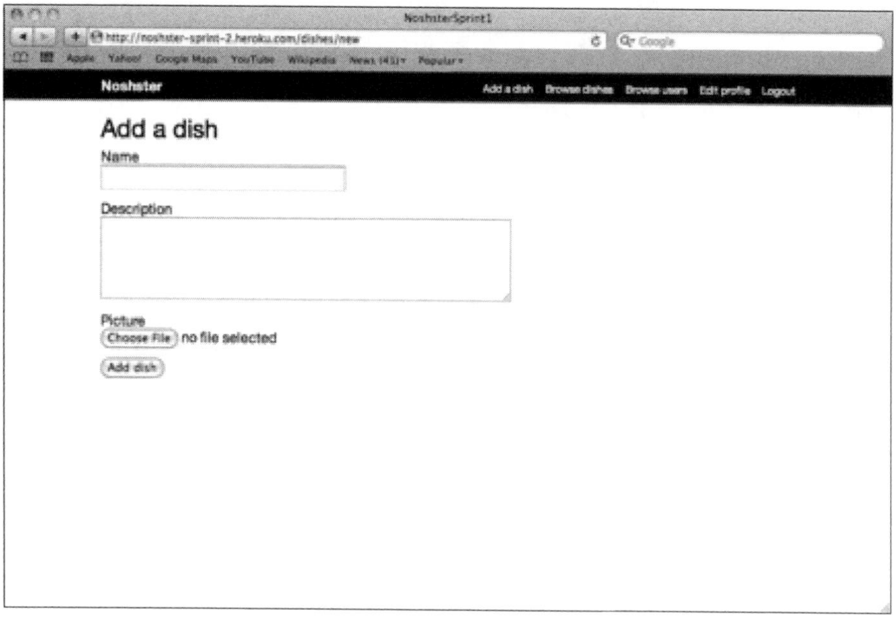

Figure A.19
Add dish page.

This page allows the user to add a dish by taking the following partial and adding extra information like a title, etc.

```
<h1>Add a dish</h1>
<%= form_for @dish, :html => { :multipart => true } do |f| %>
    <%= f.error_messages %>
    <%= render :partial => 'form', :object => f %>
    <%= f.submit 'Add dish' %>
<% end %>
```

Form partial (a form reused across add dish and edit dish pages)

This reusable form partial presents a form, which allows a user to input dish information to add a new dish or edit dish information. It is called on the line <%= render :partial => 'for', :object => f %> in the Add Dish code.

```
<p>
    <%= form.label :name %><br/>
    <%= form.text_field :name %>
</p>
<p>
    <%= form.label :description %><br/>
    <%= form.text_area :description, :rows => 5, :cols => 50 %>
</p>
<p>
    <%= form.label :picture %><br/>
    <%= form.file_field :picture %>
</p>
```

Edit dish

This page allows the user to edit a dish by taking the preceding partial and adding extra information like a title, etc.

```
<h1>Edit dish</h1>
<%= form_for @dish, :html => { :multipart => true } do |f| %>
    <%= f.error_messages %>
    <%= render :partial => 'form', :object => f %>
    <%= f.submit 'Update dish' %>
<% end %>
```

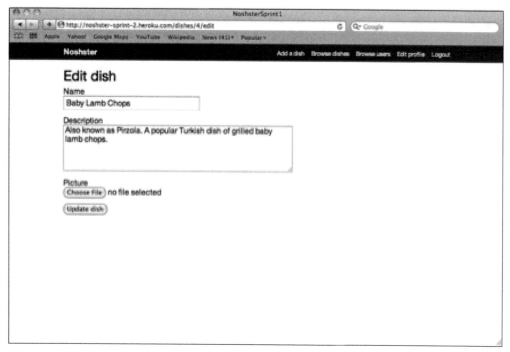

Figure A.20
Edit dish page.

Form partial (a form reused across add dish and edit dish pages)

This reusable form partial presents a form, which allows a user to input dish information to add a new dish or edit dish information. It is called on the line < %= render :partial => 'for', :object => f %> in the "Edit Dish" code.

```
<p>
    <%= form.label :name %><br/>
    <%= form.text_field :name %>
</p>
<p>
    <%= form.label :description %><br/>
    <%= form.text_area :description, :rows => 5, :cols => 50 %>
</p>
<p>
    <%= form.label :picture %><br/>
    <%= form.file_field :picture %>
</p>
```

View dish

Figure A.21
View dish page.

This page allows the user to view dish information by taking the dish object returned from the database and displaying it in a structured format on the page.

```
<h1><%= @dish.name %></h1>
<p>
    <%= image_tag @dish.picture.url(:medium), :alt => @dish.name %>
</p>
<p>
    <%= @dish.description %>
</p>
<% if signed_in? %>
    <p>
        <%= link_to 'Edit dish', edit_dish_path(@dish) %>
    </p>
<% end %>
```

Browse dishes

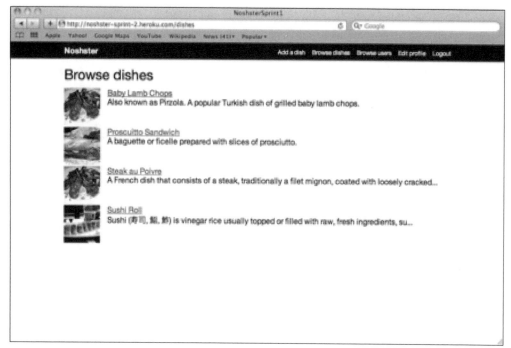

Figure A.22
Browse dishes page.

This page takes all the dishes returned from the database and presents them to the user.

```
<h1>Browse dishes</h1>
<%= render @dishes %>
```

Dish partial (to reuse showing dish details on browse dishes page)

This partial is used in the preceding page to display a single dish's information. It is called on the line <%= render @dishes %>.

```
<div class="dish">
    <div class="picture">
        <%= link_to image_tag(dish.picture.url(:thumb), :alt => dish.name),
dish %>
    </div>
```

```
<p class="details">
    <%= link_to dish.name, dish %><br/>
    <%= truncate dish.description, :length => 100 %>
</p>
</div>
```

Controllers   The DishesController controller takes a request from the user and returns the corresponding view and data from the database. For example, if a user goes to the browse dishes page, the DishesController controller finds all the dishes in the database and returns it along with the corresponding browse dishes view.

```
class DishesController < ApplicationController
  before_filter :require_user, :only => [:new, :create, :edit, :update]
  before_filter :get_dish, :only => [:show, :edit, :update]

  # the index action asks the Dish model to query the database and retrieve all of
  the dishes in alphabetical order by name.
  def index
    @dishes = Dish.order('name ASC')
  end

  # the new action instantiates a new Dish object
  def new
    @dish = Dish.new
  end

  # the create action instantiates a new Dish object and fills it with data from
  the user (params[:dish]). It then tries to save it. This may fail if the user did
  not provide all the values required by the model in its validations or provided
  incorrect data. If it succeeds, it will create a notice that will be shown to the
  user and redirect them to a new page with dish details. If it fails, it will show
  them a page with a form to retry.
  def create
    @dish = Dish.new(params[:dish])
    if @dish.save
      flash[:notice] = 'You have successfully added a dish!'
      redirect_to @dish
    else
      render :new
    end
  end
```

the show action is special in this controller. In the DishesController at the top, there is a line "before_filter :get_dish, :only => [:show, :edit, :update]". This is called a filter which, for the show, edit, and update actions, will execute the get_dish action. The get_dish action retrieves a specific dish from the database for presentation.

```
def show
end
```

the edit action is essentially the same as the show action.

```
def edit
end
```

the update action takes the dish retrieved from the get_dish action and attempts to update it with data provided by the user (params[:dish]). This may fail if the user did not provide all the values required by the model in its validations or provided incorrect data. If it succeeds, it will create a notice that will be shown to the user and redirect them to a new page with dish details. If it fails, it will show them a page with a form to retry.

```
def update
  if @dish.update_attributes(params[:dish])
    flash[:notice] = "You have successfully updated #{@dish.name}!"
    redirect_to @dish
  else
    render :edit
  end
end
```

```
private
```
the get_dish action is created to promote reusability. Since several actions in this controller require a dish to be retrieved from the database, it can be created in a separate place instead of being copied multiple times.

```
  def get_dish
    @dish = Dish.find(params[:id])
  end
end
```

Noshster Release 2—Sprint 3

The goal of the second Sprint of release 1 is to build the restaurant management features on top of the dish and user management foundation of features developed in the preceding Sprint.

Stories (Release 2—Sprint 3) The stories that will be developed during this Sprint are:

1. Add restaurant

2. Edit restaurant

3. View restaurant

4. Browse restaurants

Developing these features first will help us in the last Sprint, which must have the dish and restaurant management features already created in order to function properly.

In Figure A.23, you will find the organization of data models for Release 1— Sprint 3.

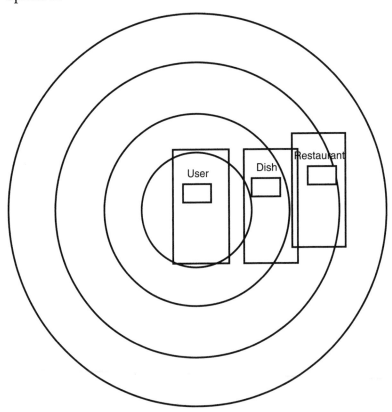

Figure A.23
The common data ring during Sprint 3.

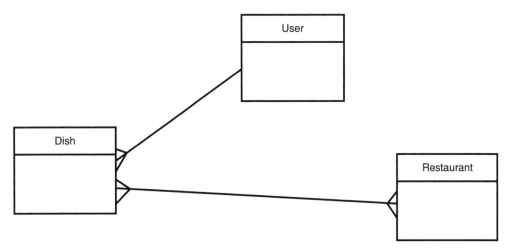

Figure A.24
Noshster's data model during Sprint 3.

In Figure A.24, you will find the relationship of data models for Release 1—Sprint 1.

Noshster Model—View—Controller (Release 2—Sprint 3) The Restaurant model allows the Noshster web application to store restaurant information and ensures that there is a name, address, city, state, and zip code passed to the database. It also ensures that the zip code is a number and that the restaurant is not a duplicate.

```ruby
class Restaurant < ActiveRecord::Base
  validates :name, :presence => true
  validates :address_1, :presence => true
  validates :city, :presence => true
  validates :state, :presence => true
  validates :zip_code, :presence => true, :numericality => true

  validate :restaurant_is_not_duplicate

  private
  def restaurant_is_not_duplicate
    if Restaurant.where(:name=>self.name, :address_1=>self.address_1).count>0
      errors[:base] << 'That restaurant already exists.'
      return false
    end
  end
end
```

Views

Add restaurant

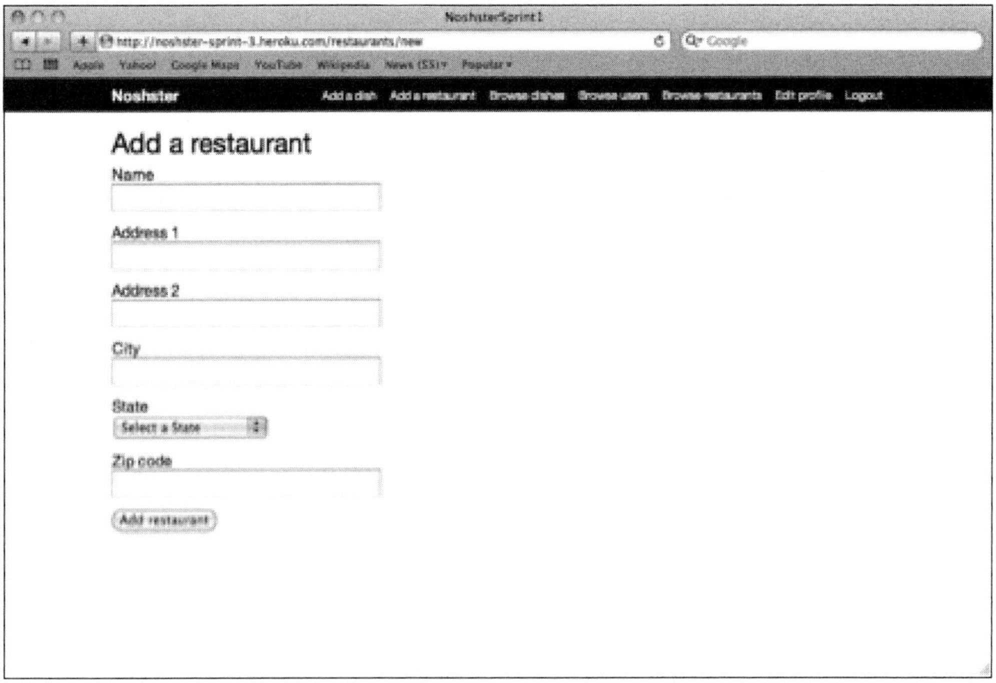

Figure A.25
Add restaurant page.

This page allows the user to add a restaurant by taking the above partial and adding extra information like a title, etc.

```
<h1>Add a restaurant</h1>
<%= form_for @restaurant do |f| %>
    <%= f.error_messages %>
    <%= render :partial => 'form', :object => f %>
    <%= f.submit 'Add restaurant' %>
<% end %>
```

Form partial (a form reused across add restaurant and edit restaurant pages)

This reusable form partial presents a form, which allows a user to input restaurant information to add a new restaurant or edit restaurant information.

It is called on the line <%= render :partial => 'form', :object => f %> in the Add Restaurant code.

```
<p>
    <%= form.label :name %><br/>
    <%= form.text_field :name %>
</p>
<p>
    <%= form.label :address_1 %><br/>
    <%= form.text_field :address_1 %>
</p>
<p>
    <%= form.label :address_2 %><br/>
    <%= form.text_field :address_2 %>
</p>
<p>
    <%= form.label :city %><br/>
    <%= form.text_field :city %>
</p>
<p>
    <%= form.label :state %><br/>
    <%= select :restaurant, :state, ['[List of states]'] %>
</p>
<p>
    <%= form.label :zip_code %><br/>
    <%= form.text_field :zip_code %>
</p>
```

Edit restaurant

This page allows the user to edit a restaurant by taking the preceding partial and adding extra information like a title, etc.

```
<h1>Edit restaurant</h1>
<%= form_for @restaurant do |f| %>
    <%= f.error_messages %>
    <%= render :partial => 'form', :object => f %>
    <%= f.submit 'Update restaurant' %>
<% end %>
```

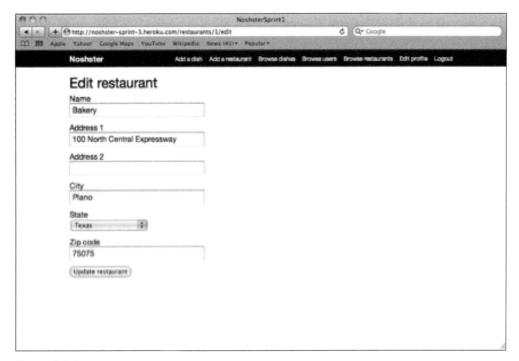

Figure A.26
Edit restaurant page.

Form partial (a form reused across add restaurant and edit restaurant pages)

This reusable form partial presents a form, which allows a user to input restaurant information to add a new restaurant or edit restaurant information. It is called on the line <%= render :partial => 'form', :object => f %> in the Edit Restaurant code.

```
<p>
    <%= form.label :name %><br/>
    <%= form.text_field :name %>
</p>
<p>
    <%= form.label :address_1 %><br/>
    <%= form.text_field :address_1 %>
</p>
<p>
    <%= form.label :address_2 %><br/>
```

```
    <%= form.text_field :address_2 %>
</p>
<p>
    <%= form.label :city %><br/>
    <%= form.text_field :city %>
</p>
<p>
    <%= form.label :state %><br/>
    <%= select :restaurant, :state, ['[List of states]'] %>
</p>
<p>
    <%= form.label :zip_code %><br/>
    <%= form.text_field :zip_code %>
</p>
```

View restaurant

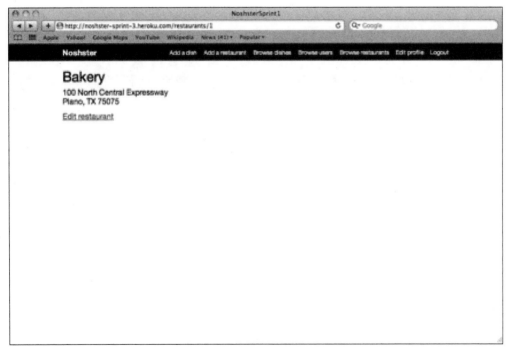

Figure A.27
View restaurant page.

This page allows the user to view restaurant information by taking the restaurant object returned from the database and displaying it in a structured format on the page.

```
<h1><%= @restaurant.name %></h1>
<p>
    <%= @restaurant.address_1 %><br/>
    <% unless @restaurant.address_2.empty? %>
        <%= @restaurant.address_2 %><br/>
    <% end %>
    <%=@restaurant.city %>, <%=@restaurant.state %> <%=@restaurant.zip_code %>
</p>
<% if signed_in? %>
    <p>
        <%= link_to 'Edit restaurant', edit_restaurant_path(@restaurant) %>
    </p>
<% end %>
```

Browse restaurants

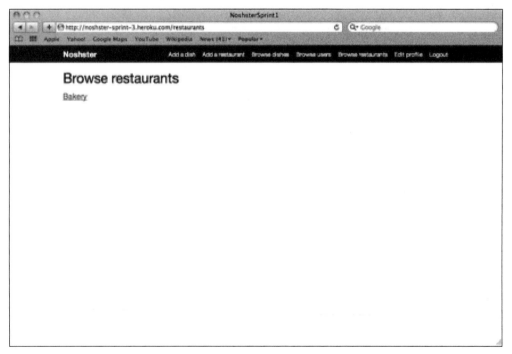

Figure A.28
Browse restaurants page.

This page takes all the restaurants returned from the database and presents them to the user.

```
<h1>Browse restaurants</h1>
<%= render @restaurants %>
```

Restaurant partial (to reuse showing restaurant details on browse restaurants page)

This partial is used in the preceding page to display a single restaurant's information. It is called on the line <%= render @restaurants %>.

```
<div class="restaurant">
    <%= link_to restaurant.name, restaurant %>
</div>
```

Controllers   The RestaurantsController controller takes a request from the user and returns the corresponding view and data from the database. For example, if a user goes to the browse restaurants page, the RestaurantsController controller finds all the restaurants in the database and returns them along with the corresponding browse restaurants view.

```
class RestaurantsController < ApplicationController
  before_filter :require_user, :only => [:new, :create, :edit, :update]
  before_filter :get_restaurant, :only => [:show, :edit, :update]

  # the index action asks the Restaurant model to query the "restaurants" table in
the database and get all the restaurants in order of alphabetical name.
  def index
    @restaurants = Restaurant.order('name ASC')
  end

  # the new action instantiates a Restaurant object
  def new
    @restaurant = Restaurant.new
  end

  # the create action instantiates a new Restaurant object, populates it with
user inputted values (params[:restaurant]), and then attempts to save it. This
may fail if the user did not provide all the values required by the model in its
validations or provided incorrect data. If it saves successfully, then it
creates a notice that will be displayed to the user and redirects them to a new
page. If not, it will render the new action, which is typically a page a form,
so that they can retry.
```

```
def create
  @restaurant = Restaurant.new(params[:restaurant])
  if @restaurant.save
    flash[:notice] = 'You have successfully added a restaurant!'
    redirect_to @restaurant
  else
    render :new
  end
end
```

the show action is special in this controller. In the RestaurantsController at the top, there is a line "before_filter :get_restaurant, :only => [:show, :edit, :update]". This is called a filter which, for the show, edit, and update actions, will execute the get_restaurant action. The get_restaurant action retrieves a specific restaurant from the database for presentation.

```
def show
end
```

the edit action is essentially the same as the show action

```
def edit
end
```

the update action takes the dish retrieved from the get_restaurant action and attempts to update it with data provided by the user (params[:restaurant]). This may fail if the user did not provide all the values required by the model in its validations or provided incorrect data. If it succeeds, it will create a notice that will be shown to the user and redirect them to a new page with restaurant details. If it fails, it will show them a page with a form to retry.

```
def update
  if @restaurant.update_attributes(params[:restaurant])
    flash[:notice] = "You have successfully updated #{@restaurant.name}!"
    redirect_to @restaurant
  else
    render :edit
  end
end
```

```
private
```
the get_restaurant action is created to promote reusability. Since several actions in this controller require a restaurant to be retrieved from the database,

it can be created in a separate place instead of being copied multiple times.

```
  def get_restaurant
    @restaurant = Restaurant.find(params[:id])
  end
end
```

Noshster Release 2—Sprint 4

The goal of the second Sprint of release 2 is to build the review management features on top of the restaurant management foundation of features developed in the preceding Sprint.

Stories (Release 2—Sprint 4)   The stories that will be developed during this Sprint are:

1. Add review

2. Edit review

3. View review

After developing all of the other features in the preceding Sprints, we are now able to develop the last "tree" of features.

In Figure A.29, you will find the organization of data models for Release 1— Sprint 4.

In Figure A.30, you will find the relationship of the data models for Release 1— Sprint 1.

Noshster Model—View—Controller (Release 2—Sprint 4)   The Review model allows the Noshster web application to store review information in the database that is connected to a user, dish, and restaurant for later reporting. It ensures that there is a body, rating, and restaurant attached to the review.

```
class Review < ActiveRecord::Base
  validates :body, :presence => true
  validates :rating, :presence => true
  validates :restaurant_id, :presence => true

  belongs_to :user
  belongs_to :dish
  belongs_to :restaurant
end
-----------------------
```

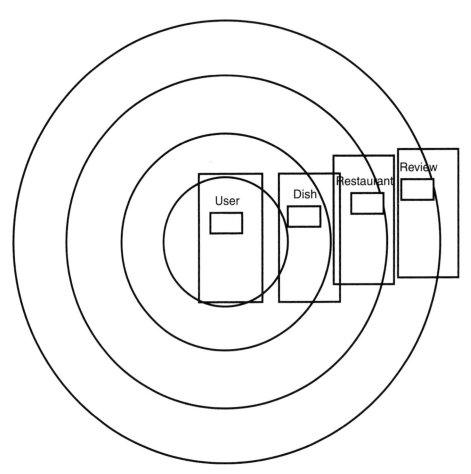

Figure A.29
Data rings during Sprint 4.

The User model is modified to form a relationship between users and reviews—
that is, a user has many reviews so that when a review is displayed, we can tell
the viewer who wrote the review.

```
class User < ActiveRecord::Base
  acts_as_authentic do |c|
    c.require_password_confirmation = false
  end

  has_many :reviews
end
----------------------
```

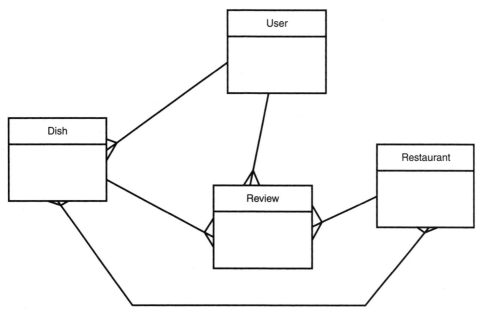

Figure A.30
Noshster's data model during Sprint 4.

The Dish model is modified to form a relationship between dishes, reviews, and restaurants so that by retrieving a dish from the database, you can also see all the related reviews and restaurants.

```
class Dish < ActiveRecord::Base
  validates :name, :presence => true, :uniqueness => true
  validates :description, :presence => true

  has_attached_file :picture, :styles => { :medium => '350x350#', :small =>
'150x150#', :thumb => '75x75#' }, :storage => :s3, :s3_credentials =>
"#{Rails.root}/config/s3.yml", :path => ":attachment/:id/:style.:extension"

  validates_attachment_presence :picture

  has_many :reviews
  has_many :restaurants, :through => :reviews
end
```

The Restaurant model is modified to be connected to reviews and dishes for the same reasons as the Dish model.

```
class Restaurant < ActiveRecord::Base
  validates :name, :presence => true
  validates :address_1, :presence => true
  validates :city, :presence => true
  validates :state, :presence => true
  validates :zip_code, :presence => true, :numericality => true

  validate :restaurant_is_not_duplicate

  has_many :reviews
  has_many :dishes, :through => :reviews

  private
  def restaurant_is_not_duplicate
    if Restaurant.where(:name => self.name, :address_1 => self.address_1).count > 0
      errors[:base] << 'That restaurant already exists.'
      return false
    end
  end
end
```

Views

Add review

This page allows the user to add a review by taking the preceding partial and adding extra information like a title, etc.

```
<% content_for :head do %>
    <%= javascript_include_tag '/restaurants' %>
    <script type="text/javascript">
        $(document).ready(function() {
            $('#restaurant_name').autocomplete(data, {
                matchContains: true,
                mustMatch: true,
                formatItem: function(item) {
                    return item.name + '<br/>' + item.address;
                },
                formatMatch: function(item) {
                    return item.name;
                },
```

```
                formatResult: function(item) {
                    return item.name;
                }
            }).result(function(event, item) {
                $('#review_restaurant_id').attr('value', item.id);
            });
        });
    </script>
<% end %>
<h1>Add a review for <%= @dish.name %></h1>
<%= form_for [@dish, @review] do |f| %>
    <%= f.error_messages %>
    <p>
        <%= label_tag "Where did you eat #{@dish.name}?" %><br/>
        <%= text_field_tag :restaurant_name, params[:restaurant_name] %><br/>
        <%= link_to 'Add a new restaurant', new_restaurant_path %>
        <%= f.hidden_field :restaurant_id %>
    </p>
    <%= render :partial => 'form', :object => f %>
    <%= f.submit 'Add review' %>
<% end %>
```

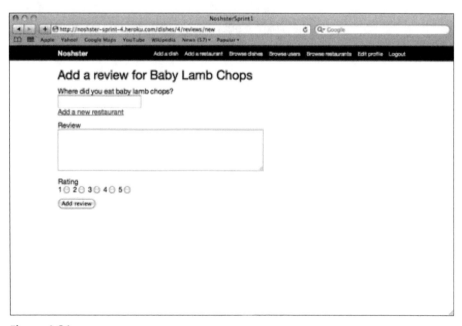

Figure A.31
Add review page.

Form partial (a form reused across add review and edit review pages)

This reusable form partial presents a form, which allows a user to input review information to add a new review or edit review information. It is used on the line <%= render :partial => 'form', :object => f %> in the "Add Review" code.

```
<p>
    <%= form.label :body, 'Review' %><br/>
    <%= form.text_area :body, :rows => 5, :cols => 50 %>
</p>
<p>
    <%= form.label :rating %><br/>
    1 <%= form.radio_button :rating, 1 %> 
    2 <%= form.radio_button :rating, 2 %> 
    3 <%= form.radio_button :rating, 3 %> 
    4 <%= form.radio_button :rating, 4 %> 
    5 <%= form.radio_button :rating, 5 %> 
</p>
```

Edit Review

Figure A.32
Edit review page.

This page allows the user to edit a review by taking the preceding partial and adding extra information like a title, etc.

```
<h1>Edit review for <%= @dish.name %></h1>
<%= form_for [@dish, @review] do |f| %>
    <%= f.error_messages %>
    <%= render :partial => 'form', :object => f %>
    <%= f.submit 'Update review' %>
<% end %>
```

Form partial (a form reused across add review and edit review pages)

This reusable form partial presents a form, which allows a user to input review information to add a new review or edit review information. It is used on the line <%= render :partial => 'form', :object => f %> in the Edit Review code.

```
<p>
    <%= form.label :body, 'Review' %><br/>
    <%= form.text_area :body, :rows => 5, :cols => 50 %>
</p>
<p>
    <%= form.label :rating %><br/>
    1 <%= form.radio_button :rating, 1 %> 
    2 <%= form.radio_button :rating, 2 %> 
    3 <%= form.radio_button :rating, 3 %> 
    4 <%= form.radio_button :rating, 4 %> 
    5 <%= form.radio_button :rating, 5 %> 
</p>
```

Review partial/delete review

This partial presents reviews in a specific format along with a delete review button that allows a user to delete their own review.

```
<div class="review">
    <p>
        <%= link_to review.user.email_address, review.user %> gave <%= link_to
review.restaurant.name, review.restaurant %> <%= review.rating %> stars for
this dish!
    </p>
```

```
    <p>
        <%= review.body %>
    </p>
    <p>
        <% if signed_in? %>
            <% if review.user == current_user %>
                <%= link_to 'Edit review', edit_dish_review_path(review.dish,
review) %>
                <%= button_to 'Delete review', dish_review_path(review.dish,
review), :method => :delete %>
            <% end %>
        <% end %>
    </p>
</div>
```

Figure A.33
Delete review page.

Controllers   The ReviewsController controller takes a request from the user and returns the corresponding view and data from the database. For example, if a user goes to the add a review page, the ReviewsController controller finds the relevant dish and restaurant in the database and an empty review object to be filled in later and returns it along with the corresponding add a review view.

```
class ReviewsController < ApplicationController
  before_filter :require_user, :only => [:new, :create, :edit, :update, :destroy]
  before_filter :get_dish
  before_filter :get_review, :only => [:edit, :update, :destroy]
  before_filter :authorize_user, :only => [:edit, :update, :destroy]


  # the new action gets the signed-in user using Authlogic's built-in
  current_user action which retrieves a signed-in user and instantiates a Review
  object.
  def new
    store_location
    @user = current_user
    @review = @user.reviews.build
  end


  # the create action gets the signed-in user and instantiates a Review object
  while populating it with data provided by the user (params[:review]). It then
  sets the parent object of that Review object to the dish retrieved by the
  database in the get_dish action. It then tries to save it. This may fail if the
  user did not provide all the values required by the model in its validations or
  provided incorrect data. If it succeeds, it will create a notice that will be
  shown to the user and redirect them to a new page with the dish details and all
  of its reviews. If it fails, it will show them a page with a form to retry.
  def create
    @user = current_user
    @review = @user.reviews.build(params[:review])
    @review.dish = @dish
    if @review.save
      flash[:notice] = "You have successfully reviewed #{@dish.name}!"
      redirect_to @dish
    else
      render :new
    end
  end
```

the edit action uses the before_filter which runs get_review in order to provide a Review object to the view.

```ruby
  def edit
  end
```

the update action uses the before_filter which runs get_review to get a review which it then attempts to update with user provided values. It then tries to save it. This may fail if the user did not provide all the values required by the model in its validations or provided incorrect data. If it succeeds, it will create a notice that will be shown to the user and redirect them to a new page with dish details. If it fails, it will show them a page with a form to retry.

```ruby
  def update
    if @review.update_attributes(params[:review])
      flash[:notice] = 'You have successfully updated your review!'
      redirect_to @dish
    else
      render :edit
    end
  end
```

the destroy action also uses the before_filter which runs get_review in order to retrieve a specific review before attempting to delete it from the database.

```ruby
def destroy
    @review.destroy
    flash[:notice] = 'You have successfully deleted your review!'
    redirect_to @dish
  end

  private
  def get_dish
    @dish = Dish.find(params[:dish_id])
  end

  def get_review
    @review = Review.find(params[:id])
  end

  def authorize_user
    unless @review.user == current_user
```

```
        flash[:notice] = 'You do not have permission to perform this action.'
        redirect_to current_user
      end
    end
end
```

Testing Noshster

Example Unit Test   An example unit test for our Dish model was:

```
class DishTest < ActiveSupport::TestCase
  test 'Dish is successfully created' do
    old_count = Dish.count
    Dish.create(:name => 'Example', :description => 'Example', :picture =>
'Example.jpg')
    new_count = Dish.count
    assert_equal(new_count, old_count + 1) # Make sure that there is 1 more dish
in the database than before
  end
end
```

The test itself ensures that you can successfully add a dish to the database given it has all the necessary properties such as a name, description, and picture.

An example functional test for our Dish controller was:

```
class DishControllerTest < ActiveSupport::TestCase
  test 'Dish is successfully created through the controller' do
    post :create, :dish => { :name => 'Example', :description => 'Example',
:picture => 'Example.jpg' }
    assert :redirect # Make sure the POST request to the create action was
successful
  end
end
```

This ensures that the controller properly accepts dish information and saves a new dish to the database and responds by redirecting the user to the right page.

Example Integration Test   An example integration test for our Add a dish feature was:

```
class DishFlowsTest < ActionController::IntegrationTest
  test 'Sign in and add a dish' do
    get '/sign_in'
    assert_response :success
```

```
    post_via_redirect '/sign_in', :username => 'example', :password =>
'example'
    assert_equal '/welcome', path

    post :create, :dish => { :name => 'Example', :description => 'Example',
:picture => 'Example.jpg' }
    assert :redirect # Make sure the POST request to the create action was
successful
  end
end
```

This test ensures that a given certain user flow (going to the sign in page, signing in, being redirected to the sign in page, and then creating a dish) works properly.

Example User Acceptance Test An example user acceptance test for the Noshster sign up feature would be:

```
Feature: Sign up
    In order to use Noshster
    As a non-member
    I want to be able to register

    Scenario: Sign up
    Given I have filled in all the form's fields username, password, and email
address with andrewpham, password, andrewpham@example.com
    When I click sign up
    Then I should be redirected to my newly created profile page


Given /^I have filled in all the form\'s required fields username, password, and
email address with (.+)$/ do |inputs|
    user_fields = inputs.split(', )
    @user = User.new
    @user.username = user_fields[0]
    @user.password = user_fields[1]
    @user.email_address = user_fields[2]
end

When /^I click sign up$/ do
    @user.save!
end
```

```
Then /^I should be redirected to my newly created profile page$/ do
  assert_response :redirect
  assert_redirected_to @user
end
```

This test emulates a real-world user and ensures that if a real-world user were to use the web application, it would work as expected.

CASE STUDY 2 (CONFEROUS)

Conferous is an online conference call management web application that allows teams and groups to easily collaborate by making the setting up of conference calls simple.

Product Vision and Goal

The product vision of Conferous is to create an extremely simple and easy-to-use online conference call management web application that can be used to create easily accessible and easily remembered conference calls that are recorded for later reference for teams and groups.

The overall goal of Conferous is to make hosting conference calls simple.

- **Who:** Corporate conference users
- **Why:** Make conference calls easy to use and remember
- **What:** Conference calls
- **Where:** Limited to the U.S.A. only
- **When:** 24×7

Requirements Gathering Using the Book's Visual Technique

Using the visual requirements gathering technique in Chapter 4, the team was able to identify the following requirements using the tree and forest analogy (Figure A.34).

Architecture Vision and Release/Sprint Planning

At first, we were presented with several requirements, which, when thrown together, looked quite overwhelming as shown in Figure A.35.

Architecture Vision

Using the approach we learned in Chapter 6, we were able to quickly see more clearly, as shown in Figure A.36.

With Conferous, we decided to horizontally slice the application; that is, instead of developing entire trees of features within the same Sprint, we decided to develop more than one tree subset of features in one Sprint, and to expand progressively into other features as we moved into subsequent Sprints.

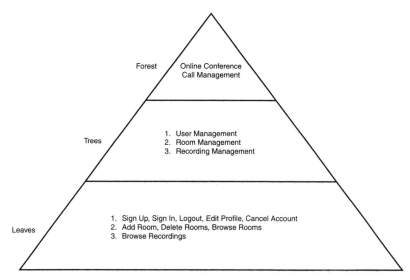

Figure A.34
The requirements pyramid for the conference management software conferous.

The reason for this was that we needed the user to be able to sign up for the basic features of a teleconference room to start using our application right away rather than having to wait for us to finish all the features of a room. And as it turned out, our calculation was correct.

Conferous Release and Sprint Planning

Forest			Trees	Leaves
Online Conference Call Management				
	Release 1			
		Sprint 1		
			User Management	Sign up, Sign in, Logout
			Room Management	Add Room, Delete Room, Browse Rooms
		Sprint 2		
			Recording Management	Browse Recordings
			User Management	Edit Profile, Cancel Account

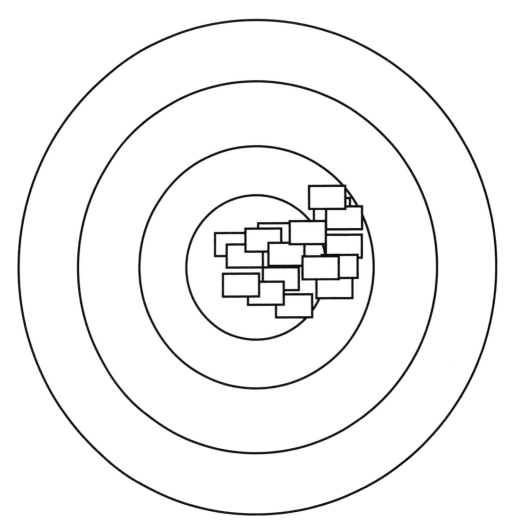

Figure A.35
When requirements list was thrown at us at first sight.

Project Estimation Using the Objective Criteria Technique

The chart below is a summary of the points estimated for each story within each Sprint using the objective criteria technique presented earlier in the book. You can find the formulas used to calculate each column in Chapter 5.

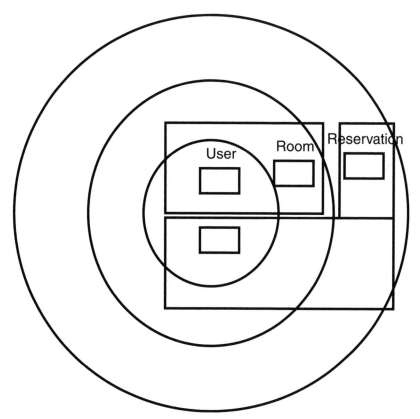

Figure A.36
Slicing the application horizontally.

| PBIs (Story) | Characteristics | | | | Total UP (Unadjusted Points) | Coefficient | AP (Adjusted Points) | ED (Environment Dimensions) | PPS (=(AP* ED)/36) |
	Interaction Type	Business Rules	Entities	Data Manipulation Type					
Sprint 1									
Sign up	3	1	1	2	7	1	7	18	3.5
Sign in	3	1	1	2	7	1	7	18	3.5
Logout	3	1	1	1	6	1	6	18	3
Add Room	3	1	1	2	7	1	7	18	3.5

(Continued)

PBIs (Story)	Characteristics				Total UP (Unadj-usted Points)	Coeffi-cient	AP (Adju-sted Points)	ED (Envi-ronment Dimens-ions)	PPS (=(AP* ED)/36)
	Inter-action Type	Busi-ness Rules	Enti-ties	Data Manipul-ation Type					
Delete Rooms	3	1	1	3	8	1	8	18	4
Browse Rooms	3	1	1	1	6	1	6	18	3
Sprint 2									
Edit Profile	3	1	1	3	8	1	8	18	4
Cancel Account	3	1	1	2	7	1	7	18	3.5
Browse Recordings	3	1	1	1	6	1	6	18	3

Conferous Development

Conferous Sprint 1

The goal of the first Sprint is to develop only the necessary features needed for the development of the later application-centric features.

Stories (Sprint 1)　The stories that will be developed during this Sprint are:

1. Sign up

2. Sign in

3. Logout

4. Add Room

5. Delete Room

6. Browse Rooms

In Figure A.37, you will find the organization of data models for Release 1— Sprint 1.

In Figure A.38, you will find the relationship of the data models for Release 1— Sprint 1.

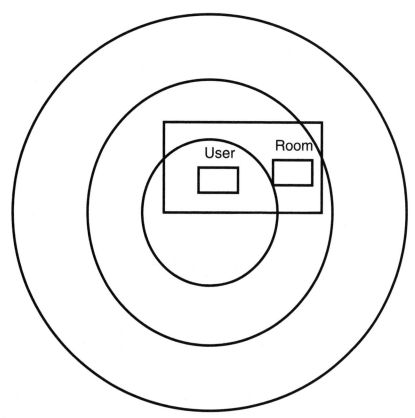

Figure A.37
Conferous data ring during Sprint 1.

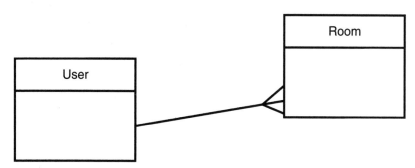

Figure A.38
Conferous data model during Sprint 1.

Conferous Model—View—Controller (Sprint 1)   The User model enables the Conferous application to store user registration information. It uses the Authlogic plugin and specifies that a potential user does not need to type in a password confirmation (only a username, password, email, etc.) to sign up.

```
class User < ActiveRecord::Base
  acts_as_authentic do |c|
    c.require_password_confirmation = false
  end

  has_many :rooms
end
```

The UserSession model enables the Conferous application to authenticate user sign ins against user registration information stored in the database. Therefore, when a user tries to sign in with invalid credentials that don't match what is in the database, the application will put out a friendly error. Otherwise, it will let the user go into what is normally a restricted area.

```
class UserSession < Authlogic::Session::Base
  def to_key
    new_record? ? nil : [ self.send(self.class.primary_key) ]
  end
end
```

The Room model enables the Conferous application to store room information. It ensures that a name and description for the room is provided and that the name for the room is unique. It also establishes a connection between the user who created it and the room itself for later reporting.

```
class Room < ActiveRecord::Base
  validates :name, :presence => true, :uniqueness => true
  validates :description, :presence => true

  belongs_to :user
end
```

Views

Sign up

This view takes the following sign up form partial and adds extra information such as a title, etc.

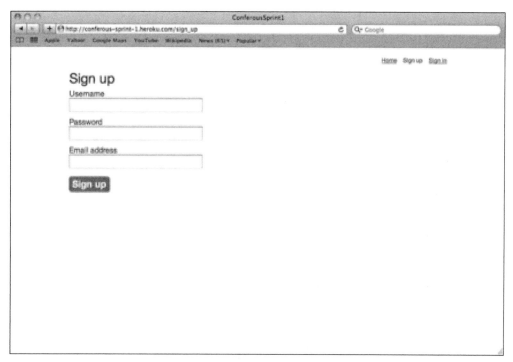

Figure A.39
Sign up page.

```
<h1>Sign up</h1>
<%= form_for @user do |f| %>
    <%= f.error_messages %>
    <%= render :partial => 'form', :object => f %>
    <%= f.submit 'Sign up' %>
<% end %>
```

Form partial—(for use in sign up and edit profile—in the future—pages)

This is a reusable form that shows users a sign up form, which they can then use to fill in their user registration information. It is called on the line <%= render : partial => 'form', :object => f %> in the Sign up code.

```
<p>
    <%= form.label :username %><br/>
    <%= form.text_field :username %>
</p>
```

```
<p>
    <%= form.label :password %><br/>
    <%= form.password_field :password %>
</p>
<p>
    <%= form.label :email_address %><br/>
    <%= form.text_field :email_address %>
</p>
```

Sign in

This view takes the sign up form, but gears it towards allowing users to use the form to sign in to the web application.

Figure A.40
Sign in page.

```
<h1>Sign in</h1>
<%= form_for @user_session do |f| %>
    <%= f.error_messages %>
    <p>
        <%= f.label :username %><br/>
        <%= f.text_field :username %>
    </p>
    <p>
        <%= f.label :password %><br/>
        <%= f.password_field :password %>
    </p>
    <%= f.submit 'Sign in' %>
<% end %>
```

Add room

This view presents the add a room form and allows it to accept user input to create a room.

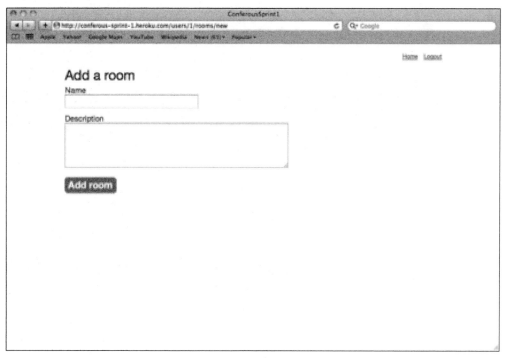

Figure A.41
Add a room page.

```
<h1>Add a room</h1>
<%= form_for [@user, @room] do |f| %>
    <%= f.error_messages %>
    <p>
        <%= f.label :name %><br/>
        <%= f.text_field :name %>
    </p>
    <p>
        <%= f.label :description %><br/>
        <%= f.text_area :description, :rows => 5, :cols => 50 %>
    </p>
    <%= f.submit 'Add room' %>
<% end %>
```

Delete room

This view presents a delete room button, which allows the user to delete a specific room.

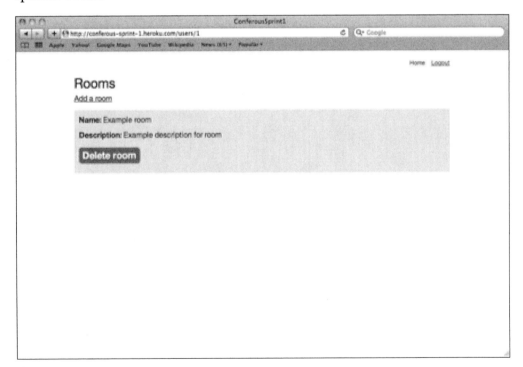

Figure A.42
Delete a room page.

```
<div class="room">
    <p>
        <span class="bold">Name:</span> <%= room.name %>
    </p>
    <p>
        <span class="bold">Description:</span> <%= room.description %>
    </p>
    <p>
        <%= button_to 'Delete room', user_room_path(@user, room), :method => :
delete %>
    </p>
</div>
```

Browse rooms

This view takes all of the rooms returned from the database in the controller and
displays them.

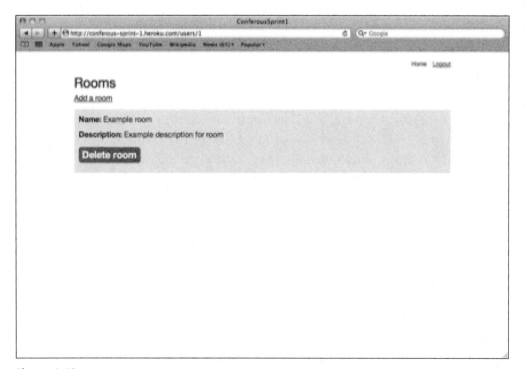

Figure A.43
Browse rooms page.

```
<h1>Rooms</h1>
<%= link_to 'Add a room', new_user_room_path(@user) %>
<div id="rooms">
    <%= render @user.rooms %>
</div>
```

Room partial—(to reuse showing room details)

This is the reusable view partial that is used in the preceding page to display room information in a specific way.

```
<div class="room">
    <p>
        <span class="bold">Name:</span> <%= room.name %>
    </p>
    <p>
        <span class="bold">Description:</span> <%= room.description %>
    </p>
    <p>
        <%= button_to 'Delete room', user_room_path(@user, room), :method => :
delete %>
    </p>
</div>
```

Controllers The UserController controller takes in the request from the browser and returns the proper view and necessary data. For example, if a user goes to the sign up page, the UserController controller returns the sign up page along with an empty User object to be filled in later. In another example, when a user actually clicks the sign up button, the controller receives the information typed into the form, puts it into the empty User object, and tells the object to save itself (this is when the model takes over and validates the data).

```
class UsersController < ApplicationController
  before_filter :require_no_user, :only => [:new, :create]

  # the new action instantiates a new User object.
  def new
    @user = User.new
  end

  # the create action instantiates a new User object and fills it with user-
provided values (params[:user]). It then tries to save it. This may fail if the
user did not provide all the values required by the model in its validations or
```

provided incorrect data. If it succeeds, it will create a notice that will be shown to the user and redirect them to a new page with user details. If it fails, it will show them a page with a form to retry.

```
  def create
    @user = User.new(params[:user])
    if @user.save
      flash[:notice] = 'Sign up successful!'
      redirect_to @user
    else
      render :new
    end
  end
```

  # the show action takes the currently signed-in user through an Authlogic-provided method and puts it into the @user variable.

```
  def show
    @user = current_user
  end
end
```

The UserSessionsController controller takes in credentials provided by the user in the sign in form, puts it into an empty UserSession object, and then tells it to save itself. It then takes the necessary action depending on whether the model object was able to save itself (meaning it was authenticated successfully). It also has the capability to log the user out of the system and return her to the homepage.

```
class UserSessionsController < ApplicationController
  before_filter :require_no_user, :only => [:new, :create]
  before_filter :require_user, :only => :destroy
```

  # the new action instantiates a new UserSession object
```
  def new
    @user_session = UserSession.new
  end
```

  # the create action instantiates a new UserSession object and fills it with user-provided values (params[:user_session]). It then tries to save it. This may fail if the user did not provide all the values required by the model in its validations or provided incorrect data. If it succeeds, it will create a notice that

will be shown to the user and redirect them to a new page with user details. If it fails, it will show them a page with a form to retry.

```
  def create
    @user_session = UserSession.new(params[:user_session])
    if @user_session.save
      flash[:notice] = 'Sign in successful!'
      redirect_back_or_default @user_session.user
    else
      render :new
    end
  end


  # the destroy method takes the current user session and deletes it from stored
  values, essentially logging out the currently signed in user.
  def destroy
    current_user_session.destroy
    flash[:notice] = 'Logout successful!'
    redirect_to root_path
  end
end
------------------------
class RoomsController < ApplicationController
  before_filter :require_user
  before_filter :get_user


  # the new action takes the currently signed-in user through the get_user
  filter, and instantiates a Room object.
  def new
    @room = @user.rooms.build
  end


  # the create action instantiates a Room object and fills it with user-provided
  values (params[:room]). It then tries to save it, which will authenticate the
  credentials provided by the user and try to match it to the values stored in the
  database. If this succeeds, it will create a notice to show the user and redirect
  them to their user page. If it fails, it will show a page with a form so that they
  may retry.
  def create
    @room = @user.rooms.build(params[:room])
```

```
    if @room.save
      flash[:notice] = 'You have successfully created a room!'
      redirect_to @user
    else
      render :new
    end
  end

  # the destroy action takes a specific room and attempts to delete it from the
database.
  def destroy
    @room = @user.rooms.find(params[:id])
    @room.destroy
    flash[:notice] = 'You have successfully deleted a room!'
    redirect_to @user
  end

  private
  def get_user
    @user = current_user
  end
end
```

Conferous Sprint 2

The goal of the second Sprint is to build upon the foundation of the first Sprint and develop valuable application-centric features.

Stories (Sprint 2)   The stories that will be developed during this Sprint are:

1. Browse recordings

2. Edit profile

3. Cancel account

In Figure A.44, you will find the organization of data models for Release 1—Sprint 2.

In Figure A.45, you will find the relationship of data models for Release 1—Sprint 2.

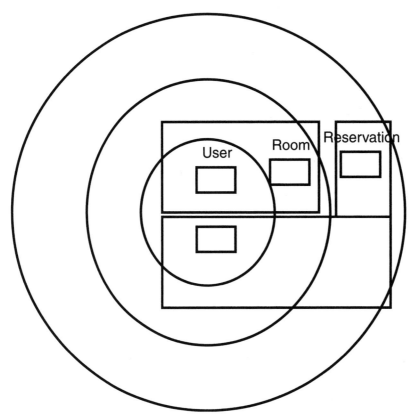

Figure A.44
Conferous data ring during Sprint 2.

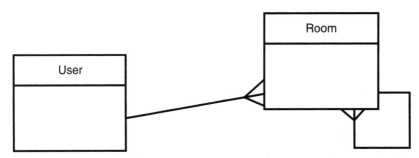

Figure A.45
Conferous data model during Sprint 2.

Conferous Model—View—Controller (Sprint 2)   The Recording model allows the Conferous web application to store recording information for each conference call made in a specific room.

```
class Recording < ActiveRecord::Base
  belongs_to :room
end
----------------------
```

The Room model is modified to create a connection between itself and corresponding recordings so that when a user tries to look at the recordings made in a specific room, they can easily be found in the database.

```
class Room < ActiveRecord::Base
  validates :name, :presence => true, :uniqueness => true
  validates :description, :presence => true

  has_many :recordings

  belongs_to :user

  after_create :setup_test_data

  private
  def setup_test_data
    1.upto(3) do
      self.recordings.create
    end
  end
end
```

Views
Browse recordings

This view takes all of the rooms returned from the database in the controller and displays them along with all of their recordings.

```
<% content_for :head do %>
    <script type="text/javascript">
        $(document).ready(function() {
            $('#view_recordings').click(function() {
                $('.recordings').slideToggle();
```

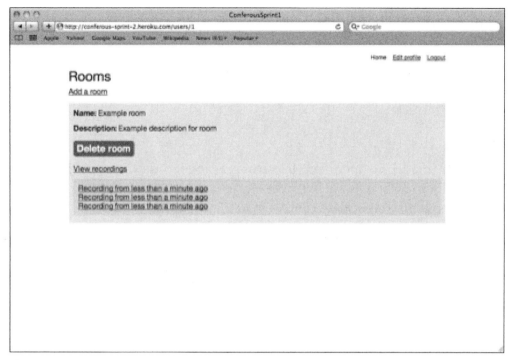

Figure A.46
Browse recordings page.

```
                return false;
            })
        });
    </script>
<% end %>
<h1>Rooms</h1>
<%= link_to 'Add a room', new_user_room_path(@user) %>
<div id="rooms">
    <%= render @user.rooms %>
</div>
```

Room partial—(to reuse showing room details)

This is the reusable view partial that is used in the preceding page to display room information in a specific way. It is modified from the previous Sprint to show recordings that are attached to the room. It is used in the line <%= render @user.rooms %> in the Browse Rooms code.

```
<div class="room">
    <p>
        <span class="bold">Name:</span> <%= room.name %>
    </p>
    <p>
        <span class="bold">Description:</span> <%= room.description %>
    </p>
    <p>
        <%= button_to 'Delete room', user_room_path(@user, room), :method =>
:delete %>
    </p>
    <p>
        <%= link_to 'View recordings', nil, :id => 'view_recordings' %>
    </p>
    <p class="recordings">
        <%= render room.recordings %>
    </p>
</div>
```

Edit profile

This view takes the following edit profile form partial and adds extra information such as a title, etc.

Figure A.47
Edit profile page.

```
<h1>Edit profile</h1>
<%= form_for @user do |f| %>
    <%= f.error_messages %>
    <%= render :partial => 'form', :object => f %>
    <%= f.submit 'Update profile' %>
<% end %>
```

Form partial—(for use in the sign up and edit profile pages)

This is a reusable form that shows users an edit profile form, which they can then use to update their user registration information. It is called on the line <%= render :partial => 'form', :object => f %> in the Edit profile code.

```
<p>
    <%= form.label :username %><br/>
    <%= form.text_field :username %>
</p>
<p>
    <%= form.label :password %><br/>
    <%= form.password_field :password %>
</p>
<p>
    <%= form.label :email_address %><br/>
    <%= form.text_field :email_address %>
</p>
```

Cancel account

This view takes the current user in the database and displays a form for him to edit his information. At the same time, it also allows him to cancel his account with a Delete account button.

```
<h1>Edit Profile</h1>
<%= form_for @user do |f| %>
    <%= f.error_messages %>
    <%= render :partial => 'form', :object => f %>
    <%= f.submit 'Update profile' %>
<% end %>
<%= button_to 'Delete account', @user, :method => :delete %>
```

Form partial—(for use in sign up and edit profile—in the future—pages)

This is a reusable form that shows the user a sign up form, which he can then use to fill in his user registration information. It is called on the line <%= render :partial => 'form', :object => f %> in the Cancel account code.

```
<p>
    <%= form.label :username %><br/>
    <%= form.text_field :username %>
</p>
<p>
    <%= form.label :password %><br/>
    <%= form.password_field :password %>
</p>
<p>
    <%= form.label :email_address %><br/>
    <%= form.text_field :email_address %>
</p>
```

Controllers   The UserController controller is modified to allow for the Cancel account feature.

```
class UsersController < ApplicationController
  before_filter :require_no_user, :only => [:new, :create]

  # the new action instantiates a new User object.
  def new
    @user = User.new
  end

  # the create action instantiates a new User object and fills it with user-
  provided values (params[:user]). It then tries to save it. This may fail if the
  user did not provide all the values required by the model in its validations or
  provided incorrect data. If it succeeds, it will create a notice that will be shown
  to the user and redirect them to a new page with user details. If it fails, it will
  show them a page with a form to retry.
  def create
    @user = User.new(params[:user])
    if @user.save
      flash[:notice] = 'Sign up successful!'
      redirect_to @user
    else
```

```
      render :new
    end
  end

# the show action takes the currently signed-in user through an Authlogic-
provided method and puts it into the @user variable.
  def show
    @user = current_user
  end

# the destroy action finds the specified user and deletes it from the database,
thereby canceling the account.
  def destroy
    @user = User.find(params[:id])
    @user.destroy
    flash[:notice] = 'You have successfully canceled your account!'
    redirect_to root_path
  end
end
```

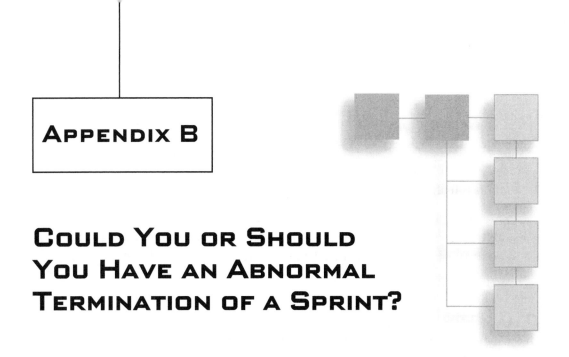

APPENDIX B

COULD YOU OR SHOULD YOU HAVE AN ABNORMAL TERMINATION OF A SPRINT?

INTRODUCTION

If you have read and followed all the suggestions we make throughout this book, you should never have to ask yourself this question or go through this ordeal, unless your Sprint termination is due to an order from management or the business.

Normally, terminating a Sprint before its terms is not something you would like to do since it is rather demoralizing for the team, but it is something you should be able to deal with because it does happen in the real world.

Before we discuss how to restart after an abnormal termination of a Sprint, let's go through three different scenarios where this could happen.

WHEN CAN A SPRINT BE TERMINATED EARLIER THAN PLANNED?

- By management order:

  An example of this is when management has to call off a project or a Sprint when they have to announce:

  1. Lay-off
  2. Plant closing
  3. Re-organization

  All of these require the termination of your project or Sprint.

- By the business:

  An example of this is when, for example, the marketing team has to re-direct their strategy towards a new segment of the market which requires the redirection of the fund that had been allocated to your project.

- By the team:

  An example of this is when the team comes to realize that it will not be able to meet its commitment, either due to a wrong technical decision or because of some conflicts that have been plaguing the team's work.

How to Avoid Terminating a Sprint Earlier Than Planned

As we have seen, terminating a Sprint is almost unavoidable if it is due to management or business decisions.

When it comes to the team's own actions or their lack of ability to reach the Sprint goal, however, there are things you can do—or should have done—to avoid having to terminate a Sprint before its term:

- Reduce the team's velocity (or scope) when first started on your Scrum project:

  When you first start with Scrum, it is always advisable to be more conservative with people's time and to schedule their time as if they would be working part-time at first.

- Do not hurry to make wrong technical or architectural decisions:

  To be straightforward, we will recommend that you follow our advice here in Chapters 6 and 7 before you make any decision regarding the future architecture of your application.

- Make sure to get management commitment to provide you with all the resources needed before you start.

  Scrum or not, there is no way you can get anything done without the appropriate resources.

- Keep track of your project one day at a time.

- Keep an eye open on your Burndown chart, one day at a time.

■ Make sure to get your management to understand that they should not get you to take care of something else during the course of a Sprint.

Classic cases of impediments still happen very often in our corporations.

HOW TO RESTART AFTER TERMINATING A SPRINT EARLIER THAN PLANNED

Whenever you re-start after an abnormal termination of a Sprint, always make sure to know the reason for the interruption of the Sprint, not just the symptoms, but the root causes of the termination. Next, what you should do is to have a new planning session to make sure you take into account the new situation and environment before you run ahead into another Sprint termination.

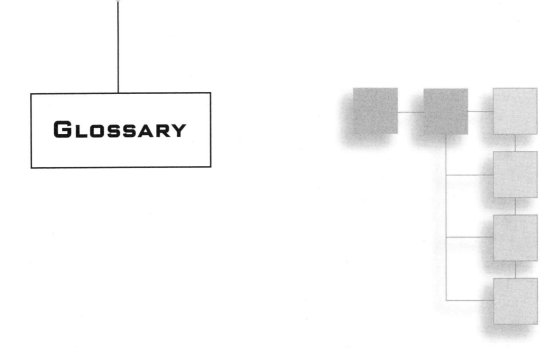

GLOSSARY

Agile. Generic name that often means the opposite of a rigid and heavyweight software development and/or project management approach or process.

Agile manifesto. Document drafted during a meeting in Utah in 2001, which initiated a more adaptive and lightweight movement in software development.

Architecture. The overall design or arrangement of the main components of a software application.

Architecture vision. Similar to what some other people call architecture intent, this is a high-level vision of what the architecture will look like once all the details are fleshed out.

Burndown chart. Diagram used by the Scrum team to display how much work remains in the Sprint.

Coaching. The art of developing someone's talents or helping someone grow or reach some specific goals by helping the person identify his own roadmap and commitments that will be required of him to get to the results.

Conflict resolution techniques. Teams are self-organizing in Scrum; these are techniques that project team members can use to resolve conflicts among themselves: Accommodating, Compromise, Competitive, Collaborating, and Avoidance.

Core business data elements. Data elements that relate to the core of the business domain or to the organization's business. Room and reservation are, for example, core data elements of a hotel, while book and patron are core data elements of a library. Designing and building software applications around these core data elements ensures the long-term stability of the software product and helps extend it more easily into the future without the excessive costs of rebuild.

CUTFIT technique. Simple rules that a Scrum team can use to validate its user stories (while gathering requirements). CUTFIT stands for Consistent, Unambiguous, Testable, Feasible, Independent, and Traceable.

The (development) team. The team that is responsible for all the software development activities within a Scrum team, from writing requirements to designing to coding and testing.

Daily Scrum (Daily Standup). A daily progress meeting where the team members get together, physically or virtually, to synchronize and learn how much they have progressed towards the Sprint goal. Three questions have to be answered during this meeting:

1. What have I been able to accomplish since yesterday's meeting?

2. What do I plan on accomplishing before tomorrow's meeting?

3. What stands in my way?

Done. Agreement by all the three parties of the Scrum team as to what the end state is supposed to be for the development team by the end of the sprint.

Enterprise Architecture. High-level blueprint of a company's eco-system that shows the relationship and inter-dependencies between its business vision, strategy, processes, software applications, data, and infrastructure.

Enterprise Architecture team. A team, which exists in many IT organizations, that is responsible for the overall architecture of the company's IT systems and with which the Scrum team often must interact to get their project's application approved and to ensure that their new application architecture fits into the overall enterprise architecture.

Iteration. Still called a Sprint in Scrum, this is a time-boxed cycle in Scrum during which the development team is asked to turn some selected (prioritized) user stories into an increment of potentially shippable product.

Kanban. A process improvement framework famous for its contribution to the Toyota Production System (TPS).

kanban (with a lower case). Denotes a card and technique, derived from the broader Kanban framework, which is used to limit work-in-process, thus, increasing workflow.

Lean. Generic name that covers all processes or techniques, which is known to eliminate waste from a system or process.

Potentially shippable product increment. An increment of working software product that was developed during a Sprint and which can be eventually shipped to customers.

Project Management Office (PMO). A team within many IT departments that is in charge of business and IT alignment and tracking IT performance, mainly in terms of project costs, benefits, and timely delivery.

Product Owner. A member of the Scrum team who is responsible for the product vision, product backlog items (requirements), and their prioritization, from a business perspective. In some cases, the product owner is required to play the mediation role between different business units within a company in order to prioritize their conflicting business needs and requirements.

Quality Assurance (QA). A team with many IT departments, which is responsible for quality assurance and testing activities of all new software development. It is not part of the Scrum process framework but is a unit with which the Scrum team must interact, even if only to get a testing professional to be loaned to the Scrum project team to create a cross-functional capability.

Release planning. Meeting during which the product owner shares with the Scrum team his product vision and what functionality, in terms of user stories, should be delivered by when. With the architectural approach we recommend in this book, the development team members could have some very positive influence on what user stories should be built first, rather than passively attending the meeting as some used to in the past.

Remaining work. Number of hours estimated to be needed for a team to finish any unfinished task during a Sprint.

Sprint retrospective. Meeting during which the Scrum team will go through what worked and what did not work during the Sprint they just finished and determine whether there is anything they can learn from their experience that will make the process even better for the next Sprint.

ScrumMaster. Scrum specialist whose responsibility it is to help the rest of the team (and the organization) understand and properly apply Scrum to a project.

The Scrum team. Generic name that covers the ScrumMaster, the product owner, and the (development) team.

Sprint. A time-boxed cycle, or iteration, during which the development team is supposed to turn some selected requirements (user stories) into a potentially shippable product increment.

Sprint backlog. List of all the tasks the development team has to do during a Sprint.

Sprint planning meeting. A two-phase meeting: during the first part, the product owner lets the team know which requirements she thinks should be part of the Sprint, and during the second part, the team decides how to turn the selected requirements into an increment of potentially shippable product.

Sprint review. Meeting during which the team provides a demonstration of what they have built to the product owner and the stakeholders.

Self-organizing team. A concept in Agile and Scrum, which dictates that the development team should be responsible for organizing itself as the members see fit to get the job done. If the team does not deliver, self-organization does not mean that the ScrumMaster or product owner could not or should not intervene, in a subtle way and indirectly, to help the team move forward.

Sprint goal. The goal that the product owner will give to the team for their Sprint, such as "laying down the foundation for US credit cards."

ScrumButs (Negative). Wrong adaptation of Scrum, often equated to an excuse to hide the organization's weaknesses.

ScrumButs (Positive). Good adaptation of Scrum that helps get the team moving forward despite some constraints they have to deal with in the real world.

Scrum readiness assessment. A quick assessment at the beginning of a Scrum project that serves to assess the team's ability to deliver on their results using Scrum. Knowing where the team stands with the assessment allows the team to know what they should do in order to improve their chance of using Scrum with success.

Servant-leadership. A leadership philosophy which considers that the leader or manager can be more successful and effective in helping the team by removing impediments rather than ordering them around as in the old command and control style.

SMART (technique). Simple technique known to be very effective in helping management and teams identify goals that they can achieve within a reasonable amount of time and with available resources. SMART stands for Measurable, Achievable, Realistic, and Time-Based.

Stakeholders. A generic name to indicate any person or team that has a stake in the Scrum project team's success.

Story card. Index card used to describe a user story, both in agile and lean processes.

Task board. Whiteboard where team tasks and assignments are recorded in all transparency.

Toyota Production System (TPS). Production system considered to be the leanest and most effective in the world.

Traits of a caring leader. Qualities that help someone be a good leader. Being honest, open, authentic, available, and caring are some examples of these qualities.

Unadjusted estimation points. Requirements estimate made before taking into account the weight of the surrounding environment.

User role. Roles played by different users during the course of the project. Sometimes one person can play more than one role; for instance, one person can be both a system administrator and a billing approver.

User story. Generic name used in agile software development to indicate user business requirements.

Velocity. Number of user stories (usually measured in points) the development team can deliver during a Sprint.

Visual requirements gathering technique. Visual technique based on the tree and forest hierarchy that can simplify the effort put into gathering user requirements for complex projects.

Waterfall. A sequential software development process that makes the assumption that all the requirements should be gathered first, then analyzed, then developed, and only then tested for user sign-off before being put into production for use.

REFERENCES

Anderson, David, *Kanban*, Blue Hole Press, 2010.

Appelo, Jurgen. *ScrumButs Are the Best Part of Scrum*, September, 2009. (http://www.noop.nl/2009/09/scrumbuts-are-the-best-part-of-scrum.html)

Augustine, Sanjiv. *Managing Agile Projects*, Prentice-Hall, 2005.

Cohn, Mike. *User Stories Applied: For Agile Software Development*, Upper Saddle River: Addison-Wesley, 2004.

Cohn, Mike. *Agile Estimating & Planning*, Boston: Prentice-Hall, 2005.

Cohn, Mike. *Succeeding with Agile: Leading a Self-Organizing Team*, August, 2009. (www.informit.com/articles/article.aspx?p=1382538).

Cohn, Mike. *Succeeding with Agile: Software Development Using Scrum,* Addison-Wesley, 2009.

Davies, Rachel, and Sedley, Liz. *Agile Coaching*, The Pragmatic Programmer, 2009.

Derby, Esther, and Larson, Diana. *Agile Retrospectives: Making Good Teams Great*, Raleigh: Pragmatic Bookshelf, 2006.

Hirotaka Takeuchi and Ikujiro Nonaka. "The New New Product Development Game." *Harvard Business Review,* 1986.

Highsmith, Jim. *Agile Software Development Ecosystems*, Addison-Wesley, 2002.

Highsmith, Jim. *Agile Project Management,* Addison-Wesley, 2004.

Japan Management Asociation. *Kanban: Just in time at Toyota*, English translation and revised edition, Productivity Inc, 1989.

Kniberg, Henrik. *Scrum and XP from the Trenches*, InfoQ, 2007.

Lencioni, Patrick. *Five Dysfunctions of Teams,* Jossey-Bass, A Wiley company, 2002.

Martin, Robert. *Agile Software Development: Principles, Patterns and Practices*, Upper Saddle River, New Jersey: Pearson Education, 2005.

Moore, Geoffrey. *Crossing the Chasm*, HarperBusiness Essentials, 2004.

Pham, Andrew. "Influence of Architecture on Team Velocity and Software Quality," Presentation at the Dallas Scrum User Group, March, 2010.

Pham, Andrew. Scrum presentation to the University of Pennsylvania, School of Medicine Information Services, June, 2010.

Poppendieck, Mary, and Poppendieck, Tom. *Lean Software Development*, Addison-Wesley Professional, 2006.

Katzenbach, Jon, and Smith, Douglas. *The Wisdom of Teams: Creating a High Performance Organization*, Collins Business, 1993.

Rising, Linda, and Manns, Mary Lynn. *Fearless Change: Patterns for Introducing New Ideas*, Addison-Wesley, 2004.

Schwaber, Ken, and Beedle, Mike. *Agile Software Development with Scrum*, Prentice Hall, 2002.

Schwaber, Ken. *Agile Project Management with Scrum,* Microsoft Press, 2004.

Schwaber, Ken, and Sutherland, Jeff. *Scrum Guide*, Feb. 2010, Scrum.org.

Shalloway, Alan; Beaver, Guy; and Trott, James. *Lean-Agile Software Development Achieving Enterprise Agility,* Addison-Wesley, 2010.

Sutherland, Jeff; Sutherland, Irene; and Hegarty, Christine. *Scrum in Church*, Agile 2009.

INDEX

Special Characters

`:` literal constructor, Ruby language, 183
5W technique, 110

A

acceptance testing, 116–118
accommodating (ACCO) technique,
129–130
accountability, on group level, 125–126
achievable goals, 49
ActiveRecord component, Ruby on Rails,
186–187
actual cost (AC), 25, 28
adapting Scrum, 145–155
  business dimension, 154
  examples of situational adaptations,
   147–154
  infrastructure dimension, 151
  organization dimension, 147–150
  process dimension, 153–154
  team dimension, 152
  technology dimension, 152–153
  without negative ScrumButs,
   146–147
adaptive project management, 13–14
Add dish feature, Noshster
  overview, 213–214
  testing, 239–240
Add restaurant page, Noshster, 222
Add review page, Noshster,
232–233
Add room view, Conferous,
251–252
adjourning stage of teams, 129
Adjusted Points (AP), 70
admitting mistakes as leadership
  quality, 143
advocate, product owner as, 112
Agile Manifesto, 3–4
Agile Project Management with Scrum, 4,
  31, 135

Agile Software Development and Project
  Management, 1–15
  application to real-world projects,
   177–180
  effectiveness of, 12–14
  foundation of, 3–5
AP (Adjusted Points), 70
Appelo, Jurgen, 146, 149
applications, aspects of, 63
architects, Keirsey Temperament Types
  Sorter, 127–128
architecture
  data, 40–45, 82–83, 87–89, 195, 197
  defined, 75–76
  enterprise, 40–45, 82–83, 89, 91–92
  software, 178
architecture vision, 75–106
  benefit of, 82–92
  Conferous case study, 242–244
  identifying, 78–82
  importance of, 77–78
  Noshster case study, 192–197
  overview, 178–179
  parallel software development, 103–105
  release and sprints planning, 93–103
arrays in Ruby language, 184
Asian cultures, planning poker in, 62
assertions, testing through, 190–191
assessment of project readiness, 157–171
  business dimension, 162
  example, 164–169
  improving score, 169–170
  infrastructure dimension, 160
  organization dimension, 160
  overview, 177, 180
  process dimension, 162
  scores, 163–164, 169–170
  simple tool for, 157–164
  team dimension, 161
  technology dimension, 161
attr_accessor method, Ruby language, 183
authentic leaders, 143

Authlogic plugin
  Conferous, 248
  Noshster, 199
automated testing
  general discussion, 118–119
  infrastructure for, 151
  team velocity, 113, 115
  Web development with Ruby on Rails,
   190–191
availability
  of leaders/managers, 143
  of product owner, 111
average score, project readiness
  self-assessment, 163–165
average-performance teams, 132
avoidance (AVOID) technique, 130

B

BAC (Budget at Completion), 28
backlog, product, 47–59
  CUTFIT rules, 51–54
  defined, 6–7
  example, 54–58
  gathering requirements for backlog,
   49–51
  identifying stakeholders and goals, 47–48
  SMART rules, 48–49
  visual requirements gathering process,
   47–54
backlog, Sprint, 7–8, 100, 102
bad ScrumButs, 146–147
balance scorecard, 34–35
belonging, in groups, 125–126
break even point, 18–19
Browse dishes page, Noshster, 217
Browse recordings view, Conferous,
259–260
Browse restaurants page, Noshster,
226–227
Browse rooms view, Conferous, 253–254
Browse users view, Noshster, 206–207

Budget at Completion (BAC), 28
budget forecasting, 27–28
    Estimate at Completion, 28
    Estimate to Complete, 28
    formulas for, 24
    Variance at Completion, 28
burndown charts, 9, 147–148
business dimension
    project readiness self-assessment, 159, 162
    Scrum adaptation for, 154
    in story point estimation, 70
business entities in story point estimation, 65–66
business management
    focusing on finance with, 177–178
    product owner, lack of, 154
    working with top, 32–35
business prioritization matrix, IT, 36
business requirements, 65
business rules in story point estimate, 63–65
business units and team management, 138
buy versus build, 19–21
buy-in, management. See project management

C

calculating project costs, 17–18
call management web application.
    See Conferous case study
Cancel account view, Conferous, 262–263
Capital One, 145
caring
    in teamwork, 132
    as trait of leader and manager, 143–144
case studies, software development, 181–264
    See also Conferous case study; Noshster case study
    Ruby language, 181–185
    Ruby on Rails as web framework, 185–189
    Web development with Ruby on Rails, 189–191
cash flow, in payback period, 18–19
CDE (Container, Difference, Exchange) concept, 138
central library system example, 94–102
champions, Keirsey Temperament Types Sorter, 128
change process, 37–39
classes, Ruby language, 182
clustering user stories, 84–85
coaching
    adapting Scrum, 150
    in leadership, 139
    by product owner, 112
    for superior performance, 141–143
code
    reusing in Ruby on Rails, 185
    version control, 189

Cohn, Mike, 135–136, 138
collaborating (COLLA) technique, 130
collaboration, in Scrum, 11. See also project management
collaboration capabilities, version control system, 189
command-and-control management, 149–150
commitment, of dual product owner/ScrumMaster, 152
common data element approach, 95–100, 150
communication skills
    of product owner, 112
    ScrumMaster, 175–176
communication with IT middle management, 38
comparable story point estimate, 61–73
    cultural problems with planning poker, 62
    example, 71–73
    objective criteria-based estimating process, 62–70, 197–198, 244–246
    overview, 178
    problems with non-comparable, 61–62
    readiness self-assessment, 167–168
competitive (COMPE) technique, 130–131
composers, Keirsey Temperament Types Sorter, 127
compromise (COMP) technique, 129–130
concurrent (parallel) software development
    architecture vision, 80, 103–105
    Noshster, 211–213
    version control systems, 189
Conferous case study, 242–264
    architecture vision, 242–244
    product vision and goal, 242
    project estimation, 244–246
    release planning, 242–244
    Sprint 1, 246–257
    Sprint 2, 257–264
    Sprint planning, 242–244
    visual requirements gathering process, 242–243
conflict resolution
    ScrumMaster skills at, 176
    techniques for, 129–131
consistent, unambiguous, testable, feasible, independent, traceable (CUTFIT) rules, 51–54
constructs, Ruby language, 182
Container, Difference, Exchange (CDE) concept, 138
continuous integration testing, 119, 151, 154
controllers, in MVC
    Conferous Sprint 1, 254–257
    Conferous Sprint 2, 263–264
    Noshster, testing, 239
    Noshster release 1—Sprint 1, 207–210
    Noshster release 1—Sprint 2, 218–219

Noshster release 2—Sprint 3, 227–229
Noshster release 2—Sprint 4, 237–239
    overview, 187–188
convention over configuration principle, Ruby on Rails, 185–186
cost performance
    Cost Performance Index, 25–26
    cost variance, 25
    formulas for, 24
Cost Performance Index (CPI), 25–26, 28
cost variance (CV), 25
costs
    calculating project, 17–18
    human resource, of project, 17–18
    payback period, 18–19
Cottmeyer, Mike, 146–147
counselors, Keirsey Temperament Types Sorter, 127
crafters, Keirsey Temperament Types Sorter, 127
Create, Read, Update, Delete (CRUD), 66
criteria-based estimating process
    Conferous case study, 244–246
    example, 71–73
    general discussion, 62–70
    Noshster case study, 197–198
    overview, 178
    readiness self-assessment, 167–168
CSM/PO internal servant-leadership quadrant, 138–139
cultural problems with planning poker, 62
Current Reality in GROW model, 142
CUTFIT Rules (consistent, unambiguous, testable, feasible, independent, traceable), 51–54
CV (cost variance), 25

D

daily builds, 154
Daily Standup (daily Scrum), 8–9, 104, 150
data architecture
    architecture vision, 82–83, 87–89
    enterprise architecture, 40–45
    Noshster, 195, 197
data entities in story point estimation, 65–66
data manipulation factor in story point estimation, 66
data models
    Conferous Sprint 1, 246–247
    Conferous Sprint 2, 257–258
    Noshster release 1—Sprint 1, 199–200
    Noshster release 1—Sprint 2, 211–212
    Noshster release 2—Sprint 3, 220–221
    Noshster release 2—Sprint 4, 229–231
data-based user stories, 79–81, 84–85
dates types, Ruby language, 183–184
debts, technical, 101, 103
Declaration of Inter-Dependence, 4–5
Delete profile page, Noshster, 206

Delete review page, Noshster, 235–236
Delete room view, Conferous, 252–253
deleting with ActiveRecord, 187
design. *See* architecture vision
development, parallel software
    architecture vision, 80, 103–105
    Noshster, 211–213
    version control systems, 189
development, Web, with Ruby on Rails,
    189–191
    testing, 189–191
    version control with Git, 189
development environment, 119–121
development example, trees and forest
    technique, 54–58
development infrastructure dimension, 68
development of software with Scrum, 1–15
    See also case studies, software
        development; project management
    application to real-world projects,
        177–180
    effectiveness of Agile and Scrum, 12–14
    foundation of Agile, 3–5
    origins of Scrum, 5
    Scrum process, 5–12
development team
    management, 31–32, 135–136
    product owner availability, 111
    suggestions to project owner, 93
    TDD, 151
Dish model, Noshster, 213, 231, 239
Dish partial, Noshster, 217–218
DishesController controller, Noshster,
    218–219
done, defining, 115–117, 153
don't repeat yourself principle, Ruby on
    Rails, 185
Ducker, Peter, 136

E

EA (enterprise architecture), 40–45, 82–83,
    89, 91–92
EAC (Estimate at Completion), 28
Earned Value (EV)
    cost variance, 25
    defined, 24
    project budget forecasting, 27
    Schedule Variance, 26–27
ED (environment dimensions)
    example, 71
    general discussion, 67–70
Edit dish page, Noshster, 214–215
Edit profile view
    Conferous, 261–262
    Noshster, 204–205
Edit restaurant page, Noshster, 223–224
Edit review page, Noshster, 234–235
elicitation process. *See* requirements
    gathering process
encryption, password, 199
engineering, TDD in, 151

enterprise architecture (EA), 40–45, 82–83,
    89, 91–92
enterprise-wide implementation, 61–73
    cultural problems with planning
        poker, 62
    example, 71–73
    objective criteria-based estimating
        process, 62–70, 197–198, 244–246
    problems with non-comparable story
        point, 61–62
entities, quantity of in story point
    estimation, 65–66
environment dimensions (ED)
    example, 71
    general discussion, 67–70
Estimate at Completion (EAC), 28
Estimate to Complete (ETC), 28
estimating comparable story point, 61–73
    Conferous case study, 244–246
    cultural problems with planning
        poker, 62
    example, 71–73
    Noshster case study, 197–198
    objective criteria-based estimating
        process, 62–70, 197–198, 244–246
    overview, 178
    problems with non-comparable story
        point, 61–62
    readiness self-assessment, 167–168
EV (Earned Value)
    cost variance, 25
    defined, 24
    project budget forecasting, 27
    Schedule Variance, 26–27
executives. *See* project management
expectations of stakeholders, product
    owner management of, 109
extended GROW model, 141–143
externally facing side of leadership,
    137–140

F

failure with Scrum, 2
feasible requirements, 52
field marshals, Keirsey Temperament
    Types Sorter, 128
finances, 17–29
    buy versus build, 19–21
    calculating project costs, 17–18
    cost performance, 25–26
    focus on, 177–178
    monitoring project performance, 24–28
    Net Present Value, 21–22
    payback period, 18–19
    project budget forecasting, 27–28
    reporting on, 149
    Return on Investment, 22–24
    schedule performance, 26–27
    selecting project investments, 18–24
Five Dysfunctions of Teams, 126, 179
5W technique, 110

fixed price, buy versus build technique,
    19–21
Fixnums, 184
forecasting, budget, 27–28
    Estimate at Completion, 28
    Estimate to Complete, 28
    formulas for, 24
    Variance at Completion, 28
Form partial
    Conferous, 249–250, 262–263
    Noshster, 202, 205, 214–215, 222–225,
        234–235
forming stage of teams, 129–130
four-week Sprints, 153
framework, web, Ruby on Rails as,
    185–189
    general discussion, 185–186
    MVC (Model-View-Controller),
        186–189
functional managers
    intervention with, 140
    as ScrumMaster, 149–150
functional tests, 190, 239
Future Value (FV), 21

G

gathering requirements, 47–54
    adapting Scrum, 153–154
    architecture vision, 78
    Conferous case study, 242–243
    CUTFIT rules, 51–54
    gathering requirements for backlog,
        49–54
    identifying stakeholders and goals,
        47–49
    Noshster case study, 192–193
    overview, 178
    product owner skill at, 111
    SMART rules, 48–49
Git version control system, 189
goal, reality, options, and will (GROW)
    model, 141–143
goals
    in groups, 125
    GROW model, 141–143
    product, 78, 109–110, 139, 192, 242
    release, 100–101
    SMART rules, 48–49
    Sprint, 100–101
    stakeholder, 47–49, 54–55
    top business management, 35
good ScrumButs, 146–147
governance, PMO IT project, 36–37
great teamwork, conditions of,
    131–132
groups, teamwork by, 125–126
GROW (goal, reality, options, and will)
    model, 141–143
guidance
    in leadership, 139
    by product owner, 112

H

hashes in Ruby language, 184
healers, Keirsey Temperament Types Sorter, 127
hierarchy of needs, 124–125
high-performance teams, 126, 132
honesty, as quality of leader, 143
horizontal data architecture, 83, 87
horizontal slicing
    Conferous case study, 242–243, 245
    overview, 96–98, 101
    versus vertical slicing, 193
human development skills, ScrumMaster, 176
human nature, 124–125
human resource cost of Scrum project, 17–18

I

impediments, removal by leaders, 139
independent requirements, 52
individuals in team, 124–125
inflation rate, 21–22
influence of leaders on team, 139
InformIT, 135
infrastructure
    organizing testing, 119–121
    team experience with, 152–153
infrastructure dimension
    project readiness self-assessment, 157, 160, 166
    Scrum adaptation for, 151
infrastructure team, 154
Inspect and Adapt cycle, Scrum, 12
inspecting properties with ActiveRecord, 187
inspectors, Keirsey Temperament Types Sorter, 126
integration tests, 116–117, 119, 190, 239–240
interaction type in story point estimate, 63–64
interest rate, 21–22
Internal Rate of Return (IRR), 22–24
internally facing side of leadership, 137–139
inventors, Keirsey Temperament Types Sorter, 128
investments, selecting project, 18–24
    buy versus build, 19–21
    Net Present Value, 21–23
    payback period, 18–19
    Return on Investment, 22–24
IT business prioritization matrix, 36
IT middle management, 36–43
    concerns of, 36–38
    enterprise architecture, 40–43
    Operations management, 39–40
    Quality Assurance, 38–39
IT top management, 35–36

J

job safety, 132, 140

K

kanban technique, 80
Keirsey Temperament Types Sorter, 126–129
Kilmann, Ralph, 129
Kniberg, Henrik, 6, 115
knowledge
    product, of product owner, 109–110
    Scrum, of ScrumMaster, 174–175

L

leadership, 135–144
    coaching with GROW model, 141–143
    versus management, 135–140
    overview, 179
    traits of caring leader, 143–144
Lencioni, Patrick, 126, 179
life cycle, software development, 12–13
Logout page, Noshster, 203
low-performance teams, 126, 132

M

management, project, 1–15, 31–45, 135–144
    See also adapting Scrum
    adapting Scrum, 149
    adaptive, 13–14
    Agile foundations, 3–5
    coaching with GROW model, 141–143
    effectiveness of Agile and Scrum, 12–14
    focusing on finance, 177–178
    IT middle management, 36–43
    versus leadership, 135–140
    overview, 179
    program management office, 35–36
    Scrum origins, 5
    Scrum process, 5–12
    top business management, 32–35
    top IT management, 35–36
    traits of caring leader and manager, 143–144
    turning management into ally, 43–44
management matrix, stakeholder, 109
manual testing, 119, 190
Maslow's Hierarchy of Needs, 124–125
Master Data Management (MDM) layer, 41, 43–45
masterminds, Keirsey Temperament Types Sorter, 127
matrices
    conflict resolution, 130
    estimation, 168, 170
    IT business prioritization, 36
    self-assessment readiness, 158, 163–165
    stakeholder management, 109
    story point estimation, 72

maximum score, project readiness self-assessment, 163–164
measurable goals, 48
measurements, stakeholder, 49, 55
mediocre-performance teams, 132
meetings
    See also Daily Standup
    adapting Scrum, 150
    ScrumMaster role in organizing, 175
    Sprint planning, 8
    Sprint retrospective, 10–11
    Sprint review, 10
mentoring
    in leadership, 139
    by product owner, 112
methods, Ruby language, 184–185
middle management, IT, 36–43
    concerns of, 36–38
    enterprise architecture, 40–43
    Operations management, 39–40
    overview, 178
    Quality Assurance, 38–39
minimum score, project readiness self-assessment, 163
mistakes, leader admission of, 143
models, in MVC
    Conferous Sprint 1, 248
    Conferous Sprint 2, 259
    Noshster, testing, 239
    Noshster release 1—Sprint 1, 199, 201–202
    Noshster release 1—Sprint 2, 213
    Noshster release 2—Sprint 3, 221
    Noshster release 2—Sprint 4, 229–232
    overview, 186–187
Model-View-Controller. *See* controllers, in MVC; models, in MVC; MVC; Views, in MVC
monitoring project performance, 24–28
    cost performance, 25–26
    overview, 24
    project budget forecasting, 27–28
    schedule performance, 26–27
monthly fees, buy versus build technique, 19–21
motivation
    framework based on, 13
    in GROW model, 142
MVC (Model-View-Controller)
    See also controllers, in MVC; models, in MVC; Views, in MVC
    Conferous Sprint 1, 248–257
    Conferous Sprint 2, 259–264
    Noshster release 1—Sprint 2, 213–219
    Noshster release 2—Sprint 3, 221–229
    Noshster release 2—Sprint 4, 229–239
    overview, 186–189

N

needs, hierarchy of, 124–125
negative ScrumButs, 146–147

Net Present Value (NPV), 21–23
new method, Ruby, 182
"The New New Product Development
     Game" paper, 5
Nonaka, Ikujiro, 5
non-comparable story point, problems
     with, 61–62
non-Western cultures, planning
     poker in, 62
norming stage of teams, 129–130
Noshster case study, 192–241
     5W technique, 110
     architecture vision, 192–197
     product vision and goal, 192
     project estimation, 197–198
     release 1-Sprint 1, 199–210
     release 1-Sprint 2, 210–219
     release 2-Sprint 3, 219–229
     release 2-Sprint 4, 229–239
     release planning, 192–197
     Sprint planning, 192–197
     testing, 239–241
     visual requirements gathering,
          192–193
NPV (Net Present Value), 21–23
numbers in Ruby language, 184

O

objective criteria-based estimating process
     Conferous case study, 244–246
     example, 71–73
     general discussion, 62–70
     Noshster case study, 197–198
     overview, 178
     readiness self-assessment, 167–168
Object-Oriented Analysis and Design
     (OOAD), UML for, 76
object-oriented programming languages,
     182
object-relational mapping, 186–187
objects, Ruby language, 182
open mindset
     of leaders, 143
     in teamwork, 131–132
open-source version control
     system, 189
operational management, IT, 36–43
     concerns of, 36–38
     enterprise architecture, 40–43
     Operations management, 39–40
     Quality Assurance, 38–39
Operations management, 39–40
options, GROW model, 142
organization dimension
     project readiness self-assessment, 157,
          160, 165
     Scrum adaptation for, 147–150
     in story point estimation, 68
organizational skills,
     ScrumMaster, 175
organizer, product owner as, 111

P

parallel (concurrent) software
     development
     architecture vision, 80, 103–105
     Noshster, 211–213
     version control systems, 189
participation, product owner, 111
password encryption, 199
payback period, 18–19
PBIs (Product Backlog Items)
     See also story point estimate; user stories
     building in concurrence, 85
     defined, 47
performance, coaching for superior,
     141–143
performance, monitoring project, 24–28
     cost performance, 25–26
     project budget forecasting, 27–28
     schedule performance, 26–27
performers, Keirsey Temperament Types
     Sorter, 128
performing stage of teams, 129–130
personality types, 126–127
phases, specialized Scrum, 153
Planned Value (PV), 26–27
planning, release/Sprint
     architecture vision, 93–103
     Conferous case study, 242–244
     Noshster case study, 192–197
     overview, 7–8
planning poker, 61–62
PMO (program management office), 35–36
positive ScrumButs, 146–147
PPS (Points per Story), 70–71
practical knowledge of Scrum,
     ScrumMaster, 174–175
Present Value (PV), 21–22
presentation skills, ScrumMaster, 176
price difference, buy versus build
     technique, 19–21
pride, framework based on, 13
prioritization
     changing product, 81, 86
     of stakeholders, product owner
          management of, 109
prioritization matrix, IT business, 36
Private Room Reservation software
     product example, 54–58
process dimension
     project readiness self-assessment, 159,
          162, 167
     Scrum adaptation for, 153–154
     in story point estimation, 70
product backlog, 47–59
     CUTFIT rules, 51–54
     defined, 6–7
     example, 54–58
     gathering requirements for backlog,
          49–51
     identifying stakeholders and goals, 47–48
     product owner skill at gathering
          requirements for, 111

SMART rules, 48–49
     visual requirements gathering process,
          47–54
Product Backlog Items (PBIs)
     See also story point estimate; user
          stories
     building in concurrence, 85
     defined, 47
product owner, 107–112
     architecture vision, 81
     availability of, 111
     collaboration for release and sprint
          planning, 105
     communication skills, 112
     conflict resolution, 131
     CUTFIT rules, 50
     defined, 6–7
     as good organizer, 111
     job safety of team members, 132
     lack of, adapting to, 154
     management and leadership, 135–140
     overview, 179
     product backlog, skill at gathering
          requirements for, 111
     product vision and knowledge, 109–110
     project management, 31, 33
     responsibilities of, 11
     as ScrumMaster, 152
     ScrumMaster role in helping, 176
     servant leadership, 112
     Sprint review, 10
     stakeholder expectations and
          prioritization, managing, 109
     suggestions from development team, 93
product prioritization, changing, 81, 86
product vision and goals
     architecture vision, 78
     Conferous case study, 242
     Noshster case study, 192
     of product owner, 109–110, 139
production environment, 119–120
profit margin in ROI, 23
program management office (PMO),
     35–36
progress, reporting team, 147–148
project budget forecasting, 27–28
     Estimate at Completion, 28
     Estimate to Complete, 28
     formulas for, 24
     Variance at Completion, 28
project costs, calculating, 17–18
project governance, PMO IT, 36–37
project investments, selecting, 18–24
     buy versus build, 19–21
     Net Present Value, 21–22
     payback period, 18–19
     Return on Investment, 22–24
project management, 1–15, 31–45,
     135–144
     adapting Scrum, 149
     adaptive, 13–14
     Agile foundations, 3–5

project management (*continued*)
 coaching with GROW model, 141–143
 effectiveness of Agile and Scrum, 12–14
 focusing on finance, 177–178
 IT middle management, 36–43
 versus leadership, 135–140
 overview, 179
 program management office, 35–36
 Scrum origins, 5
 Scrum process, 5–12
 top business management, 32–35
 top IT management, 35–36
 traits of caring leader and manager,
   143–144
 turning management into ally, 43–44
project performance, monitoring, 24–28
 cost performance, 25–26
 project budget forecasting, 27–28
 schedule performance, 26–27
project readiness self-assessment, 157–171
 business dimension, 162
 example, 164–170
 improving score, 169–170
 infrastructure dimension, 160
 organization dimension, 160
 overview, 177, 180
 process dimension, 162
 scores, 163–164, 169–170
 simple tool for, 157–164
 team dimension, 161
 technology dimension, 161
project status, reporting, 147–148
**promoters, Keirsey Temperament Types
  Sorter, 128**
**protectors, Keirsey Temperament Types
  Sorter, 127**
**providers, Keirsey Temperament Types
  Sorter, 128**
PV (Planned Value), 26–27
PV (Present Value), 21–22
pyramid of needs, 124–125

Q

**QA (Quality Assurance) management,
  38–39, 154**
qualities, product owner
 availability of, 111
 communication skills, 112
 as good organizer, 111
 overview, 107–109
 product backlog, skill at gathering
   requirements for, 111
 product vision and knowledge, 109–110
 servant leadership, 112
 stakeholder expectations and
   prioritization, managing, 109
qualities, ScrumMaster, 173–176
 communication skills, 175–176
 conflict resolution skills, 176
 human development skills, 176
 knowledge of Scrum, 174–175

 organizational skills, 175
 presentation skills, 176
 servant-leadership ability, 175
**Quality Assurance (QA) management,
  38–39, 154**
**questionnaires, readiness self-assessment,
  159–164, 177**

R

readiness self-assessment, project, 157–171
 business dimension, 162
 example, 164–169
 improving score, 169–170
 infrastructure dimension, 160
 organization dimension, 160
 overview, 177, 180
 process dimension, 162
 scores, 163–164, 169–170
 simple tool for, 157–164
 team dimension, 161
 technology dimension, 161
realistic goals, 49
Reality, in GROW model, 142
**real-world software product development
  case studies, 181–264**
 See also Conferous case study; Noshster
   case study
 Ruby language, 181–185
 Ruby on Rails as web framework,
   185–189
 Web development with Ruby on Rails,
   189–191
Recording model, Conferous Sprint 2, 259
regression testing, 190–191
release planning
 architecture vision, 93–103
 Conferous case study, 242–244
 Noshster case study, 192–197
 overview, 7
requirements, business, 65
requirements gathering process, 47–54
 adapting Scrum, 153–154
 architecture vision, 78
 Conferous case study, 242–243
 CUTFIT rules, 51–54
 identifying stakeholders and goals, 47–49
 Noshster case study, 192–193
 overview, 49–54, 178
 product owner skill at, 111
 SMART rules, 48–49
respect
 in teamwork, 132
 towards leaders, 143
Restaurant model, Noshster, 221, 232
Restaurant partial, Noshster, 227
**RestaurantsController controller,
  Noshster, 227–229**
**results, reviewing in GROW model,
  142–143**
retrospective, Sprint, 10–11
Return on Investment (ROI), 22–24

returns, calculating project, 18–24
 buy versus build, 19–21
 Net Present Value, 21–22
 payback period, 18–19
 Return on Investment, 22–24
reusing code in Ruby on Rails, 185
revenue, payback period, 18–19
review, Sprint, 10
Review model, Noshster, 229
Review partial, Noshster, 235–236
reviewing results in GROW model, 142–143
**ReviewsController controller, Noshster,
  237–239**
risk reduction mechanism, Scrum, 12
ROI (Return on Investment), 22–24
Room model, Conferous, 248, 259
Room partial, Conferous, 254, 260–261
Ruby language, 181–185
 classes, 182
 constructs, 182
 dates types, 183–184
 methods, 184–185
 objects, 182
 syntax, 182
 variables, 182–183
Ruby on Rails (RoR)
 MVC, 186–189
 testing, 189–191
 version control with Git, 189
 Web development with, 189–191
 as web framework, 185–189
**rules, business, in story point estimate,
  63–65**

S

saving with ActiveRecord, 187
schedule performance, 26–27
 formulas for, 24
 Schedule Performance Index, 27
 Schedule Variance, 26–27
Schedule Performance Index (SPI), 27
Schedule Variance (SV), 26–27
Schwaber, Ken, 4–5, 31, 135, 146
scorecard, balance, 34–35
**scores, project readiness self-assessment,
  159, 163–170**
Scrum, 1–15
 application to real-world projects,
   177–180
 effectiveness in project management,
   12–14
 general discussion, 5–12
 origins of, 5
"Scrum and the Perfect Storm" article, 5
Scrum and XP from the Trenches, 6, 115
"Scrum in the Church" article, 146, 150
ScrumButs, 146–147, 152. *See also*
  adapting Scrum
ScrumMaster, 173–176
 adapting Scrum in absence of, 149
 burndown chart, 9

collaboration for release and sprint
    planning, 105
communication skills, 175–176
conflict resolution, 131, 176
functional managers as, 149–150
human development skills, 176
job safety of team members, 132
knowledge of Scrum, 174–175
lack of, adapting to, 152
management and leadership, 135–140
organizational skills, 175
overview, 180
presentation skills, 176
as product owner, 152
project management, 31, 33
responsibilities of, 11
servant-leadership ability, 175
Sprint review, 10
SDLC (Software Development Life
    Cycle), 154
self-actualization, 124
self-assessment, project readiness, 157–171
    business dimension, 162
    example, 164–169
    improving score, 169–170
    infrastructure dimension, 160
    organization dimension, 160
    overview, 177, 180
    process dimension, 162
    scores, 163–164, 169–170
    simple tool for, 157–164
    team dimension, 161
    technology dimension, 161
self-esteem, 124
self-organization, team, 126, 149
semicolons in Ruby language, 182
servant leadership
    internally facing leadership, 138–139
    by product owner, 112
    by ScrumMaster, 150, 175
Service-Oriented Architecture (SOA), 40–41
Sign in view
    Conferous, 250–251
    Noshster, 202–203
Sign up view
    Conferous, 248–249
    Noshster, 201–202
sign-ins, Noshster, 201
situational Scrum adaptation examples,
    147–154
    business dimension, 154
    infrastructure dimension, 151
    organization dimension, 147–150
    process dimension, 153–154
    team dimension, 152
    technology dimension, 152–153
SMART (specific, measurable, achievable,
    realistic, time-based) rules, 48–49,
    141
SOA (Service-Oriented Architecture), 40–41
social network case study. See Noshster
    case study

software architecture, 178
software development case studies, 181–264
    See also Conferous case study; Noshster
        case study
    Ruby language, 181–185
    Ruby on Rails as web framework,
        185–189
    Web development with Ruby on Rails,
        189–191
software development example, trees and
    forest technique, 54–58
Software Development Life Cycle
    (SDLC), 154
software development, parallel
    architecture vision, 80, 103–105
    Noshster, 211–213
    version control systems, 189
software development with Scrum, 1–15
    See also project management
    application to real-world projects,
        177–180
    effectiveness of Agile and Scrum, 12–14
    foundation of Agile, 3–5
    origins of Scrum, 5
    Scrum process, 5–12
software project management. See project
    management
software quality, and technical debt, 103.
    See also architecture vision
specialized Scrum phases, 153
specific, measurable, achievable, realistic,
    time-based (SMART) rules, 48–49, 141
SPI (Schedule Performance Index), 27
Sprint backlog, 7–8, 100, 102
Sprint planning
    architecture vision, 93–103
    Conferous case study, 242–244
    Noshster case study, 192–197
    overview, 7–8
Sprint retrospective, 10–11
Sprint review, 10
Sprints
    See also Conferous case study; Noshster
        case study
    defined, 8–9
    length of, 153
    ScrumMaster role during, 175
stages, team, 129–130
stakeholders
    identifying, 47–49
    management matrix, 109
    product owner management of, 109
    SMART rules, 48–49
    visual requirements gathering process,
        54–55
star schema, 89
status of project, reporting, 147–148
stories, user
    See also story point estimate; visual
        requirements gathering process
    architecture vision, 77–86, 94–96
    Conferous case study, 246–247, 257–258

CUTFIT rules, 51–54
    example of, 57–58
    gathering, 49–51
    Noshster case study, 199, 210–212,
        220–221, 229
    parallel software development, 103–104
    product owner skill at gathering, 111
    reporting on progress of, 147–148
    Sprint planning meeting, 8
storming stage of teams, 129–130
story bar charts, 147–148
story card, 57–58, 71, 73
story point estimate, 61–73
    Conferous case study, 244–246
    cultural problems with planning
        poker, 62
    example, 71–73
    Noshster case study, 197–198
    objective criteria-based estimating
        process, 62–70
    overview, 178
    problems with non-comparable, 61–62
    readiness self-assessment, 167–168
strategy, top business management, 35
strings in Ruby language, 184
sub-teams, 103–104
"Succeeding with Agile Using Scrum"
    article, 138
success, predicting. See project readiness
    self-assessment
supervisors, Keirsey Temperament Types
    Sorter, 128
support
    in leadership, 139
    by product owner, 112
Sutherland, Arline C., 146, 150
Sutherland, Jeff, 5, 146, 150
SV (Schedule Variance), 26–27
symbols in Ruby language, 184
syntax, Ruby language, 182

T

Takeuchi, Hirotaka, 5
Task Board, 8
TDD (Test-Driven Development), 151
teachers, Keirsey Temperament Types
    Sorter, 128
team, defined, 126
team, Scrum
    See also development team; leadership;
        teamwork
    architecture vision, 93–103
    general discussion, 5–7
    objective criteria-based estimating
        process, 71
    parallel software development, 103–105
    problems with non-comparable story
        point, 61–62
    product owner as advocate of, 112
    project management, 31, 33
    release planning, 93–103

team, Scrum (*continued*)
   responsibilities of, 11
   ScrumMaster conflict resolution
     skills, 176
   size of, 150
   Sprints planning, 93–103
team dimension
   project readiness self-assessment, 158,
     161, 166
   Scrum adaptation for, 152
   in story point estimation, 69
team velocity
   architecture vision, 76–78, 178
   automated testing, 113, 115
   defined, 17–18
teamwork, 123–133
   conditions of great, 131–132
   conflict resolution techniques, 129–131
   group, 125–126
   individuals, 124–125
   Keirsey temperament types, 126–129
   overview, 179
   team, defined, 126
   team stages, 129
technical debts, 101, 103
technology dimension
   project readiness self-assessment, 158,
     161, 167
   Scrum adaptation for, 152–153
   in story point estimation, 69
teleconferences. *See* Conferous case study
temperament types, Keirsey, 126–129
test cases, in TDD, 151
testable requirements, 52
Test-Driven Development (TDD), 151
testing, 113–122
   acceptance, 116–118
   adapting Scrum, 151
   automated, 113, 115, 118–119, 151,
     190–191
   continuous integration, 119, 151, 154
   done, definition of, 115–117
   functional, 190, 239
   integration, 116–117, 119, 190, 239–240
   manual, 119, 190
   Noshster case study, 239–241
   organizing infrastructure, 119–121
   overview, 179
   Quality Assurance management, 39
   regression, 190–191
   Test::Unit framework, 191
   unit, 115–116, 151, 190, 239
   user acceptance, 116–118, 191, 240–241
   Web development with Ruby on Rails,
     189–191
Test::Unit testing framework, 190–191
theoretical knowledge of Scrum,
   ScrumMaster, 174–175
Thomas, Kenneth, 129
three-tiered structure, MVC, 186

time value of money, 21–22
time-based goals, 49
top business management, 32–35
top IT management, 35–36
traceable requirements, 52
training, technology, 152–153
traits of caring leader and manager,
   143–144. *See also* qualities, product
   owner; qualities, ScrumMaster
transactional data model, 89–90
trees and forest technique
   Conferous case study, 242–243
   example of, 54–58
   Noshster case study, 192–193
   overview, 49–53
trust, in teamwork, 132
Tuckman, Bruce, 129

U

UML for Object-Oriented Analysis and
   Design (OOAD), 76
Unadjusted Points (UP), 67
unambiguous requirements, 52
unit testing
   defined, 190
   done, definition of, 115–116
   Noshster, 239
   in TDD, 151
updates, 39–40
user acceptance testing
   done, definition of, 116–118
   Noshster, 240–241
   Web development with Ruby on
     Rails, 191
User Management Tree, 56
User model
   Conferous, 248
   Noshster, 199, 201, 230
User partial view, Noshster, 207
user sign-ins, Noshster, 201
user stories
   See also story point estimate; visual
     requirements gathering process
   architecture vision, 77–86, 94–96
   Conferous case study, 246–247, 257–
     258
   CUTFIT rules, 51–54
   example of, 57–58
   gathering, 49–51
   Noshster case study, 199, 210–212,
     220–221, 229
   parallel software development, 103–104
   product owner skill at gathering, 111
   reporting on progress of, 147–148
   Sprint planning meeting, 8
user validation, 199
UserController controller
   Conferous, 254–255, 263–264
   Noshster, 207–209

UserSession model
   Conferous, 248
   Noshster, 201
UserSessionsController controller
   Conferous, 255–257
   Noshster, 209–210

V

validation, user, 199
variables, Ruby language, 182–183
Variance at Completion (VAC), 28
velocity, in ROI, 23
velocity, team
   architecture vision, 76–78, 178
   automated testing, 113, 115
   defined, 17–18
version control systems, 189, 212–213
vertical data architecture, 83, 88
vertical slicing, 98–100, 192–193, 195–196
View dish page, Noshster, 216
View restaurant page, Noshster, 225–226
View/delete profile page, Noshster, 204
Views, in MVC
   Conferous, 248–254, 259–263
   Noshster, 201–207, 213–218, 222–227,
     232–236
   overview, 186
vision, in leadership, 139
vision, product
   architecture vision, 78
   Conferous case study, 242
   Noshster case study, 192
   of product owner, 109–110, 139
visual requirements gathering process,
   47–54
   adapting Scrum, 153–154
   architecture vision, 78
   Conferous case study, 242–243
   CUTFIT rules, 51–54
   gathering requirements for backlog,
     49–54
   identifying stakeholders and goals,
     47–49
   Noshster case study, 192–193
   overview, 178
   product owner skill at, 111
   SMART rules, 48–49

W

waterfall software process, 113–114, 154
Web development with Ruby on Rails,
   189–191
   testing, 189–191
   version control with Git, 189
web framework, Ruby on Rails as,
   185–189
whole numbers in Ruby language, 184
will, in GROW model, 142